Paris and the River Seine

ALSO BY HUNT JANIN
(SOME WITH COAUTHORS)
AND FROM MCFARLAND

Medieval Monks and Monasteries (Ursula Carlson, 2023)

Yellowstone: The History, Ecology and Future of America's First National Park (Nicole Sheehan, 2022)

Overland Explorations of the Trans-Mississippi West: Expeditions and Writers of the American Frontier (Ursula Carlson, 2020)

Historic Nevada Waters: Four Rivers, Three Lakes, Past and Present (Ursula Carlson, 2019)

The Californios: A History, 1769–1890 (Ursula Carlson, 2017)

The California Campaigns of the U.S.–Mexican War, 1846–1848 (Ursula Carlson, 2015)

The India-China Opium Trade in the Nineteenth Century (1999; paperback 2014)

Mercenaries in Medieval and Renaissance Europe (Ursula Carlson, 2013)

Rising Sea Levels: An Introduction to Cause and Impact (Scott A. Mandia, 2012)

Trails of Historic New Mexico: Routes Used by Indian, Spanish and American Travelers through 1886 (Ursula Carlson, 2010)

Medieval Justice: Cases and Laws in France, England and Germany, 500–1500 (2004; paperback 2009)

The University in Medieval Life, 1179–1499 (2008)

Islamic Law: The Sharia from Muhammad's Time to the Present (André Kahlmeyer, 2007)

The Pursuit of Learning in the Islamic World, 610–2003 (2005; paperback 2006)

Four Paths to Jerusalem: Jewish, Christian, Muslim, and Secular Pilgrimages, 1000 BCE to 2001 CE (2002; paperback 2006)

Fort Bridger, Wyoming: Trading Post for Indians, Mountain Men and Westward Migrants (2001; paperback 2006)

Claiming the American Wilderness: International Rivalry in the Trans-Mississippi West, 1528–1803 (2006)

Paris and the River Seine
A History

Hunt Janin *and*
Nicole Sheehan

McFarland & Company, Inc., Publishers
Jefferson, North Carolina

All photographs are by Michele Janin

ISBN (print) 978-1-4766-9037-7
ISBN (ebook) 978-1-4766-5278-8

LIBRARY OF CONGRESS AND BRITISH LIBRARY
CATALOGUING DATA ARE AVAILABLE

Library of Congress Control Number 2024012796

© 2024 Hunt Janin and Nicole Sheehan. All rights reserved

No part of this book may be reproduced or transmitted in any form or by any means, electronic or mechanical, including photocopying or recording, or by any information storage and retrieval system, without permission in writing from the publisher.

Front cover image: © Funny Solution Studio/Shutterstock

Printed in the United States of America

*McFarland & Company, Inc., Publishers
Box 611, Jefferson, North Carolina 28640
www.mcfarlandpub.com*

In memory of all the historians
who have gone before me.—HJ

For my "Four Lights,"
Alexander, Justin, Laynie & Julian.
I love you to Paris and the moon and beyond.—NS

"Paris is a veritable ocean. Here you will always
encounter a virgin place—an unknown lair,
something unheard of and forgotten by literary
divers.... You may cast a sounding-line,
but you will never fathom its depth."[1]
—French novelist Honoré de Balzac (1799–1850)

Table of Contents

Preface	1
Introduction: Setting the Stage	5
1. Welcome to the Seine	13
2. From the Beginnings of Paris	25
3. Viking Raids in France	41
4. Money Changes Hands	46
5. The Seine in the Hundred Years War	53
6. A World Heritage Cultural Site and the Bridges (Ponts) Over the Seine in Paris	63
7. Île Saint-Louis	83
8. The Glory of Notre-Dame de Paris	86
9. The Sainte-Chapelle	94
10. Pont Neuf	96
11. The Louvre	100
12. The Musée d'Orsay	106
13. The Place de la Concorde and Louis XVI	108
14. The Petit Palais	111
15. The Grand Palais	113
16. The Eiffel Tower	114
17. *Bateau Mouche* Excursion Boats	117
18. Illustrations and Descriptions of the River Seine	120
19. The Latin Quarter and Peter Abelard	123

20. The Riverbanks (*Berges*) of the Seine in Paris	126
21. The *Brigade Fluviale* (River Police) of Paris	135
22. The Bloody Seine	138
23. The Unknown Woman of the Seine	140
24. The "Thirty Glorious Years"	142
25. Paris and the Man-Made Evolution of the Seine Basin	144
26. The Old Ports of Paris	150
27. Haropa Port: The Combined Ports of Le Havre, Rouen, and Paris	156
28. The Likely Future of the Seine	164
29. The Seine and the English Channel	168
30. Suburban Villages Along the Seine	171
31. New Crews for European River Transport	173
Conclusions: The Jewel in the Crown	176
A Chronology	181
Appendix 1: The Seine and Architecture in Paris	187
Appendix 2: The Mona Lisa	191
Appendix 3: The Paris-Area Canals	193
Appendix 4: Tug Boats on the Seine	196
Appendix 5: Shipping Along the Seine in Paris	197
Appendix 6: The Tidal Wave of the Seine	202
Appendix 7: Medieval Transport of Wine and Grain by River	203
Appendix 8: The First Iron Steamship to Reach Paris	205
Appendix 9: The Inland Waterways Museum on the Seine	207
Appendix 10: Mercenaries Along the Seine	208
Chapter Notes	211
Bibliography	219
Index	223

Preface

The intertwined histories of the city of Paris and of the Seine are quite complicated. It is the Seine, though, with all its ports, bridges, boats, commerce, monuments, and vistas, that has always been the keystone in the arch of Paris life, both in the past and now in the present.

Crossing France from east to west for about 482 miles, the Seine—a name which in Old French means "fishing net"—is the second-longest river in France (after the Loire). In this book, our focus will be on the Seine in the Paris area. A modern map of Paris looks much like the shell of a snail: the Seine forms the heart of the city, and all the *arrondissements* (the districts or neighborhoods) of Paris uncoil around it.

There has always been what one modern French writer has called "a magic link between the Seine and Paris."[1] Very much earlier, Claude Fauchet (1530–1602), a French magistrate, humanist, and historian, explained that the Seine was so important because "helped by seventeen local rivers which can carry cargo shipments, Paris has access to all the commodities available in France."[2]

The great French medievalist Jean Favier (1932–2014) put it even more forcefully. The first three words of the first chapter of his magisterial 1,007-page book on the history of Paris are simply these: "*Paris est né de la Seine*" ("Paris is born of the Seine"). He goes on to add that the Seine is a flatland river with a large basin containing other rivers, too, all of which converge precisely or very close to where Paris is today.[3]

Almost all the best studies on the past, the present, and the likely future of the Seine are in French; very few of them have been written in English or translated into English. All the French and the English books on these subjects that have been used in writing this book are listed in the bibliography.

With about 2.2 million people living in its densely populated central area and almost 12 million people living in its surrounding region, Paris—famously known as *la Ville Lumière* ("the City of Light")[4]—is located on a very fertile plain with easy axes of communication. It has long been the chief commercial hub of France and its leader in many other fields as well.

A Seine-born and Seine-blessed city, Paris grew up in northern France along a bend in the Seine between the Marne River and the Oise River. The Seine eventually empties into the English Channel at Le Havre ("The Harbor" in French), which has traditionally been the key commercial deep-water port for Paris, with goods being transferred there to and from ocean-going ships and barges bound for Paris via the Seine. Le Havre, the Seine port of Rouen, and the English Channel itself will all be discussed in this book.

The focal point of the book, however, is modern and historical Paris, which is now the world's most popular tourist destination and which hosts about 45 million visitors each year. While focusing on the Seine in Paris, the book also discusses several other parts of the Seine river basin in different eras. This basin now totals 25,096 square miles and is extremely rich in cartographic documents generated over the past two centuries. These include general maps describing the territory, fiscal land registries, and navigation charts.[5]

In general, about 62 percent of this river basin is now used for agriculture; it also hosts up to 30 percent of the national industrial activity of France. About 55 percent of the water used in the basin comes from pumped groundwater, with the remaining share coming from surface water such as the Seine and other rivers. The Seine basin groundwater system itself consists of ten major aquifers developed over the ages in karstic Jurassic limestone, lower Cretaceous sand, and Upper Cretaceous chalk.

Today, in overall terms, the Seine basin is significantly affected by pollution ultimately sourced to intensive agriculture. Excessive fertilization and organic pollution are the chief sources of nitrogen in the groundwater and in the surface water. Any cleanup measures, however, are not likely to improve groundwater quality in the short term because, once nitrates get into groundwater, they will stay there for a long time.

The Seine now furnishes Paris and its outlying area with about half of the treated drinking water it needs each day and provides the essential cooling water for many thermal and nuclear power plants in central and western France. Equally important, however, is the fact that the Seine is still a major *commercial maritime highway*: indeed, in earlier times, it was the French equivalent of the interstate highway system in the United States today. Historically, it has always been the most important single factor in the rise and flourishing of Paris itself.

The river's extensive past is, however, more interesting to us as historians and photographers than its modern, heavily regulated, thoroughly documented, and high-tech present. For this reason, the book you now have in your hands has a great deal to say about the Seine and Paris in years long gone by.

For example, King Richard I of England attached so much importance to this river that in 1196 he ordered a special fleet of very fast, state-of-the-art, oar-powered boats known as galleys to be built in order to defend English interests along the Seine.

Much more recently, in the 1830s, the 3,300-year-old, 72-foot-long, 220-ton, red granite obelisk of Luxor was transported by ship from Egypt up the Seine to the Place (the Square) de la Concorde in Paris, where it now stands upright in all its ancient glory.

This is not a beginner-level introductory guidebook that focuses only on the most popular tourist sites of Paris. The French poet Jacques Prévert (1900–1977) hit the most upbeat and touristy note possible when he wrote of the Seine in these translated lines:

> The Seine has very good luck, and never a care in the world. She flows sweetly, both night and day, and she comes out of her source without noise, and without foaming, without getting out of her bed. She goes to the sea by way of Paris, and she walks around all along her quays with her beautiful green dress and her gilded lights: the jealous Notre-Dame, immobile and severe, from the top of all its stones looking the other way.
>
> But the Seine … has no worries; she flows smoothly, day and night, and goes to Le Havre and then goes to the sea, passing by like a dream in the midst of the miseries of Paris.[6]

In fact, however, the Seine has seen very high levels of violence and suffering, too. Despite the scenic qualities of many of its banks and monuments which are discussed here, its few critics would say that it is little more than a cold river with long-standing pollution problems that do not lend themselves to easy solutions.

In this book we will discuss, among many other things: key environmental matters, and historical accounts of both the rich and the famous, and the poor and the *inconnus de la Seine* ("the unknowns of the Seine"). These "unknown people" were the now-long-forgotten and thus nameless men and women of the Seine river basin.

Examples of these "unknowns" include traders; subsistence-level workers; officials supervising the boatmen; police officers; prostitutes; charlatans; monkey handlers; jugglers; millers; carpenters; water-carriers; fishermen; customs officers; and, finally, the lowest of the low, the down-on-their-luck men searching through the cold mud of the Seine with rakes or with their bare hands and feet, desperately hoping to find an earring, a ring, or any other small gold ornament carelessly lost by a rich traveler passing by in a boat.

In 1993 François Beaudouin (1929–2013), the founder of the French inland waterways museum on the Seine, namely, said that "the destiny of Paris is, above all, that of a river-city."[7]

Presented here in approximate chronological order and with a good deal of local French history and local color added, this account of the co-mingled stories of Paris and the Seine will offer the reader unique insights into the river's roles in earlier eras. It also speculates on its likely future in the years to come and provides information on the training today of apprentices in river navigation.

The chapters that follow are usually kept short for ease of reading but vary in length depending on the importance or the complexity of the subjects they discuss. Some chapters contain human interest or historical sketches that focus on a specific moment in time or give a unique insight into a character, an idea, or a setting. Probably the best example of such a sketch is on Joan of Arc (c. 1412–1431).

More than 250 endnotes are provided in this book for attribution and explanation. For simplicity and ease of reading, however, the endnotes are all presented in an informal format rather than in a dense scholarly format. Specifically, most of them are identified as being "after"—that is, following the work of, but not necessarily quoting *verbatim*, a given author. They appear here in English, often translated from the original French.

Ten short appendices offer information that is relevant and interesting but is best presented apart from the text itself in order to keep the text flowing smoothly.

Our only regret in writing this book is that it has been impossible because of the costs involved to include any of the many excellent maps and illustrations, often in vivid color, which visually document the history of the Seine in Paris. For this reason, although some of them are mentioned in the text, they have not been endnoted.

Introduction
Setting the Stage

Paris has a kaleidoscopic history. For example, a modern outline map tracing the story of Paris shows that the Seine has always divided it into two roughly equal halves. This reflects the ceaseless expansion of the city from its tiny beginnings in the 3rd century BC down to the present day.

Bird's-eye view engravings of the heart of Paris, for example, dating from 1619 and depicting the Seine upstream of the Louvre, reveal both a bustling commercial capital and a river very busy with boats large and small with their crews, and with longshoremen (manual workers in the ports) on the banks waiting to load or unload boat cargoes.[1]

It is worth noting that the word "port," as used in this book, means both "points on the bank of a river were ships and boats can unload and load their cargoes" and "maritime facilities located on the sea or in an estuary."

It is also important to remember that, in the Middle Ages, the word "boat" could refer to many different craft, ranging from a small eight-oared "cockboat," either used on its own or carried on the deck of a ship, to a 26-oared "great boat" that was towed behind a big ship. Oared boats were used extensively, both in business for transporting cargo and passengers, and in war for carrying soldiers from big ships to combat beaches.[2]

Although rarely documented in surviving illustrations or by archeological remains, the French rivers were also the scenes of a good deal of pleasure-boating for the aristocracy during the Middle Ages. These outings in summer usually included a professional boatman, a few passengers, and perhaps a lady singing and accompanying herself with a type of guitar, or by a musician playing a flute or some other small wind instrument.[3]

This high level of historic activity reminds us that among its many modern charms, Paris also has the merit of antiquity. In 2008, for example, a team of French archeologists, who were excavating a district of Paris close to the left bank of the Seine, discovered there the oldest human remains and the traces of the earliest known hunter-gatherer settlement in Paris. These early residents relied very heavily on the Seine for fishing and for transportation by dugout canoes, rafts, or other rudimentary watercraft. Fishing must have been very productive: as late as 1738, for example, a huge seven-foot-long sturgeon was netted in the Seine in downtown Paris, just off the cathedral of Notre-Dame.[4]

Archeological finds date the lives of these residents to the middle Neolithic period (4200–3500 BC), to the early Bronze Age (3500–1500 BC), and to the Iron Age (800–500 BC). The relevance of the Seine to Parisians has continued down to our own day and will certainly extend far beyond it.

From the Louvre to the Eiffel Tower, on the one hand, and from the Place de la Concorde to the Grand Palais and the Petit Palais, on the other, the evolution of Paris can best be seen and appreciated from the many vantage points offered by the Seine and especially by its 37 bridges and four footbridges, the latter, as the name indicates, being for pedestrian use only. Most of the bridges have starred, too, in the numerous international expositions held in Paris.

In this book, we have used these Paris bridges as convenient pegs on which to hang related historical events. This is appropriate because, as the modern French historians and atlas-writers Philippe Lorentz and Dany Sandron have pointed out, "Les ponts constituent l'un des facteurs déterminants du développement de Paris au cours de son histoire."[5] ("The bridges constitute one of determining factors in the development of Paris during the course of its history.")

Bridges have been one of the key factors encouraging the rise of Parisian power and influence throughout many centuries. By 1615, when one of the best early and relatively accurate maps of Paris was drawn up, there were already 12 bridges or other crossing-points shown over the Seine. Little by little, the purely commercial role they had played ever since the Middle Ages was expanded as they took on new and more modern duties instead as paths of communication, ideas, and urbanization. Most of our comments on them will be summarized in later pages of this book.

Due to the many floods (between 1733 and 1882 alone there were 55 floods of varying sizes), to thick ice in winter (an engraving of 1873 shows men harvesting ice from the Seine), to road and river accidents, and to occasional military conflicts, nearly all the original bridges in Paris have been replaced several times over the course of the passing years.[6] That said, all of them are worth mentioning briefly in this book because, without exception, they are all of some architectural or historical interest.

Setting the Stage

This famous river and its crossing-points have played key roles in the life of Paris ever since the earliest days of the first settlers, known as the Parisii. At that time, the Seine was much shallower in many places and was twice as wide as it is today. At what is now Paris, the river was very easy to bridge with timber and, perhaps equally important, this area did not attract any well-armed hostile forces.

The current there was slow, the banks were naturally low-lying and densely vegetated, and, in the absence of any external threat, the Parisii saw no need to exert themselves strenuously by building up any defenses. In short, it was easy enough for them to pursue a modest existence with their dugout canoes, first during the Iron Age and then, after 52 BCE, during the Roman era. In fact, Caesar mentions them in his commentary on the Gallic War; the modern city of Paris is named after them.

They initially used the Seine as their sole source of drinking water. Later, however, the Romans living there built an aqueduct that carried water down to the city by gravity-feed from the higher and less limestone-rich hills. Since pre–Roman times the Seine has always been an integral and colorful part of Paris life.

It has provided endless opportunities for commerce, travel, fishing, social life, art, literature, entertainment, and, more recently, anti-pollution studies. Today there are numerous iconic sights in Paris that can easily be seen from a tour boat on the Seine and which will be discussed later. They include the Eiffel Tower; the Île de la Cité (the "Island of the City"), including Notre-Dame and the Conciergerie; the Louvre; the Musée d'Orsay; and the Grand Palais and Petit Palais.

The Paris "water merchants" (the businessmen who bought and sold goods to be transported along the rivers of France), eventually formed a rich and politically powerful corporation, which was approved by the French king himself in 1170. It was given the major and highly valued monopoly of having "the sole right of commercial navigation" on the Seine between Paris and Mantes-la-Jolie, a key river port 30 miles downstream of Paris. Over time, it gradually won the right to conduct trade, too, on the higher reaches of the Seine upstream from Paris, e.g., at Nogent-sur-Seine.

It must be remembered here that, in France and elsewhere in Western Europe, the far-flung, large-scale, interlocking medieval network of rivers and roads led goods and people into and out of port cities, which in turn connected European communities to the rest of the world via international trade and financial exchanges.

It was in fact the widespread use of large numbers of small shallow-draft cargo boats that made heavy reliance on the Seine and other rivers possible at all. These boats also required constant maintenance of both the channels of the waterways themselves and their banks to make sure that the river's varying current could flow without any obstructions. This maintenance was vital not only for the cargo vessels themselves but also for all the watermill operators, fishermen and hunters, washerwomen, tanners and dyers, blacksmiths, and low-level administrative officers who depended on the Seine for their income.

In France, the official medieval seal of the water merchants depicted a Nordic-style river boat (a double-ended boat with a high bow and a high stern) rigged for sailing. Remarkably, this same seal is still used today on the official coat of arms of the city of Paris. It still bears the original Latin motto *Fluctuat nec mergitur* ("She [Paris] is tossed [by the waves], but does not sink").

The banks of the Seine are also the locations of many of the finest buildings of Paris. This book contains a good deal of information on the past and present status of these banks, which in Paris have for hundreds of years been exceptionally busy in handling cargo of all kinds, ranging from food products, wine, and hay to charcoal, firewood, and building materials. They have long been carefully documented, probably beginning with the Bâle map of 1552 which gave an extremely careful and detailed picture of the banks of Seine around the Île de la Cité.[7]

Today most of these banks are also wonderful places to stroll idly; to *boire un verre* ("to have a drink") at a local bar; to admire the old houseboats, e.g., the converted Freycinet 126-foot-long barges; and to experience what has been aptly called *la magie de la Seine* ("the magic of the Seine").[8]

It must not be forgotten that in Paris the traditional names of the "left bank" and the "right bank" of the river still carry a great deal of geographic, social, and political baggage. The left bank was initially devoted chiefly to activities centered on the making and distribution of wines, but beginning, in about the year 1200, it gradually evolved into a world-famous and much-beloved university complex as students and their professors began to settle there.

For example, in the Middle Ages, one English visitor, whose name has come down to us in French as Barthélemy l'Anglais (Barthelemy the Englishman), had these good things to say about the left bank:

> In Paris, clerics, bishops, professors, and students all lived only on the left bank. There Paris welcomed the newcomers from around the world who arrived there. Paris is a city where riches and consumer goods abound, well-presented and well-laid out for the clerics shopping there. The city also has fine lawns, fields, and hills full of beauty which refresh the students when their work tires them. The scholars live in beautiful homes set on lovely streets.[9]

The right bank, on the other hand, devoted itself to less scholarly but more lucrative and business undertakings. Both banks have been on

UNESCO's World Heritage List since 1991 and will be discussed again briefly in later pages.

By about 1870s, the Seine itself was both a watery social and political frontier between these two very different banks, and an exceptionally busy commercial channel—rolling through the very heart of Paris and always densely packed with peoples and vessels of various kinds who were setting off on their own missions.

Finally, we can note that along the Seine there were some very important traditional landing-spots (*grèves* in French), which were gently sloping curves in the sedimentary banks of the river where boats could moor safely to load or unload cargo or passengers. In the medieval era, boats arriving in or passing through Paris would always use these then-undeveloped coves. They became so useful over time, however, that their banks were inevitably built up and proper landing docks gradually appeared there.

From early times, the two banks of the Seine in Paris have been closely linked by bridges. The right bank, which was first settled by Parisians in about the year 1000, developed into a more conservative district than the left bank, which now attracts a younger, more artistic, and less affluent crowd. Ironically, at first the right bank was so muddy and so low-lying that it was sometimes *underwater* during big floods. Indeed, this now-elegant neighborhood was, and today part of it still is, known as *le Marais* (the Marsh).

An interesting footnote here is that much like the Seine in the Paris region, during the Roman era the lower part of the River Thames in England was also only a shallow waterway winding through the marshes. In the case of both rivers, many later centuries of human intervention have created what is now in effect a canal flowing between miles of solid stone walls. This development has transformed a former floodplain into a region where millions of people now very much want to live, work, and play.

Fundamentally, the physical setting of Paris has always been very appealing. Writing in about 1190, for example, the well-traveled visitor Guido de Bazoches, who will be described later, depicted it along the following lines:

> I am in Paris in that royal city where abundance of natural wealth not only holds those who live there, but also attracts those from afar. Just as the moon outshines the stars in brilliance, so does this city, the seat of the monarchy, lift her proud head above the rest. She lies in the embrace of an enchanting valley, surrounded by a crown of hills which Ceres and Bacchus [the gods of grain and wine] make fruitful.
>
> The Seine, proud river of the East, runs there in a brimming stream, and holds in its arms an island [the Île de la Cité] which is the head, the heart, the marrow of the whole city. Two suburbs extend to right and left, of which the

lesser alone rivals many cities. Each of these suburbs communicates with the island by two bridges of stone; the Grand Pont towards the north, on the side of the English Channel, and the Petit Pont towards the Loire.

The first—great, rich, trading—is the scene of seething [commercial] activity; innumerable ships surround it, filled with merchandise and riches. The Petit Pont belongs to the dialecticians [scholars], who walk there deep in argument. [The University of Paris was founded on the left bank in about 1200.] In the island [the Île de la Cité], by the side of the King's palace that dominates the whole city, is seen the palace of philosophy, where study reigns as the sole sovereign in a citadel of light and immortality.[10]

The Seine has always been used very heavily throughout the ages. For example, illustrations of the Seine off Pont Neuf (one of its most famous bridges) which were made in the first half of the 17th century show that then the river was already choked with large numbers of boats variously powered by oars, sails, and, in more confined waters, simply by paddling or poling.[11]

By 1715, the Seine was already clearly the lifeblood of Paris. Wine and, perhaps even more essentially, grain for making bread (the staple of the French diet) were brought into the city either by small boats known as *flettes* (these were tenders, or assistant-boats, to larger ships) or, more commonly, by large convoys of bigger boats 52 to 59 feet long.[12] These were so long and so cumbersome that they had to be pulled up the river by teams of 24 horses. Because they had such a small crew, they could neither repel any thieves nor force them to open any narrow passageways in the river which the thieves had blocked to immobilize the boats.

Listed from its source to its mouth, the Seine has 25 tributaries of various sizes. Some of the boats used on the upper Seine and on the Aube River, one of the biggest tributaries of the Seine, were quite remarkable. "Margotats," for example, were 32 feet to 42 feet long but only 5 feet wide. They were so long and so narrow, in fact, that they could only be navigated in *pairs*—that is, by being lashed together to prevent them from capsizing. Running downstream with the current, they could carry 26 tons of assorted cargo, but only 8 tons when being sailed, rowed, or hauled upstream by horses or by men.

At certain times of the year, however, (probably at times of low water to avoid any strong currents) some reaches of the Seine were dominated by the *marnois* ("Marne River boats"). These undecked ships varied in size. They could be up to 127 feet long by 22 feet wide, with rising bows and sterns, and could carry up to 50 tons of general cargo.

To help the steersman navigate them safely when they were very heavily laden, e.g., with tons of charcoal, some of them had unusually big rudders with extended tillers. They could also transport cereals and timber as separate cargoes. Marne boats could be propelled by poling, rowing, or towing by horses or by men.

The Seine was used, too, from the 16th century on, for transporting long "trains" of timber (*bois flotté*, that is, floating logs) down-river to market areas. These "trains" were flexible wooden rafts, assembled by using logs trimmed of their branches; cut into more-manageable 3-foot to 5-foot lengths in the riverside forests and then lashed or chained together to form rudimentary but unsinkable rafts which could easily be disassembled and sold upon reaching markets.[13] These are often depicted in c. 1800 paintings of the Seine near Pont-Neuf and elsewhere.

The first documented effort in France to turn this process into a sustainable and organized business seems to date from 1547. Whereas large amounts of wine and wheat could be produced on demand every year under good weather conditions, it required as much as 20 years for a harvested forest to regenerate itself fully.[14]

Moreover, transport of timber was not a very easy business because it required just the right amount of water in the river and involved many hazards. If the river was in full flood, for example, logs might get lodged so high up wooded hillsides that they could never be recovered economically. If, on the other hand, there was not enough water, however, either because there was a drought or because the river was iced up, it might take too long for very slow-moving logs to reach a marketplace in time for them to be sold at a good price.

There was no centralized headquarters in the logging business and there were no effective national or regional police forces in France. As a result, energetic petty thieves could easily intercept and dismantle these "trains" and then sell the logs. Moreover, at the end of their long, dangerous, and badly paid journeys, the raftsmen themselves—always poor and often in poor health, too, because they had to spend so much time tending logs by wading into cold rivers in all weathers—had no choice but to walk all the way uphill back to their simple homes.

At the very bottom of the Seine's economic and social pecking order were what we today might call the "homeless men." These were men who, for one reason or another, managed to survive—but then only barely—by searching through the cold mud of the Seine shoreline, hoping to find small bits of broken or lost gold buttons or, indeed, any metallic items that had some market value. In a French newspaper article of 1843, they were dismissed by successful longshoremen simply as being "pests."[15]

Today, over 60 percent of the Seine's length can be navigated by large commercial barges and by most tour boats as far upriver as Burgundy (a province about 200 miles upstream of Paris). Smaller recreational vessels can travel nearly its entire length.

For our purposes here, by far the most interesting part of the Seine in Paris itself lies between the Pont de Sully in the east, and the Pont d'Iéna near the Eiffel Tower in the west. Roughly 3½ miles long and totaling 901 acres in size, this stretch of the river includes 23 of the 37 famous bridges and footbridges in Paris over the Seine.

In 1991, UNESCO named this section of the Seine a World Heritage Cultural Site; it will be discussed at some length in the later pages. An excellent multicolor outline map of it and of 22 of the 37 bridges and footbridges over the Seine can be found on pp. 94–95 of the *Waterways Guide* to the Seine which is listed in the bibliography. A similar map appears on pp. 274–275 of the Eighth Edition of David Edward-May's account of *Inland Waterways of France*, which is also listed.

1

Welcome to the Seine

The Seine is a 485-mile-long river located in northern France. It drains an extensive lowland geographic region known as the Paris basin, which extends over most of northern France, includes part of Belgium, and in much of Paris is only about 90 feet above sea level. The Seine in Paris is an integral part of the landscape of this most famous capital city.

It was chiefly the Seine that encouraged and made it possible for France to centralize its political, economic, and cultural power by means of a network of rivers and canals spread throughout the country. The French historian Maxime du Camp (1822–1894) spelled out in detail in 1869 just why this was so.

The Seine, he wrote,

> is in communication with the Champagne region and Normandy; via the canals of the Loire and the Centre region it connects to the Loire and the Saône; via the Canal de Bourgogne, the Yonne and the Saône, it reaches the Rhône and from the Rhône to the Rhine; via the Canal de Saint-Quentin and the Oise, it is linked to the North; via the Canal Saint-Denis and the Canal de l'Ourcq; it corrects and cancels out the sharpest bends of its course, in the same way through the Canal Saint-Maur, the Marne avoids a slow detour and arrives at the large warehouses of Paris more quickly. As can be seen, through the canals the Seine has [access to] the East and the West; via the sea, coastal shipping and her mouth at Le Havre it has [access to] the West to which the South is reached by canals.[1]

The left bank of the Seine in Paris is higher and dryer than the right bank, and thus was populated much earlier. In Paris itself, the Seine has carved a big inverted "C"-shaped channel through a gentle low-lying valley which is bordered on the north and northeast, and on the south and southwest, by modest elevations known as *monceaux* (literally "heaps of earth").

A higher hill known as the *montagne Sainte-Geneviève* ("the mountain of Saint Geneviève") is located near where the River Bièvre had been diverted from its original course in 1148 by the monks of the abbey of Saint-Victor. After earlier decades of heavy pollution from the textile industry near Paris, this river now forms an unpolluted rainwater-control system and flows into the Seine near the Latin Quarter.

In rivers, sediments frequently accumulate in their beds. In modern times, they can harbor many persistent chemicals that harm both people and the environment. Today some parts of the Seine river basin are still polluted by industrial activities, by urban runoff, by the continuing growth of the city of Paris itself and its suburbs, and by the residues of partygoers after romantic Saturday nights.

To ensure safe navigable waters, the rivers and other waterways of Paris must be dredged. The polluted sediments must then be carried by barges to a wet disposal site, where the dredged material is mixed with cleaner Seine water and is then pumped into a receiving site. A significant problem with this process is that such pumping-and-dumping may release into cleaner waters some of the contaminants held in the original polluted sediments.[2]

Historically, the Seine was exceptionally difficult to navigate under its original free-flowing conditions, both due to its very limited depths during times of low flows, to the strength of the river's current in times of high water, and to the places where it runs under narrow bridges even in times of normal flows.[3]

The average depth of the Seine today in Paris is about 31 feet. Until locks were built in the 1800s to raise the water level, the river within Paris itself, as shown by many contemporary illustrations, was much shallower, consisting only of one small channel of gently flowing water, bordered by low sandy banks.

Indeed, at that time, teams of up to two dozen heavy horses had to be used to drag convoys of 59-foot-long cargo-carrying river boats upstream through the Seine's shallows. More rarely, two-oxen teams could be used instead.

These ox teams had the great advantage of having the hauling-rope attached to the top of the boat's mast, rather than to the bow of the boat as was necessary when using horses. This gave the boatman much more flexibility in steering and meant that he would not always be blocked by small obstacles in the river directly in front of his vessel but could steer around them. Not infrequently, any of these convoys could easily be robbed when their passage on the river was blocked by thieves.

In any case, transport upstream was never very easy. Near the Seine-side town of Vernon, for example, before 1854 up to 30 horses and 100 human haulers were sometimes needed to pull a boat upstream under a bridge against a stiff current.

Several proposals were put forward to dredge a reliable all-weather channel in the Seine during the late 18th century, but no progress was made until after a moveable weir had been invented in 1820 and could then be used to regulate the depth of the river at any given time or place.

This was a critically important development. It permitted construction work to be undertaken to canalize the Seine and other rivers, thus giving cargo boats invaluable access to many other parts of the river and canal network.

As shown in some of the historical illustrations, canalization of the Seine was already well underway by 1830. When it was finally accomplished, it was very likely that there would always be enough water in the canal "to float your boat," even when the water level in the Seine was low. Moreover, its now well-defined safe channel prevented boats from venturing out onto shallow parts of the waterway where they were likely to run aground.

Canalization came none too soon. An illustration from about 1830, for example, shows a very peaceful bucolic scene in which cows are grazing on the muddy banks and in the very shallow waters of the Seine. However, the cows are right next to cargo boats moored there "three up," which means that they are moored side-to-side at right angles to the shoreline and thus protrude out into the river.

The problem here was that in the shallowest parts of the Seine that were still too deep for cattle to graze, these curves encouraged grass to grow in them, thus effectively reducing both the width and the depth of the navigable channel. By making grazing impossible, mooring "three-up" could have the same effect.[4]

Five locks and weirs were built on the Lower Seine, beginning in the 1840s, which guaranteed that there would always be more than 5 feet of water on that part of the river. Much more river-engineering work was done over the coming years, culminating in 1957–1964 with new lock chambers having a cill depth of over 16 feet all the way to Paris. (A cill, also spelled sill, is a narrow horizontal ledge protruding a short way into a lock chamber from below the upper gates of the lock. The greater the cill depth, the bigger a boat that such a lock can handle safely.)

The Seine itself rises very gently and unobtrusively in the low hills of the Côte d'Or ("Gold Coast" so named for the golden color of the grapevines there in the autumn) at a spot known as Source-Seine ("Source of the Seine"). The nascent river lies in a field of many small springs about 19 miles northwest of the city of Dijon (famous for its mustard) in northeastern France.

A grotto has been built on the field on land owned by the city of Paris since 1864. Ancient small statues of a nymph, a dog, and a dragon have been found there, as have the buried remains of a Gallo-Roman temple dedicated to the *dea Sequana*, namely, the "Seine goddess." The little statues of this divinity also found there are now on public exhibition in the archaeological museum of Dijon.

During the Gallo-Roman era, the mini-city of Paris, nestled along the Seine and centered on the island known as the Île de la Cité, had only a handful of attractions. These were limited to a temple on the island; three public baths; a theater; a forum; and an amphitheater, all linked by well-built Roman roads. The River Bièvre flowed through the city at that time and ran into the Seine.[5]

The infant Seine now grows slowly from its headwaters and then, usually gradually, flows through the very heart of Paris, finally discharging into the English Channel near the major French port-city of Le Havre. The length of the Seine from Paris to the seaward limit of the Seine estuary near Le Havre on the English Channel is about 216 miles.

Compared with the major rivers of the world, the Seine is never of very impressive proportions. Its highest point is just 79 feet above sea level, some 277 miles upstream from the mouth of the river. Thanks to its many locks and weirs, it is usually slow-flowing and it is not hard for well-trained and well-equipped boatmen to navigate it safely, except during the rare times of very high water, when it is legally necessary for all boats to stay off the river.

Traditionally, Parisians know the river is in flood when the feet and legs of "the Zouave"—a large stone statue, made in 1856 of a French soldier in a regiment in North Africa and now installed under the Pont de l'Alma of the Seine—are underwater. During the huge flood of 1910, the Seine was even lapping at his head, having risen to 28 feet above its normal level.

A contemporary photo of this flood shows a wrecked and flooded boat-rental office—with a plaintive sign still on it advertising "Pianos on board." During this event, so many official buildings in Paris were flooded that senior civil servants had be taken around the city in rowboats so that they could discharge their duties.

Because of the poor state of roads in rural France and despite the risks variously posed by floods, low water, or ice, the Seine was for many generations the most practical, the cheapest, and the fastest way to transport a great many essential items throughout the Seine basin.

These included foodstuffs and wine; wood for the innumerable fireplaces; hay for horses and other livestock (about 200 horses were brought into Paris early each morning to be harnessed to carts delivering foodstuffs and other supplies within the city); building materials and supplies for an ever-growing population; and sizeable numbers of travelers themselves.

A contemporary tabulation in 1899, for example, showed that 294 boats went up the Seine every day, and 291 boats came down it. These included 210 passenger steam boats which, together with other boats powered by currents, winds, oars, horses, or by even steam-driven chains lying on the bed of the river, could carry an average of 10,000 passengers in 12 working hours.[6]

Today, the Seine is artificially and for purposes of navigational convenience divided into five sequential parts. Their names, counting downstream from their sources to the river's merger with the English Channel, are as follows:

- The *Petite Seine* ("Small Seine"), from the river's sources to Montereau-Fault-Yonne.
- The *Haute Seine* ("Upper Seine"), from Montereau-Fault-Yonne to Paris.
- The 8-mile-long *Traversée de Paris* ("the crossing of Paris" or "the Paris waterway") is the most important section of the Seine for the purposes of this book. Its depth varies, especially after heavy rain, but usually ranges there from about 8.5 feet to 12.7 feet. The navigation channel is usually dredged to a minimum depth of about 11.5 feet.
- A modern guidebook on this reach of the river—the text of which has been lightly annotated here to stress safety issues—warns the skipper as follows:

    This trip on the Seine provides magic moments and an unforgettable spectacle—*provided that* it is done only under the best navigating conditions. The background is magnificent, and each of the buildings beside the river is usually more stunning than the next.

    But this spectacular scenery is very popular not only with tourists but also with all the intense river traffic of *the working Seine itself*, e.g., barges; push-tow convoys, up to 590 feet long and often heavily laden with sand for construction purposes; crowded passenger vessels; and low-profile coasters (ships that usually trade with nearby coastal ports). Most of these ships can generate very heavy wakes, thus making small-boat navigation difficult and sometimes very dangerous.

    As a result, navigation in the middle of all this dense traffic must always be done with the greatest care and precision. The skipper must always keep a constant eye on surrounding boats. No question here of "playing the tourist" by slowing down or zigzagging to take photos while also steering the boat!

    At the same time, the crew must keep a very sharp eye on boats coming up from astern. The skipper is most strongly advised to abide by all the navigational rules carefully laid out by the City of Paris.[7]

- The *Basse Seine* ("Lower Seine"), from Paris to Rouen, which was fully canalized by the end of the 19th century, permitting

- a high degree of the industrialization generated by ships and railroads.
- The *Seine maritime* ("Maritime Seine"), from Rouen to the English Channel.

The Seine is now navigable by ocean-going ships as far upriver as Rouen, which is 75 miles from the English Channel, and then much further upstream only by a variety of shallow-draft barges, tour boats, and private recreational vessels. In Paris itself, excursion boats offer many sightseeing tours of the Seine and are extremely popular with visitors.

In its progress toward the sea, the Seine meanders by former ancient nomadic campsites, Roman towns, Viking forts, medieval chateaux, monastic abbeys, landscapes treasured by artists, and World War II battlefields. Its importance to France prompted the French leader Napoleon Bonaparte to assert, in 1802, that the three key cities of Paris, Rouen, and Le Havre "are all the same city, of which the Seine is the major highway."[8]

Today the Seine flows about eight miles through central Paris, where, as noted earlier, its average depth is about 31 feet. In some reaches, its width ranges from about 65 feet to 656 feet. Until locks were installed in the 1800s to raise the level of the river and thus make it more navigable, however, the Seine was much shallower and much narrower than it is now. Because of its shallows during the frequent periods of low flows, navigation on it was historically very difficult. As mentioned earlier, teams of strong horses had to be used to tug the heavily laden cargo boats through the shallowest reaches.

A later French report of 1910 on "Les Ports de Paris" ("The Ports of Paris") mentions some long-standing problems encountered when navigating the Seine at that time, which the report tells us were not overcome until river-control measures were undertaken in the middle of the 19th century.

These problems included the following:

1. Difficulties affecting water levels, namely, floods, freezing conditions, and droughts. During the dry season of August, Parisians could often simply wade across the Seine at the shallow arm of the river known as *le bras de la Monnaie* because the current was so weak there. That said, at times of high water, boatmen feared this same arm of the river because it was so dangerous then.
2. The silting-up of the Seine downstream of the Île de la Cité. This led to related problems: e.g., the greater power of the current in certain narrower sections of the river, and the erosion of the banks of the river, which narrowed the navigable channel and made it harder

for boatmen to land safely at formal ports, such as the Louvre, or at the makeshift ports, in order to load or unload their cargo or passengers.

3. Navigation problems caused by population densities arose as well. With ever-more people in Paris, more bridges were needed. The pillars of these bridges could cause new problems, for example, the infamous *arche au Diable* ("the Devil's arch") of the bridge of Notre-Dame during the second half of the 19th century. In addition, the numerous watermills installed on and under the bridges, and the huge pumps built there to provide water for Paris, also reduced the space needed for safe boat transit close to them. Finally, the many "laundry boats" moored in the Seine (there were about 100 of them in the 19th century) were hazards to navigation, too. They will be discussed in a later endnote.

On the plus side of the coin, the decision to dredge and thus deepen the bed of the Seine to limit the impacts of floods also made navigation safer because so much sand was removed during this process. After about 1846, the decision to raise the height of the quays helped, too, as did the building the Suresnes lock in 1866, which permitted a higher level of the river there.

Although the average flow of the river in Paris is relatively slow (only a few cubic meters per second) it must be remembered that much higher flows do occur during times of heavy rain and heavy runoff.

For example, in 1296, a flood of epic proportions carried away virtually all the bridges of Paris, which at that point had many heavy, multi-storied, densely occupied houses built right on top them, side-by-side. A surviving illustration from that era shows both the Grand Pont and the Petit Pont of Paris being swept downstream by this flood, resulting in a heavy loss of life.[9] Another illustration, this time from 1576, shows that more than 30 houses were still being built side-by-side right on the Pont Notre-Dame.[10]

Nevertheless, such river-lessons fell on deaf ears: the bridges of Paris would remain covered by such vulnerable cheek-by-jowl housing until the 1780s.

In more modern times, extensive flooding has occurred in 1801–1802, 1910, 1924, 1955, 1982, 1999–2000, 2016, and 2018. The 2018 rise of the Seine was chiefly caused by more rainfall due climate change, which is a broader and more accurate term than global warming. This is certain to be an ever-increasing world-wide problem, not only for Paris but also for many other cities and countries as well.

Major dredging work and the construction of bigger locks and weirs did not begin on the Seine until the 1840s and continued at least through

1957–1964. Today, only the highest upriver section of the Seine remains to be upgraded to modern and deeper French river standards.

For many years the Seine in Paris was very seriously polluted—indeed, it was even declared to be "environmentally dead"—and was a great health hazard and a real eyesore. In 1853, however, Baron Georges Eugène Haussmann (1809–1891) was named to be *Préfect de la Seine*, that is, the official in charge of the river.

Under the auspices of Emperor Napoleon III (1808–1873), Haussmann embarked on a very ambitious plan to upgrade both the Seine itself in Paris and many of the pestilential old narrow adjacent streets adjacent to it. His modernizing improvements were in fact so extensive that both his contemporaries and later generations would accurately refer to them as the "haussmannization" of the city—and not always in a flattering light.

When he began his work, the mid–nineteenth-century historic center of Paris along the Seine had not changed very much since the Middle Ages. The streets were still charming from a visitor's point of view but, more objectively, were also narrow, filthy, unlit at night and therefore dangerous, and a wonderful breeding ground for all kinds of disease.

The major catalyst for radical change was Emperor Louis-Napoleon Bonaparte's exile in England from 1846 to 1848, where he was greatly impressed by the western districts of London, which had been entirely rebuilt in the wake of the great fire of 1666.

London would subsequently become the poster child for good hygiene and for modern urban planning affecting the Seine. The emperor wanted to make Paris just as prestigious as London. Haussmann therefore set to work at once to make this happen, taking his cue from the motto of his French campaign, which promised "Paris embellished, Paris enlarged, Paris cleansed."

As part of this massive and expensive project, Haussmann built or rebuilt three major sites near the Seine on the Île de la Cité.

The most impressive of these was the big Hôtel-Dieu hospital, an earlier version of which had been destroyed by a great fire in 1772. Under the leadership of the cathedral of Notre-Dame, this had become by far the largest hospital in France by the end of the Middle Ages. It was staffed by 110 religious brothers and sisters, who cared for between 400 and 500 patients (often two patients to one bed), organized into five wings of the establishment.

This hospital was also the subject of a dramatic painting by the Seine-based French artist Raguenet, who is still celebrated today for the fullness, precision, and beautiful coloring of his many works set on the Seine.[11]

Haussmann also built or rebuilt on the Île de la Cité both the Préfecture of Police and the Tribunal de Commerce. He was in fact a creator of the still much-admired architecture of Paris, which imposed very strict esthetic and construction standards on mansions and other expensive buildings rising in Paris.

These same standards were in fact so good that they were applied, too, in many other French and foreign cities, e.g., in Marseille, Algiers (then a French colony), Brussels, Rome, Barcelona, Madrid, Buenos Aires, and Stockholm.

Haussmann began reconstructing Paris by demolishing most of the rundown medieval houses still standing along the Seine, which were really nothing more than unhealthy slums, and replacing them with wide, long, straight boulevards graced by grand and uniform buildings. In addition, he built or repaired 18 bridges over the Seine in only 20 years (1848–1877). The net result of his herculean efforts was that Paris could now take its rightful place as one of the greatest capitals of Europe.[12]

Haussmann and his successors also committed themselves to the challenging job of building formidable quays (wharfs) along the Seine in Paris itself. Earlier quays, such as the simple fifteenth-century version shown in the illuminated manuscript *Très riches Heures du duc de Berry*, which will be discussed later, might well have had a few stone steps running down from an adjacent castle to the river's edge, but they lacked any facilities to handle cargo or numerous passengers.

People and architecture. A different view of architecture and people relaxing along the Seine. In Paris, the Seine and the buildings go well together.

By the end of the 18th century, the quays along some of the key points in the Seine, e.g., near the Pont-au-Change, were already at least 15 feet high, designed both to prevent flooding and to stabilize the soil along the river.

Haussmann's vastly improved quays were strong stone platforms built alongside the banks of the river and projecting out into the Seine itself. They were very well-designed for loading and unloading cargo from moored ships; for facilitating, as staging platforms, the building of bridges, locks, and dams; and for making it much easier and safer to dredge the channel of the river to improve navigation for deeper-draft ships.

Indeed, it was widely said that Haussmann and his men had successfully "domesticated" the river in Paris (except in times of great floods) by narrowing it down and by forcing it to flow only between his monumental stone quays.

In point of historical fact, he and other French officials succeeded quite magnificently in their efforts. As mentioned in the Preface, the central part of the Seine, located in Paris between the Pont d'Iéna near the Eiffel Tower in the west and the Pont de Sully in the east, is by far the most famous and the most scenic section of the river.

Many other parts of the river are home to a wide range of highly developed commercial, industrial, or agricultural enterprises. These are, of course, economically very important but, visually, they can be very depressing to a visitor's eye: they also degrade the environmental quality of the river wherever they exist.

Although water purification measures began in the 1990s and some significant improvements in water quality have been made since then, the urban sections of the Seine can still be heavily polluted by sanitary sewer overflows, industrial activity, and surface runoff.

Every summer since 2002, from the end of July to the end of August an event known as Paris-Plages ("Paris Beaches") has been held on the banks of the Seine.

This is the result of a campaign, initially headed by the then-mayor of Paris Bertrand Delanoë. He wanted to transform these banks, which had been totally "confiscated" by the very dense motor vehicle traffic of Paris, which ranges from heavy trucks to light motor scooters, into a more pedestrian-and-environmental-friendly asset for Parisians and for visitors to the city. Paris-Plages therefore brings in truckloads of sand to transform 1.9 miles of the paved banks of the river into a sandy public beach to be used for sunbathing and entertainment.

One chief purpose of this program is to make it possible for Parisians who might not be able themselves to afford to go to a real beach during the summer to enjoy a modest but still quite enjoyable "beach scene" in Paris

1. Welcome to the Seine

Gaily decorated classic Vespa motor scooter. Because road traffic in Paris is so congested and parking there is so difficult, scooters, motorcycles, or bikes are preferred by many commuters.

itself. Paris-Plages is in fact part of a broader program designed "to return the banks of the river to pedestrians, to diversify use of the river, and to organize a range of activities relating to sports, culture, and nature."[13]

As one of its supporters has written:

> Paris Plages: a day at the beach in the heart of the city! All that matters is the present moment; activities are ruled by the rhythm of the stroll and the course of the sun. The visitor becomes an actor on a scene offered to other visitors, discovering enchanted places and the pleasure of spontaneous encounters, drifting with the stream....[14]

Many supporters of the Seine, including the present Mayor of Paris, Anne Hidalgo, hope that the Seine itself will be clean enough to permit swimming and diving competitions to be held in Paris after the 2024 Summer Olympics.

Mayor Hidalgo's plans are to have three river bathing areas open to the public in 2225. These sites—opposite the central Île Saint-Louis in central Paris, by the Quai de Grenelle in the 15th arrondissement to the West, and at Bercy in the eastern 12th arrondissement—will be monitored by lifeguards and marked by buoys. The bathing zones will also provide places for swimmers to shower, change their clothes, and keep their belongings safe.

Regardless of how this remarkable experiment fares, it is clear today that the hub of inland waterways transport for non-ocean-going ships in the Seine basin will continue to be the river port of Conflans-Sainte Honorine, located about 22 miles downstream of Paris.

According to local legend, Honorine was a young virgin who had converted to the Christian faith and who was martyred in what is now Normandy. Her body was thrown into the Seine but was recovered and was buried somewhere downstream.

In 876, fleeing the Vikings, who at various times were both pirates and explorers, the local residents transported her remains to the confluence of the Seine and the River Oise, where a chapel was built in her honor. Buried beside Saint Nicholas, she is now the patron saint of the "barge people" (the men and women who work on the Seine) and is believed to keep a compassionate and watchful eye on all the users of the rivers of France.[15]

Perhaps a more-modern day miracle about the Seine is that it was only this river that saved Notre-Dame de Paris, the world-famous cathedral of Paris, from certain and total destruction during the raging fire of 2019. Both this horrific blaze, which destroyed a large part of the roof and the spire of the cathedral, and the history of the cathedral itself, will be discussed in later pages.

2

From the Beginnings of Paris

Some of the lands bordering the Seine have been continuously if only lightly inhabited since the Middle Paleolithic era from 130,000 to 40,000 years ago. This proves them to be among the first human settlements anywhere in Europe.

In this chapter we can draw on, albeit it only very briefly, many centuries of Parisian history. Early highlights in this story include the first human settlements in France; dugout canoes; a river goddess; Romans; Vikings; and the growth of Paris itself during the Middle Ages.

French scholars have been studying the first human settlements in Europe, which have been found at Éricourt-Manancourt, a small town located in the Somme department in Hauts-de-France near the northeast coast of France.

Their research is part of the work being done by the French government's inland waterways agency, which is the largest in Europe. Known as Voies Navigables de France (VNF, meaning "Navigable Waterways of France"), it is also focusing on preparations for the construction of the new and ambitious cross-border Seine-Nord Europe Canal. This canal, which will be discussed in later pages, will connect the Seine and the Scheldt rivers and will provide continuous wide-gauge inland navigation from Le Havre to the Belgian port city of Antwerp.

VNF is the French navigation authority responsible for the management of the majority of France's extensive inland waterway network and all of its associated facilities, e.g., towpaths, commercial and leisure ports, lock-keepers' houses, and related structures. The headquarters of VNF are in Béthune, Pas-de-Calais, with local offices throughout France.

The VNF's open-air archeological site at Erincourt-Manancourt consists of at least five prehistoric levels extending over a period of 300,000 to 80,000 years ago. The most recent level, dated to 80,000 years ago, shows that Neanderthals lived there during the late phase Middle Paleolithic period. About 20 sites from this era have already been found in northern France.

The oldest and richest archeological level at Erincourt-Manancourt is dated to 300,000 years ago and contains several hundred flaked flint artifacts, including bifaces, the most emblematic tool type of this era. (A biface is a stone that has had flakes chipped off from both sides, thus turning it into a primitive two-sided hand-held blade.)

Numerous bifaces were made by local hominids (the first modern humans evolved from these hominid predecessors between 200,000 and 300,000 years ago), who used them to cut up animals they had killed and then threw the bifaces away when they had become too dull to cut any more.

The Neolithic period stretched from 12,000 to 2,000 years ago. In 1991, when Paris undertook a large-scale urban-renewal project in the Bercy neighborhood along the eastern edge of the right bank of the Seine about two miles from Paris, traces of Neolithic wooden huts and jetties were unearthed. Even more marvelous to relate, the remains of 10 long shallow Neolithic dugout canoes, known as pirogues, were found there, too.[1]

One of these surviving pirogues, labeled by modern curators as Number PO6, was carved by stone tools from a single piece of oak between 6,400 and 6,800 years ago. It is the first boat known to have been used on the Seine, and was made and used by hunter-gatherers who lived in the Seine and Yonne River basins. These Neolithic men and women are considered to have been the first Europeans to settle down and build primitive camps along these rivers. Today, experts believe that there they farmed, raised livestock, fished, and hunted such animals as wild boar, deer, beavers, turtles, and wolves.

A small Gallic island-settlement, then known as Lutetia (or Lutèce in French) and now known as Paris, existed in the middle of the Seine on the Île de la Cité at least since the 3rd century BC. It has been jokingly described by a modern French scholar as "a bit of Mediterranean urbanism implanted on the banks of the Seine."[2] One example of this charming urbanism today is the *Quai aux Fleurs* ("Quay or wharf of flowers") in Paris, so named for its proximity to a flower market.

The Île de la Cité was the birthplace of Paris and is still, without any possible doubt, one of the most magnificent and most beautiful parts of the city. In its early years because of its central geographic location, the Île de la Cité had to defend itself against attacks. It could do this most easily by stretching two long heavy chains, supported by floats to make them visible and easier to handle, across the Seine between (1) the Tour (Tower) de Nesle and the Tour du Coin in the west, and between (2) La Tournelle and

2. From the Beginnings of Paris

Flowers left by a bridge on a lock speak to the importance of the Seine for social and emotional reasons.

the Tour Barbeau in the east. The purpose of these chains was two-fold: to stop any ship-borne military assault on the city, and to regulate the flow of commercial ship traffic in the Seine if need be.

Remarkably, at a time when Paris street and city lighting—let alone

Seine river lighting—did not exist, a big lantern hanging over the river permitted both the river and its nearby banks to be kept under surveillance at night by the authorities.

The Île de la Cité played a leading role in medieval illustrations—most notably, for example, in a very fine illuminated manuscript of 1317 dealing with the Seine, which has been conserved in Paris in the Bibliothèque national (the National Library) under the title of *Vie de saint Denis (Life of Saint Denis)*.[3]

It has some unique and truly excellent color illustrations of contemporary boats and bridges, such as those transporting and selling wine, wood, and fish on the Seine. It also shows the watermills built on the bridge itself, designed to grind grain into flour for Paris millers, plus many other remarkable depictions of pre-modern, Seine-centered, life in Paris.

For example, one such illustration shows that, on an upstairs floor of an impressive building overlooking the Seine, prosperous Parisians are living an elegant lifestyle, while down at the river's edge, far below them physically and socially, common laborers are working hard carrying up bundles of firewood to keep their "elders and betters" upstairs dry and warm.

In another illustration, *Prédication de saint Denis aux Parisiens qui brisent leurs idoles* ("Saint Denis preaching to Parisians who are breaking their idols"), the words of Saint Denis in favor of Christianity have had such a strong impact on the "pagan" Parisians listening to them that they respond by breaking the idols they had previously worshiped.[4]

The attractions of this location were that it was on the main river trade route (via the Seine and the Rhone rivers) between Britain and the rich Roman colony of Provence on the Mediterranean Sea. Moreover, it was also the easiest place to cross the Seine (being both relatively narrow and shallow) and was thus the ideal site on which to build simple bridges and to make travelers pay to use them.

The Roman Emperor Julian, who ruled from 361 to 363, was a noted philosopher and an author in Greek. His advocacy of Neoplatonic Hellenism (Greek philosophic thought), however, led him to reject Christianity. This earned him the name by which he now is best known in Christian history, namely, as Julian the Apostate.

Julian took great comfort from being stationed at Lutetia before he came to power, and he wrote very warmly about it in 358 along the following lines:

> I was at that time living in winter quarters at my dear Lutetia: this is what the Celts [the local inhabitants] call this tiny village of the Parisii. It is a little island sticking out into the Seine, which surrounds it on all sides, and has two wooden bridges linking it to the mainland.

The river is very constant: the flow rarely diminishes or increases. Its water is limpid and pretty to see and good to drink. Because Lututia is an island, the inhabitants must draw their drinking water directly from the river....

They have also good vineyards and some of the locals even have fig trees, which they keep from freezing during the winter by wrapping them in a mantle of straw or some other substance to keep out the cold air.[5]

The inhabitants of Lutetia were sufficiently prosperous and were so well known that their gold coins were accepted for use in trade across Europe. This trade was an international business: coins from cities along the Rhine and the Danube, as well as from Spain, have been found in excavations of Lutetia. The workmanship and good taste of Lutetia's artisans, who also fabricated jewelry and fine ornaments, spread throughout the Roman province of Gaul (modern-day France and some of its adjacent areas).

Even before Rome ruled Gaul beginning in the 1st century BC, however, pilgrims came to the river's source to worship and to leave their offerings at the temple of the river goddess, who was known as Sequana. This Latin name was given to the river as well: both divinity and river were therefore known as "Sequana."

When Rome ruled the Seine basin, the Greek geographer, philosopher, and historian Strabo (64 or 63 BC–c. 24 AD) defined the Seine in very appreciative terms. It was, he tells us, "one of most beautiful commercial-pathways ever formed by nature," linking regions in what is now France with markets on the Mediterranean, the English Channel, and the North Sea.[6]

A long paved Roman road, known locally as "the highway of Julius Caesar," extended from Harfleur on the English Channel to Paris. Many other but lesser Roman roads also threaded their way throughout the Seine basin.

The abbey of Sainte-Geneviève in Paris, said to have been built in 502 by Clovis, the king of the Franks, and his queen, Clotilde, was a center of religious scholarship in the Middle Ages. Clovis and his wife were both buried there, and the patron saint of Paris, Saint Geneviève, often went there to pray. When she died in 512, her remains were buried in the abbey church near the tomb of Clovis and were brought out of the tomb only when they were believed to be needed as spiritual props to deter the ferocious Vikings or other mortal dangers threatened Paris itself.

A fine painting of Saint Geneviève symbolically praying while kneeling on top of the two towers of the cathedral of Notre-Dame—a work by Maître de Dunois of about 1440—clearly shows the layout of the very busy Île de la Cité, as well as some of its citizens and a passenger-boat on the Seine downstream from one of the three bridges there across the river. These bridges are Pont Notre-Dame, Pont au Meuniers, and Pont Saint-Michel.[7]

During the reign of Clovis, in 508 Paris became the capital of the kingdom of the Franks. Thanks to its favorable geographic location, it was economically very active. It not only profited from a key river but also from a far-flung network of trade routes. These trade routes served the north (the English Channel); the west (Rouen, Nantes, and Tours); the south (Orléans and Italy); and the east (Metz and Germany).[8]

Nevertheless, despite spiritual precautions by the Parisians which will be discussed later in this book, the Vikings still managed to raid Paris three times during the 9th century. Luckily, the very heart of Paris, the Île de la Cité, was protected by the river itself. This gave the undefended abbey a little bit of protection, but not enough: it was sacked and all the books of its library were destroyed, carried away, or were otherwise lost forever.

The Viking incursions also had a more positive aspect, however. By 911, the Viking chieftain Rolf, also known as Rollo, already had a long career as a Viking raider, not only in France but in Scotland and Ireland, too.

He and his followers now exercised, by right of conquest, *de facto* control of a considerable amount of land in the valley of the lower Seine. As a result, in 911 he was formally accepted by the Carolingian king, Charles the Simple (here "Simple" means "straightforward"), as the Duke of Normandy. Rollo and his followers agreed to convert to Christianity, to settle near the mouth of the Seine, and to protect the area against other Vikings. Under the terms of their agreement, this part of Aquitaine thus became a virtually independent kingdom. However, Rollo still recognized, if only in theory, the suzerainty (the formal overlordship) of the king himself over Aquitaine.

Furthermore, as proof of his now being officially accepted by the French government, Rollo became a Christian and had himself baptized by the archbishop of Rouen. He and his Vikings thus became permanent Christian residents, rather than just temporary pagan invaders, in what is still known today as Normandy.

By the 10th century, Paris itself was still only a very modest provincial cathedral city of no major political or economic importance whatsoever. However, under the leadership of the kings of the Capetian dynasty, who were in power in France between 987 and 1328, the city burgeoned into the dominant commercial, religious, and royal center of the whole of France.

Commerce, not agriculture or military conquest, was the now the major source of wealth in medieval Paris. It was usually generated—or at least considerably helped along—by the presence of the Seine.

In 1053, for example, a large religious fair in the Paris area, known as the Lendit fair, first welcomed the public. Its name derives from the Latin word *indictum*, that is, a proclamation of when the fair would be held.[9]

The fair owed its start to the public display of some of the most important religious relics of Christ, which were kept in the medieval Benedictine monastery of Saint-Denis, located in a northern section of Paris along the Seine. Special "indulgences" (remissions of sins) were granted to all who came to the monastery to see them.

This monastery, which had been the burial place of the kings of France, is still of major importance today in the history of architecture, being the first major building to herald the transition from the Romanesque style to the Gothic style. Because of the enormous visual and historical importance of the architecture of Paris, some of its highlights will be discussed separately in Appendix 1 so that they do not overshadow the rest of text.

The initial display of the relics at this monastery proved to be so popular that it was expanded in scope over the coming years and gradually evolved into a major fair that attracted a great many merchants. They happily used the Seine (and overland transport, too) in order to provide sufficient food, goods, and household items to satisfy the needs of the growing number of pilgrims.

The opening of this fair was traditionally announced by the Bishop of Paris, who blessed the pilgrims while he was symbolically standing on the Tournelle, a small low building erected in the center of the fairground. A poem from the first half of the 14th century lists the many towns from which the merchants came. These were chiefly towns in northern France that specialized in producing cloth, but the Lendit fair was also a key market for horses, livestock, and for the sheep needed for local wool-making.

Later, this open-air fair would be superseded by a large covered market on the right bank of the Seine known as *Les Halles* ("The Halls"). In Paris, *Les Halles* was only about 500 yards from the Seine. Many goods and services both from local ports and from local shops were actively bought and sold in or close to *Les Halles*. These included barber services, leather goods, pottery, cutlery, armor, textiles, wheat, meats, hay, wine, apples, salt, and fish.

This became one of the richest and most densely populated *quartiers* (neighborhoods) of Paris, not only because of all the products being offered for sale there but also because the *Fontaine des Innocents* (a historical fountain of drinking water probably drawn from a well dug into one of the banks of the Seine) was a central meeting-and-greeting point there.[10]

During this time, too, cargo-carrying boats on the Seine became much more important. In 1121, for example, King Louis VI granted to the leaders of the boatmen of Paris a sizeable bonus (60 *sous*) for each boatload of wine that arrived safely in the city during the wine harvest.

In 1210, these entrepreneurs, using the image of a single-masted medieval river ship known as a *nef* as their official seal and coat of arms, set up the *Hanse des marchands de l'eau* ("Corporation of merchants trading goods via the waterways"), which would later expand into many other lines of business.

A later version of this seal and coat of arms, dating from about 1358, again shows a *nef*—but now with much more complicated rigging and even with a Viking-style carving of a dragon's head mounted on its bow. By 1416, a *nef* was also being shown on the official stationery of the City of Paris as proof of the authenticity of any document so marked.

The *Hanse* gradually amassed more and more power as membership in it was deemed to be essential for successful trading along the Seine. Indeed, by 1260–1261, the *Hanse* had evolved into a political body—what today we would term "an interest group"—represented by the chief of the merchant guild. It also held a seat in the influential *Parloir aux bourgeois* (the senior Chamber of Commerce for the businessmen of Paris) and was specifically approved by King Philippe Augustus, who reigned from 1180 to 1223 and who himself was deeply interested in conditions in Paris—in order to be sure that he remained in power.

His desire to improve living conditions there extended even to the streets of the city. It is said that he loved to contemplate the flowing Seine from the windows of his palace, which overlooked it, but that he was so offended by the terrible smells emanating from the streets, which were nothing more than semi-open muddy and garbage-strewn sewers, that he gave orders that the streets should be paved.

The *Hanse* itself won even more power under the leadership of Étienne Boileau, the *Prévôt* (leader) of the merchants, who did a great deal of work to support the king.

For example, he compiled a *Livre des métiers* ("Official list of occupations in Paris"). Centers of these occupations were often located within or close to the Île de la Cité, the heart of political and commercial life in Paris.

Even more importantly, Boileau always assigned competent officials to the ports to oversee the flow of food and other items into Paris; supervised improvements to the quays of the Seine; and regulated the imports coming into Paris. Official documents from the City of Paris to its officials and to citizens had to be authenticated by images on them of the river ship, a *nef*, shown on the official seal of Paris.

In 1170, King Louis VII had expanded the river-borne income from the Seine by decreeing that traders could only carry on business between the downstream bridge at Mantes-la-Jolie on the Seine, and the two bridges over the Seine located in Paris itself. Any traders violating this edict would have their cargoes confiscated.

The king's hand-in-glove agreement with the league of Paris river merchants was accompanied by a general expansion of commerce and a rapid population increase on the right bank of Paris. By about 1200, the right bank was crowded with the shops of various artisans and traders, as shown by the names of many of the local streets. Street names proclaimed the presence of mortar makers, potters, glassmakers, tanners of both strong leather for belts and of very soft and supple leather for gloves and stockings, hemp makers, coopers, iron smiths, and cartwrights.

All these men and women valued their privacy and were very wary of strangers. Paris residents could instantly recognize a stranger (who they feared might be a tax collector) because, in the absence of maps, any outsider invariably had to ask a resident how to find a given place or person. This fact provided the locals with some protection against inquisitive officials.

Most of these people benefited directly or indirectly by the thriving commerce generated by the Seine river trade in Paris. For some examples, let us look briefly at three typical Parisian occupations, namely, the tanners, the fishermen, and the millers and their watermills.[11]

The Tanners

By the end of the Middle Ages, the community of the tanners of Paris had congregated along the right bank of the Seine on *Rue de la Tannerie*, a street named after them. It was conveniently close to the bridge of Notre-Dame; to the key port of Grève, the sandy slope of which made it ideal for loading and unloading traders' cargoes; and to the *Grande Boucherie,* the central and biggest meat market in Paris, which provided meat and hides for consumers and artisans.

This location on the river was critically important for the tanners and also for the butchers and washerwomen because of its never-failing and always-free supply of running water from the Seine.

Tanning was an extremely polluting business which elicited many official protests from the lawmakers, the merchants, and the police. A regulation of 1416 gave local authorities the power to correct some small abuses, e.g., removing sunken boats or driftwood that was impeding navigation, and regulated the working hours of tanners. For example, they were not permitted to rinse skins in the Seine before 5:00 a.m.

In practice, however, tanning was such an important local business that no one wanted to curtail it very vigorously. Indeed, it was not until

1673 that the tanners, the cloth dyers, and the fullers—all major polluters of the Seine—were finally forced, chiefly due to growing concerns about the risks they posed to public health, to move elsewhere.

Illustrations dating from about 1690 show some of the tanners' very charming but very ramshackle timber-frame houses built along the Seine near the Pont-au-Change and the Pont Notre-Dame.[12]

The Fishermen

The medieval Catholic Church taught the faithful that they must abstain from eating meat on Fridays. In Paris alone, this admonition affected the rapidly growing number of residents (up from about 25,000 people in 1180 to about 220,000 in the middle of the 14th century) and thus greatly increased the Friday demand for fish.

The Seine itself, augmented both by herring and by other fish from the sea, and helped by the supply of freshwater carp from monasteries and other waterways spread across the countryside, provided much of the fish consumed in Paris. Medieval sources, however, do not give us many details on this process.

What is clear, however, is that fish in the Seine in Paris had many potential owners. For example, downstream of the Petit Pont on the southern arm of the Seine, and at the Grand Pont on the northern arm, the Abbey of Saint-Germain itself had certain specific fishing rights. The king and other dignitaries had their own but very different rights.

The bottom line for our purposes is that in the Middle Ages there were in fact a great many fish of various types in the Seine, but the fishermen themselves were all subject to and limited by numerous rights and obligations.

There were nevertheless many ways to catch fish, e.g., by lines, by nets, by boats with all their assorted gear, and simply by poaching. In summary, it appears that although the Seine fishermen of Paris worked very hard, fared averagely well in financial terms, and certainly filled a religious need, their profession was never one that, unlike domestic and foreign trade, was of the utmost economic importance to the city itself and could therefore generate sizeable incomes for its practitioners.

The Millers and Their Watermills

In 1292, there were 56 millers registered in downtown Paris. They rented but did not own the mills they used, which were the property of abbeys or great lords. Nevertheless, as the tenant of a powerful landowner, the miller was a very influential man in his local community.

In medieval times, millers often unpopular, frequently being accused of charging too much for grinding grain to make flour for bread, or of mixing inferior grain with a more expensive variety. Their customers could use "dirty tricks" themselves, too. In 1432, for example, a Parisian named Pierre Rousseau was arrested for tampering with the public scale used to weigh grain.

A miller could hire servants or apprentices, which permitted his mill to work during the night as well as in the day. It could be open on Sunday mornings, too, until 10:00 a.m.—a cut-off time reflecting the hour at which holy water was being blessed in the nearby church. The mill could then resume work at about 6:00 p.m. on Sunday.

The mills came in various shapes and sizes. One of the most interesting variants was the *moulin pendu* ("hanging mill"). Its main floor was set very high on wooden supports, considerably above the normal level of the river, to make sure that its operating mechanism would not be damaged by big floods.

The modern French scholar Karine Berthier has focused on Seine-related jobs, e.g., on the millers and their mills, which were in the 9th century were first mentioned as playing an important role in French life. One of the bridges over the Seine was known as the *pont aux Meuniers* ["The Millers' Bridge"], which had many watermills built into it but which collapsed in 1596, killing 150 people in the process.

Berthier wrote:

> The Seine played a predominant role in the lives of Parisians. It was a major axis in the movement of many kinds of merchandise and was thus vital to the overall prosperity of Paris. For these reasons, many land-based artisans and many water-dependent workers, e.g., millers and their carpenters, boatmen, porters of drinking water, and fishermen, all found it necessary to live along the Seine.[13]

At the end of the 13th century—the heyday of watermills on this river—there were about 50 of them in operation. Some were located on the bridges across the Seine, and others were stationed on boats moored in the river.

In 1564, however, three of the last watermills were demolished to improve navigation, and in 1631 the Archbishop of Paris, François de Gondi, lord of one of the two major arms or major branches of the Seine, declared it was now no longer necessary or permissible to have any watermills at all on the Seine itself.

Not long thereafter, in Paris in about 1650 a nice sense of humor seeps into the otherwise-very-straightforward business of milling. It has to do with an *anneau* (a large iron mooring ring to which the bow line of a cargo boat was attached at a port). This tale runs along the following lines, following the French text:

> One hot summer day in the *place de Grève* mooring area, when the sun was beating down fiercely, a potbellied miller who was a little bit drunk, declared loudly that his big tummy was only an illusion.
>
> Not at all convinced by this claim, however, his drinking buddies challenged him to back up his boast by squeezing his body through a big iron mooring ring which was solidly fixed to the land and was used to tie up big boats.
>
> The miller claimed that because he was so thin he could slip through this ring as easily as a snake, and dared them to bet that he could not do it. They quickly piled up their money and accepted his challenge.
>
> The miller, who was known to be not very bright, vaguely remembered that he had heard somewhere that if you could first get your head through such a ring, the rest of your body would follow through it very easily. He therefore thrust his head through the ring.
>
> He got his shoulders through, too, but then his big stomach got stuck fast and, despite his greatest and most sweaty efforts, he was totally unable either to get himself through the ring or to back out of it.
>
> A big crowd quickly gathered around and made great fun of him. It got hotter and hotter, and the miller got weaker and weaker. Clearly, something had to be done to save him!
>
> At last, one spectator suggested that someone run and find an expert who had a good file so that the ring could be cut off. The local police, however, insisted that filing the ring off would be *illegal* because the ring was government property and must not be destroyed without high-level official permission!
>
> Fortunately, the Town Hall of Paris was very close at hand and the senior official there gave permission for the filing to be done—and it was done successfully.
>
> At that moment, the big crowd began to laugh uproariously: the sun's heat had made the metal ring so hot that it had left burn marks on the miller's body, which looked exactly like the roast marks on barbequed pork!
>
> Despite no end of ridicule from the crowd, which joked about "smelling roast pork," it was agreed that *le gros imbécile* ("the big imbecile," namely, the miller himself) could not simply be left alone to die in the sun. So, once the ring had been filed off, he was doused with water and given some water to drink.
>
> He was then set free to go home—but for many months thereafter, jokers would yell at him in the streets: "To the mooring ring! To the mooring ring!"[14]

Paris had become the most important city in Europe by about 1213. Its population in 1348 was about 200,000 people, which put it far ahead of rivals such as Florence, Venice, Ghent, and London. As early as the 15th century, separate ports had already been built along the Seine to make it easier to deliver all the wine, grain, plaster, paving stones, hay, fish, and charcoal for cooking that was needed by the Parisians every day.

The Seine was critically important for transporting "*les pondéreux,*" that is, the very heavy items that could not be shipped overland at tolerable cost. These included lumber and the heavy stones needed for quays, urban construction, monuments, and boulevard paving.

Charcoal for cooking was so important to citizens that the men who delivered it to their homes were licensed by Paris and wore on the back of their coat a special insignia to this effect. Before the 18th century, charcoal legally could be sold only from the boat that brought it to a port, often the Grève, but the merchant was required to sell it within three days to prevent speculators from profiting on price rises due to delays.

To sell it as quickly as possible, the charcoal merchants had to hire criers to shout out loudly in public places:

Charcoal, fine charcoal from young trees!
It only cost a few coins for a big sackful!
It has just arrived on a boat now docked at the Grève—
Come see it there![15]

As will be described later in the chapter on the old ports of Paris, firewood for heating homes was sent to one port, while lumber for building homes and larger structures was directed to a nearby port. A good number of educated supervisory officials, plus many more unschooled longshoremen, found good jobs in these medieval ports.

An illustration dating from about 1500, for example, shows two of these longshoremen hard at work, helping the crew of an incoming ship by using a strong rope to pull their ship, which was heavily laden with lumber, alongside a dock. An accompanying illustration of the same year shows both a local official at the dock measuring the tonnage (a measure of the cargo-carrying capacity of the ship), and another boat which was carrying many casks of wine.[16] Each cask of wine held 252 gallons.[17]

Paris merchants depended heavily on the Seine and on other rivers in their unceasing efforts to supply many of the foodstuffs and the other goods which the city of Paris needed every day, and then to distribute them there. These men set up their shops at the river ports which were most geared to their own trades.

By the 15th century, separate ports had been established along the Seine in Paris to handle the delivery of wine, grain, plaster, paving stones, hay, fish, and charcoal. Wood for cooking fires and heating was unloaded at one port: wood for construction arrived at a nearby port.

In 1421, for example, there were already 21 wine merchants officially registered in Paris: 11 of them were clustered between the Pont

Notre-Dame, on the one hand, and the Hôtel Saint-Paul on the left bank, on the other. This was the neighborhood where, not surprisingly, their favorite port was located.

After the Gréve, which was the biggest and most important port, the second-largest port in Paris was located close to the church of Saint-Germain-l'Auxerois, where incoming ships unloaded fresh fish from the coast, wood from the forests along the Aisne and the Oise Rivers, hay from the valley of the Seine, and cider from Normandy.

During the early years of Middle Ages, the principal market of Paris was located on the parvis, that is, on the big paved square which had no houses on it and which was built in front of the cathedral of Notre-Dame, adjacent to the Seine. Smaller markets were also set up near two Paris bridges over the Seine—the Grand Pont and the Petit Pont. Later, during the life of Napoleon (1769–1821), more hygienic *covered markets* rather than open air markets, were established in Paris, often along or not far from the Seine.

The Grand Pont, built by Louis VI, lasted until 1280 when it was destroyed by a flood. It was then rebuilt in stone and was packed high with houses. Thirteen of the 14 arches of the bridge also became sites for watermills; the last arch was the biggest and was reserved for navigation. In 1296, however, a flood carried away the bridge, which was later rebuilt at the king's expense. After 1305, the Grand Pont played an essential role in the economy of Paris as a major site for money changers.

The narrow Petit Pont became famous because of the very loud shouts of the colorful market women there, each claiming to have for sale on the bridge only the very best and the cheapest vegetables and other foods.[18]

Writing in 1782, the French author Louis Sébastien Mercier captured the market clamor in Paris and the shouts of the market women there in these lightly annotated words:

> Look! Here is a fine mackerel that is still alive: it just arrived! Over there are herrings on ice—nice fresh new herrings! See here our chilled snacks: a pleasure for the ladies! Look, too, at these lovely croquettes! More ships are arriving just now: bring the scales! See the fine oysters here! Lovely oranges from Portugal![19]

It must have been with this cacophony in mind that, in his "Ballad of the Women of Paris," the medieval poet François Villon assured his readers that "*The only really good chatter is the Paris market chatter!,*" with its own argot (jargon), unique vocabulary, and street-wise pronunciations.

A gentler point about life in Paris was made by the famous French poet Pierre de Ronsard (1524–1585), who wrote to the city of Paris:

> It's YOU, Paris, admirable city,
> Grand ornament of the inhabited world....
> You have your back divided by the Seine,
> A wide river-course with large and fruitful ports.

Similar praise came from by another French writer—Antoine de Saint-Amant—when he wrote in 1653 that it was only in the "superb city of Paris" that he learned how to use "words sharper than blades."[20]

The most important market arose as early as 1137 when Louis VI, in order to create a grain market for Paris, bought a plot of land called Les Champeaux. It consisted of former marshes that had been drained and turned into fields and was not far from the Seine.

Over the course of the Middle Ages, separate food halls for meat, fish, fruits, vegetables, and other food products sprang up around the grain market. Known as the Les Halles market, this would continue to be updated until the late 20th century, when it was finally moved to Rungis is the Paris suburbs.

Money-changers were active on the banks of Paris at least since 1141. Their job was to know the exact values of the many different silver and gold coins then circulating in Western Europe. Their desks were often located on the Grand Pont itself, which thanks to their busy hands, first became known as the Pont aux Changeurs and then simply as the Pont-au-Change.

During the Middle Ages and long thereafter, pollution was a major problem along the Seine in Paris. In 1698, for example, Martin Lister, an English doctor visiting Paris with a group of his friends, made these points in his book on the trip:

- Beginning with our arrival in Paris, we prepared ourselves to deal with the unsanitary conditions of the Seine, and never to drink its water. Nevertheless, it was nearly impossible for us to avoid bad effects. In the month we were there, two-thirds of our company had diarrhea, and several had dysentery, which made them quite ill.
- The French who come to Paris from elsewhere suffer just as much as the foreigners do. We were told to boil the water to improve it, but this is just a tall tale.... Dysentery is one of the most common diseases in Paris.[21]

Butchers and tripe-dealers simply dumped their unwanted lumps of fat, meat trimmings, and other offal directly onto the city's streets, or into the river near the Pont-au-Change and other bridges. In addition, the semi-congealed blood from local abattoirs slowly oozed down the streets and into the river.

Nevertheless, no matter how fetid the Seine became near the meat markets, as a practical matter, river pollution was usually ignored by the merchants and traders of Paris. Engravings made at the end of the 17th century and again in 1850 show this section of the Seine as always being very full of boats of many different shapes, sizes, and functions.[22]

There were so many, in fact, that a French official variously known either as the "evaluator of ships" or as the "master of the bridges" had to go out among them in his own small boat, known as a *flette*, to guide the bigger boats safely through the arches of bridges.

One of the arches of this early bridge was called "l'arche de Diable" ("the Devil's arch"). It earned this nickname because it was so close to the arch of another bridge just a bit further downstream and, visually, was so perfectly lined up with this downstream arch when viewed from the Seine, that there was a great danger a boat heading downstream on a strong current would crash headlong into it.[23]

A nineteenth-century lithograph shows a partial and probably ineffective solution to this problem: stationing an experienced crewman in the bow of the boat heading downstream, equipped with a short strong wooden pole known as a *bâton de marine* ("waterways baton"). This crewman could try to use his pole to force the bow of his boat just far enough to one side avoid a head-on collision with the arch. Even if he managed to do this, however, anything but a very light glancing contact with the arch, given the speed and the weight of the boat, might well have severely damaged the boat.[24]

On the economic front, Paris tax records show that in 1423 the money-changers were among the richest people in the city. Of the 20 Parisians with the highest incomes, fully half were money-changers. Indeed, between 1412 and 1450, four former money-changers rose in turn to become the most powerful financial official in Paris, namely, the *Prévôt des marchands* (who was the chief merchant and their representative when dealing with the king).

This official had very far-reaching powers. He supervised conditions on the quays and at the ports, as well as the haulage paths used by horses, and sometimes by men, to pull cargo boats upstream. He was responsible for the proper functioning of walls, drainage ditches, and local streams. Finally, he was also charged with protecting the local waterways from the deplorable habits of local residents, e.g., by throwing garbage into them.[25]

But times do change. By the end of 15th century, the richest Parisians were no longer the money-changers on the bridges over the Seine, but were instead the forward-thinking Parisians who were politically very close to the King, who had invested in land, or who had bought their way into high offices in the royal administration.

3

Viking Raids in France

The Vikings were very hardy and self-reliant bands of sea-borne Scandinavian explorers, traders, looters, and pirates—*often all at the same time*—during the ninth to the eleventh centuries, a period now often referred to simply as "the Viking Age."

The actual origin of the term "Viking" is still unclear but in written Scandinavian sources, *viking* means "piracy" or "a piracy raid," and a man taking part in such a conflict was known as a *vikingr*.[1]

Although they left almost no physical traces in what is now France except for a few weapons and other objects recovered from the Seine near Normandy, both the fact and the fiction of their depredations have become an exciting chapter in European history. It is therefore worth briefly summarizing a few of their adventures in France.

In their own time, the Vikings, who came from Norway, Denmark, and sometimes Sweden, were variously known as the "Normans," that is, the "men of the North" (*Normani*), or as the "Danes" (*Dani*). Their raids on France and elsewhere were often recorded in chronicles written by clerics who were highly literate but who could not defend themselves in any way. They were therefore quite prone to exaggerate the savagery, size, and importance of the fierce, unexpected, and repeated Viking attacks.

Monks could not defend themselves for three reasons: (1) they had no training in self-defense; (2) they had no weapons of any kind; and (3) for religious reasons, they were forbidden to shed blood. Lacking any local or national police forces, rural French men and women were in much the same helpless condition. Indeed, they were simply reduced to praying fervently: "Oh Lord, from the fury of the Northmen please deliver us!"

The Vikings used "longships." These boats were lengthy, very fast, and so light and shallow draft that they could be portaged overland by a strong crew from one river basin to another. During one siege of Paris, the Vikings even dragged their boats 2,000 feet further upstream to get a tactical advantage over the French defenders.

They usually walked rather than rode: horses were not easy to obtain and were ill-suited to battle by boat. Viking boats were powered by oars, helped sometimes by woven wool sails. Basically, they were double-ended wooden boats with rounded bottoms, flaring sides, and very high bows and sterns.[2] Until the appearance of the medieval cog in the 12th and 13th centuries, Viking boats were the very best in the world for both war and for peace.[3]

The earliest attacks of the Vikings were on undefended and very lucrative locations, e.g., on monasteries, that were located far from any possible armed help. Vikings were initially the masters of what today we would call "smash and grab" raids, but later these would evolve into more complex military operations.

The Vikings successfully plundered the English Channel, parts of the Atlantic coastline, and then, using navigable rivers such as the Seine, the Loire, and the Garonne, also attacked prosperous French monasteries and cities located well inland. They attacked Paris three times.

Although a Scandinavian fleet had plundered a monastery in Aquitaine in France in 799, the first significant Viking incursion into western France appears to date from 820, when royal annals show that a fleet of 13 ships from *"Nordmannia,"* (Scandinavia) tried to plunder the coasts of Flanders, an area then defined as including parts of modern Belgium, France, and the Netherlands, but were driven off by local forces there.

Another armed but smaller scale clash took place that same year in the English Channel at the mouth of the Seine, where five Viking men were killed and their comrades were driven off without being able to seize anything of value from the French defenders.

By about 830, however, using the rivers, larger groups of Vikings were beginning to make their way deeper and deeper into the French countryside. They seized rich, high-ranking people and held them for ransom; poor French men were captured, too, but they were either killed on the spot or were held indefinitely as slaves. French women were certainly raped or killed.

In 841, the Vikings penetrated the Seine for the first time, burning and looting Rouen and the rich abbeys of Jumièges and Saint-Ouen before returning to their longships.

Today, the two white towers of the beautiful old ruins of Jumièges Abbey, located in the middle of a forest of the same name, can still be seen from the Seine. Founded in 654 by Saint Philibert, this was one of the oldest and grandest monasteries in the region and marked the high point of Norman monasticism in the Seine Valley.

In 654–676, Saint Philibert writes of the trade and fishing fleets that supplied it with wheat, wine, salt, fish, and oil for lamps. In the 12th century, the monks profited by importing ship cargoes of French wine that much exceeded their own modest needs, selling the surplus far inland along the Seine or in England.

In 843, the Vikings sailed up the Loire to Nantes, one of the most important trading cities of the Carolingian Empire and plundered the city while the inhabitants were busy celebrating a religious holiday there. The Vikings massacred many helpless and hapless people—clerics, laity, and even the bishop himself in his church. After setting up a Viking base in the area, they then ravaged the fertile Duchy of Aquitaine for ten years.

In 845, a band of Vikings coming from Denmark and led by Ragner Lodbrok invaded the Seine with a flotilla of 120 ships carrying as many as 6,000 men. The contemporary French historian, poet, preacher, and monk Abbon de Saint-Germain-des-Prés (c. 850–c. 923) tells us in his account of *Le siège de Paris par les Normands en 885 et 886* ("The siege of Paris by the Normans in 885 and 886") that these Vikings, swarming out of their ships, spread out far and wide into the countryside and "massacred a great multitude of both sexes, burned villages, monasteries, and churches, and exercised against the people of God all the excesses of their boundless fury."[4]

They seized Rouen, devastated it and its surroundings, and finally reached Paris on the eve of Easter, one of the most important religious holidays. There they faced no resistance at all from the French, most of whom had fled up the Seine, and all their monasteries had been abandoned by the monks.

The only fortified part of Paris was the Île de la Cité itself, the other parts of city having no troops, walls, or defensive protection of any kind. The French king, Charles the Bald, therefore quickly realized that he therefore had no choice but to buy off the Vikings. This he did by giving them 7,000 pounds of silver to persuade them to leave in peace.

We learn from the Frankish historian Nithard (c. 795–844) that, in 841, Charles tried to prevent his enemy Lothar and his army from crossing the Seine between Paris and Melun, located 25 miles southeast of Paris, by stationing troops in the most likely places where the river could best be forded.

Charles judged that he could resist any effort by Lothar to cross it because his own military units were in very close communication with each other thanks to a system of sentry-posts, which could visually pass information from one to another by using special signals, much like ships at sea. However, Lothar understood this state of affairs and easily dodged the problem simply by finding another and more secure place to cross the Seine.[5]

In 850, Charles gave the Viking leader, Horik, some land near the

Seine in hopes of stopping the Viking advance. The men of Normandy, however, were not strong enough to resist the tide of Viking invaders: they either joined the looters themselves or simply became looters on their own.

The next year, 851, the Viking leader Hasting marched at the head of his troops to attack Rouen and Beauvais, spending the winter months near the Seine. When they were defeated at Vardes, these Vikings simply fanned out all over the countryside and attacked cities, buildings, and abbeys near Paris, including the famous abbey of Sainte-Geneviève de Paris.

Despite being so powerful at close quarters, the Vikings were not supermen and did indeed suffer some defeats. In 854, for example, Bishop Agius of Orleans and Bishop Burchard organized both a fleet and an army that saved Orleans from the Vikings. According to a chronicle known as the Annals of Fulda, in that year, too, many of the Vikings who were fighting in France simply abandoned their conquests there in order to take part in a civil war that was raging in Denmark itself. In that war, almost every member of the Viking royal family was killed, except for one child named Horace II.

By 855, Vikings arrived at the mouth of the Loire, invaded Bordeaux, and attacked Poitiers by land. They were driven off there but conquered Nantes and then went on up the Seine until they were defeated by troops of Charles the Bald.

In 856, the Vikings of the Loire captured and plundered Orleans while some of their fellow warriors went up the Seine, spent the winter there, and on 28 December 856 invaded and burned Paris. This second attack on Paris did much more damage than the first one and gave rise to bitter complaints to Paschase Radbert, a local abbot, which were said to have run along these lines:

> Who could have ever believed that pirates [the Vikings] gathered from different nations would have come to humiliate a kingdom so glorious, so powerful, so populous as France? No king would have hoped, no inhabitant of the earth would have believed, that an enemy could ever enter our Paris![6]

In 861 the Vikings returned for the third time to Paris, where they burned the abbey of Saint-Germain, pursued the merchants of the city, who were fleeing up the Seine, took some of them prisoner, and were finally bought off only by a "present" of 6,000 pounds of bullion, half in gold and half in silver.

By 864, the fury of the Vikings of the Seine seemed to be slackening, but the Vikings on the Loire continued their own ravages. The Vikings of the Seine did send 200 of their men into Paris to get supplies of wine. Charles the Bald bought off the raiders yet again, this time with 4,000 pounds of silver, but the Vikings always violated his peace-gestures and simply continued to mount their attacks.

Now, to make the long and repetitive "Vikings-in-France" story very short, we will conclude here by noting that Vikings under their leader Rollo entered the Seine in 876 in 100 boats and remained in the Rouen area. Their persistence finally paid off.

In 911, Rollo was officially given the lands that he had seized by force and on which he and his followers had now settled permanently as farmers or traders. These men, coupling with local French women, would become the future French Duchy of Normandy.

The Viking raids on France itself finally ended in 1017, after they landed on the coast of Poitou at Saint-Michel-en-l'Herm. This seems to have been their last act in France.

Their attacks on France ended only because the domestic politics and the growing prosperity of Scandinavian countries themselves had by then stabilized to the point where constant Viking raids abroad to win ever-more wealth, tribute, and men-at-arms were no longer considered to be necessary. They therefore ceased, but memories of the raids would persist along the Seine for many generations.

4

Money Changes Hands

Perhaps the easiest way to outline the rapid growth of Paris is to focus on the prosperity described by the modern French medievalists Boris Bove and Claude Gauvard in their 2014 book, *Le Paris du Moyen Âge* [*Paris in the Middle Ages*].

Lightly annotated and translated into English, their views can be summarized as follows:

> It was the physical location of Paris as a river-based economic and cultural crossroad that most strongly favored the rapid growth of the city during the Middle Ages.
>
> The historic island in the Seine known as the Île de la Cité permitted a succession of bridges to be built across the river there. These would play an essential role as part of the important north-south trade route linking the French cities of Senlis and Orleans.
>
> At the same time, the confluence, near Paris, of the Oise, Marne, and Yerres Rivers also channeled toward the city all the products of a very fertile and very extensive agricultural hinterland, which was rich in wheat fields, vineyards, and well-managed forests [wood was essential both for heating and for construction purposes], and which was staffed by large numbers of experienced, disciplined, low-cost agricultural workers, often led by monks.
>
> This influx of skilled agricultural production was chiefly responsible for the ever-growing and prosperous population of the Île de France itself and, by extension, of other nearby parts of Paris, too.[1]

One of the most important factors involved in the economic rise of Paris over all the years has thus been the Seine, which greatly facilitated the movement of goods and people. Its favorable impact was made possible by the many bridges built across the river from the earliest days until modern times. These will be discussed in later pages.

In overview, historians tell us that by the end of the 16th century the most important industry in Paris was no longer money-changing but, instead, the making and processing of textiles. This profitable but highly polluting trade revolved around the weaving, dyeing, and transportation of cloth, plus the related production and shipment of bonnets, belts, ribbons, and other pieces of clothing for rich and poor alike.

The dyeing business was chiefly located along the River Bièvre, a short (21-mile-long) river that ultimately flowed into the left bank of the Seine at the Latin Quarter of Paris, close to the Île de la Cité. Together with the Seine, the Bièvre was at first a main source of drinking water for the Parisians, augmented by potable water drawn from numerous small-scale wells dug into the left and right banks of the Seine.

An illustration of 1815 shows a "curator of wells" (an employee equipped only with a long wooden pole) whose job it was to keep these wells open and easy to use.[2] The wells usually had to be about 12 feet to 15 feet deep on the right bank, and 18 feet to 21 feet deep on the left bank.

Later, the Bièrve, which had become very narrow and highly polluted due to the many textile works crowded along its banks, was bridged by nearly continuous boardwalks in about 1860 to make travel by foot easier.[3] Contemporary photos show that it then looked more like a desolate industrial slum—or even like an abandoned battlefield—rather than the prosperous working waterway it really was.

At last fully covered-over and finally diverted from its original course after 1877, this river has been swallowed up by the exponential growth of Paris but is still clearly visible on the oldest detailed map of the city, dating from about 1550. It became most important market-area in Paris for fine textiles and other luxury goods.

The largest and most successful textile workshops along the Bièvre used huge dye vats which, taken collectively, could in the mid–16th century dye up to 600,000 pieces of cloth per year. It was from this highly polluting but very lucrative industrial process that sprang the vast fortunes of the Gobelins and other dyers and textile-based families.

The Bièvre also played an important role in transporting building stones for the great cathedral of Notre-Dame, where construction began in 1163 and continued beyond 1345. The reason is that there was never a shortage of the best-quality limestone building-blocks which, relatively easily, could be cut out of the extensive quarries on the left bank of the Seine, sent by the river, and used to build the cathedral.

One very strong type of Lutetian limestone, known as lias, that was used in building Notre-Dame was extracted from underground quarries dug between what are now the fifth and twelfth *arrondissements* of Paris. Lias was also used to build the Chateau of Versailles and the Vaux-le-Vicomte (both in the Paris region), the Reims cathedral in northeastern France, and, very likely, La Sainte-Chapelle (the Holy Chapel) in Paris, too. Such blocks were also used to face the high anti-flood walls lining the banks of the Seine in Paris.

Ferries were very important on the rivers of the Middle Ages. In 1297, for example, there were more than 60 of them in Paris alone, and not only for the transport of people. Parisians needed easy and reliable access to running water for drinking, for washing clothes, for cleaning, and for keeping alive the large numbers of horses, pigs, and other domestic animals living in or being driven through the city.

In 1148, the Bièvre had been diverted from its original course by the monks of the nearby Abbey of St-Victor, located about 300 yards from the Seine. Together with the Paris schools of Ste Geneviève and of Notre-Dame, it and other nearby sections of the left bank of the Seine would eventually become the cradle of the University of Paris.

This university would become world-famous and would attract such students, scholars, and intellectuals as Hugh of St. Victor, Peter Lombard, and Thomas Becket. During the 13th and 14th centuries the left bank of the Seine became the site of more than 30 colleges, convents, residences, and other institutions of higher learning.

Ironically, the Seine may well have been responsible for saving some students' lives, too. During a serious university riot in 1381, some students jumped into the Seine to avoid being beaten to death by the heavy-handed police who were breaking up the riot.[4]

Jean de Jandun (c. 1280–1328) was a well-regarded philosopher, political theorist, and university professor. His work was an essential part of a debate begun in French and Italian universities of the 13th century following the rediscovery of ancient Greek philosophy. It was, in essence, a debate between the relative importance of reason and faith—a debate which is still going on in our own day.

Jean de Jandun has left to posterity his detailed evocations of such famous Paris buildings as Notre-Dame, the Sainte-Chapelle, and the palace of Philip the Fair. He documents the contemporary reception of Gothic architecture, praising these buildings for their size, elegance, varied decoration, and color.

He is also the author of a eulogy to Paris itself, composed in 1323, which provides us with a fourteenth-century response to the now-lost comments of an anonymous specialist in the art of "dictation," which at that time meant giving an eloquent description of current events.

Jean de Jandun tells us, for example, that it is the Seine itself which was responsible for all the excellent foodstuffs and the other good things delivered so abundantly to Paris. He says that it is impossible for him to describe fully how this process works, but he sees that the people of Paris always have exactly what they need when they need it, and at acceptable prices. This is, he remarks, "a miracle" for such a densely populated city.[5]

There was a downside, however, to such river-borne good news. The

4. Money Changes Hands

many totally unregulated tanneries, butcher shops, dye-making enterprises, and water mills built along the narrow banks of the sinuous Bièvre had the effect of straightening the river, but they also produced very serious pollution problems.

As a result of all this commercial activity, beginning in the 18th century, sections of the Bièvre were gradually, step-by-step, being culverted, canalized, and then finally concealed permanently under heavy stone slabs. Indeed, some stretches of it have disappeared forever under all the rubble produced by the non-stop urbanization of Paris.

In our own times, however, this river has now become a new part of the rainwater drainage system of Paris. Under this system, drain water plans call for rain falling on Paris, in the future, to flow directly into the Seine rather than first being put through a wastewater treatment plant. This will significantly reducing local wastewater treatment costs.

During most of the 18th century, the economy of Paris was based on thousands of very modest workshops, where skilled workers laboriously made many different products entirely by hand. There were not very many industrial-scale enterprises then.

One of them and probably the best-remembered today, was the dye factory of the Gobelin family. Located on the Bièvre, it produced scarlet dye for the Gobelin royal tapestry workshop, which was the oldest factory in Paris, having been founded at the end of the 17th century.

In the second half of the 18th century, new technologies began to enlarge the scale of some Paris industries. First, between about 1608 and 1786, for example, large-scale water-powered pumps appeared, e.g., the very tall "Samaritaine" pump, which was built in 1608 and powered a large waterwheel 8½ feet in diameter with huge blades to move water, and was housed in a magnificently ornate building set alongside the Seine. Second, later on, large steam-driven pumps (*pompes à feu*, literally "fire-pumps") were used to deliver significant amounts of water to Paris directly from the Seine itself.

In the days when the concept of getting potable drinking water from a tap in one's own home was far beyond the reach of even the most fertile imagination, it must have seemed miraculous to Parisians be able to get river water from big pumps, at least indirectly, via the water carriers who will be described in later pages.

The first of the new steam-driven pumps was put into service in Paris in 1781. Some of the publicity surrounding it can be quoted and translated along the following lines:

Plan for Providing and Installing Steam-Driven Pumps for the Waters of the Seine

Far superior to water-powered pumps such as those now used at the bridges of Notre-Dame and Pont-Neuf, which are thought to be first-rate even though they cannot be regulated to cope with floods or droughts or icy conditions, the new pumps will never stop, neither because of ice nor of drought, provided they are equipped with a pipe that extends into the water underneath the ice.[6]

These were vast improvements compared to the earlier reliance on water then being sold in city streets only in small quantities by human-powered or animal-powered transport, e.g., in hand-carried pails or by horse-drawn wagons, neither of which was in any way hygienic. Still, this process continued to work in Paris tolerably well.

A sketch done in about 1820, for example, entitled the equivalent of "Three ways to get water at home," shows three well-dressed water carriers using both their pails and a hand-powered water-wagon to deliver water to homes in a French city.[7]

Writing much earlier, in 1599, the French author Platter the Younger gives us a good introduction to the *porteurs d'eau* ("water carriers") who were a very familiar fixture of Paris life until about 1880, when water became so cheap that these men had to find other jobs, e.g., as dealers in charcoal or in wine.

Interestingly, at first, many of the water carriers in Paris in the Middle Ages were *Englishmen* but, as time went on, poor Frenchmen from Auvergne in the hills of central France began to replace them.

There is today no reliable official count of their initial numbers, which reportedly varied from 58 in 1292 to less than 20 in 1313, by the 16th century the many water carriers in Paris came from a wide range of different regions—a fact which often struck strangers passing through the capital.[8]

In their heyday, this is what Platter the Younger says about them:

- In all of Paris there were only 16 fountains of running water. Since many of the most prosperous citizens lived in big houses with a large number of floors, they always needed a male or female servant assigned to carry into their homes, every day at an agreed time, an adequate supply of drinking water.
- These water carriers received for their service only the pittance of two francs per month. Because they had to work night and day to get the water, to make sure they didn't lose a single drop of it, they always carried it into houses the first thing in the morning, that is, before the household became too active and began to use the stairs. Some of the water carriers had so many clients that they themselves became rich and could afford to give their daughter a very generous dowry.[9]

The most striking water carrier was instantly known because he wore a *bretelle*—a unique, circular, strong, harness-arrangement made of leather and wood which allowed him to carry a full pail of water on each side of his body, steadying them with his hands. The weight of the water was distributed to his shoulders by means of a broad leather strap. Sometimes a couple carried water as well, each party being equipped with a *bretelle*. This was at best a very tiring and very tedious way of life.

Since he had to be outdoors most of the time in all weathers, a water carrier often wore a hat with a huge brim to keep the sun off his face. Another distinguishing characteristic was that he and his colleagues were very often great troublemakers, harassing not only each other in the marketplace but also the servants of their homeowner clients as well.

Tempers ran so high, in fact, during some of these encounters that blood was often spilled as a result. In a legal directive of 1688, for example, both men and women were most sternly ordered to behave properly at the water fountain; if they did not, they could be fined, sent to prison, and whipped.[10]

Steam was of course used, too, in boats as well as in water pumps. The age of wood-hulled steamboats dawned in the Seine in 1816, when the French paddle steamer *L'Élise* arrived in Paris from London via the English Channel, having successfully navigated the Seine all the way up to the capital.

The first iron-hulled steamboat to go into use, however, was the British ship *Aaron Manby*, which, as will be described in Appendix 8, made a voyage from the Thames to Paris in 1822. The advantages of using steam-power rather than horses or men to haul boats were so pronounced that by 1830, if not even earlier, scheduled steamboat runs were carrying passengers from Paris to other ports along the Seine.

The new technology, however, also brought new problems to the Seine. Steamboats were much bigger, faster, and heavier than their predecessors: accidents involving them and other ships were not uncommon and were often very serious. A dramatic but untitled nineteenth-century painting of a boating accident on the Seine is a good case in point here.

We do not know the details, but judging from the painting, a yellow steamship ran at cruising speed over a coal-carrying barge, and then continued on to smash into the side of the passenger vessel *Le Ville de Montereau* ("*The City of Montereau*"), which was chock-full of terrified passengers.

The painting shows that two crewmen of this latter ship have already been knocked overboard: one is swimming in the Seine, and the other is still up in the air and is about to hit the water head-first. At the same time and in another part of the picture, three other crewmen from the coal barge are trying hard to escape the accident in a small rowboat.[11]

Greatly aided by the now much-improved steam engines, during the nineteenth-century Paris became the cradle of the Industrial Revolution in France. The textile industry was installed, for example, in the Saint-Denis area (discussed earlier in terms of the Lendit fair), and many new factories were built along the Seine. These manufactured a wide range of products but, in the absence of any laws designed to protect the environment, they also polluted the river very heavily.

We shall now go back in history and enjoy the nineteenth-century bird's-eye point of view of medieval Paris as the great French novelist Victor Hugo imagined it.

In 1831, Hugo describes the Paris of the Middle Ages, where all this economic growth first began, in the following words (translated from French), which reflect his vivid imagination:

> The spectator arriving breathless at the summit [at the top of the twin towers of Notre-Dame] was met first by a dizzy confusion of roofs, chimneys, bridges, spires, steeples. Everything caught the eye at once, the carved gable, the steep roof, the turret suspended at the corner of the walls, the stone pyramid of the eleventh century, the slate obelisk of the fifteenth, the bare, round tower of the castle keep, the square decorated tower of the church, the big, the small, the airy.
>
> The eye lingered at every level of this labyrinth, where there was nothing without its originality, its reason, its beauty, nothing which did not derive from art, from the humblest house with carved and painted front, external timbers, low doorway, overhanging storeys, to the royal Louvre, which at that time had a colonnade of towers.[12]

5

The Seine in the Hundred Years War

This war was, in essence, a very long-running, bitter, and intermittent conflict between England and France and their allies for control of the French throne. It lasted from about 1300 to about 1450 and was finally won by France, in large part because the French were at last able to wear the English down by avoiding pitched battles and frontal assaults, relying instead on a long, gradual war of attrition.[1]

Although during the Middle Ages the city of Bruges, located in what is now Belgium, was the financial headquarters of western and northern Europe, it was in fact *the Seine basin* that became the most important regional commercial center during the Hundred Years War.[2] The war ended in an ignominious defeat for the English.

One phase of this conflict started in 1415 with King Henry V's of England expedition into Normandy and his capture of then-undefended port of Harfleur (near the mouth of the Seine near the English Channel) as a preliminary base for English military operations. In 1416, a more important English naval victory in Normandy established a strong beachhead in France at Harfleur—a battle that will be discussed in later pages.

In 1417, Henry V began a more serious conquest of Normandy. In 1418–1419, his forces used three Portuguese galleys, on loan from king of Portugal, to "patrol the waters of the Seine" during the siege of Rouen. By early 1419, this key port city had fallen to the English and Henry V's name had become part of the English military successes in France. By means of the treaty of Troyes of 1420, the crown of France was formally vested not in the French royal family but in Henry V and his heirs.[3]

Late fourteenth-century French chronicles give the modern readers good insights into the bloodshed during the war. For example, English skirmishes and pillaging along the Seine near the town of Vitry just south of Paris are recorded in the *Chronicles of France and Saint Denis*. This was a vernacular royal compilation of the history of France, most manuscripts of which are luxury copies that are heavily illuminated and were produced between the 13th and 15th centuries.

The ferocity of this conflict left little to chance. One illustration in this work depicts knights fighting along an arched timber bridge. Not only is great slaughter being done by their bows and arrows, swords, and pikes, but the bridge itself has been designed with what are called "drawbridge ends." This means that one or both ends of the bridge can be raised up out of the water to make it impossible for a knight to cross the bridge unless he is first willing to wade into the water in his heavy armor—which would be very foolish for him to do in a combat situation.[4]

The Hundred Years War was chronicled by many contemporary writers, perhaps best by the French historian, poet, and priest Jean Froissart. He had this to say about the Seine region:

> After taking a great deal of plunder, the English marched through the country [that is the region] of Evreux [50 miles west of Paris], burning everything except the fortified towns and castles, which the English king Edward left alone, in order to save his men and artillery.
>
> He then made for the Seine, not marching directly to Rouen, but burning the towns of Gisors, Vernon, Mantes, and Meulan on the way, and ravaging the countryside. King Edward advanced to Poissy [less than 20 miles from Paris], where he found the bridge over the Seine broken down, with the beams and posts lying scattered in the river. The King waited for five days, until the bridge was repaired and his army could cross over. His marshals advanced very close to Paris, burning Saint-Germain-en-Laye, Saint Cloud, and Bourg-la-Reine. The people of Paris were terrified, for the city was not at that time fortified.[5]

Contemporary illustrations show that military forces used a relatively long, low, flat-bottomed vessel that might then have been called a "balenger" and that today nautical experts might call a "barge." In any case, it was certain to have been a slow, sturdy vessel capable of carrying about 40 armed men and was propelled by oars or by a single sail.

One of the highlights—or, perhaps more fittingly—one of the lowest points—of the war was the widespread use of mercenaries. Writing in about 1360 in Leicester Abbey, the English monk Henry Knighton describes these men as follows:

> At this time was organized a certain company of strong men called the Company of Fortune ... which some called the Great Company. It was composed of men from different parts who, now that there was peace ... had no means of livelihood other than through their own efforts. They were bold and warlike fellows, experienced and strenuous, who congregated together from different nations, and lived by war since in peace they had nothing.[6]

5. The Seine in the Hundred Years War

In France, such mercenaries were very active in the upper Seine valley and elsewhere, e.g., on the lands situated between the rivers Seine and Loire. Of these men, a bandit named Ruffin was one of the most notorious. This is what medieval chronicler Jean Froissart tells us about him in 1367–1369:

> At this time, also, there was another company of men-at-arms, or robbers, collected from all parts, who stationed themselves between the rivers Loire and Seine, so that no one dared travel between Paris and Orleans, or even to remain in the country; the inhabitants on the plains had all fled to Paris and Orleans.
> This company had chosen for their leader a Welshman named Ruffin, whom they had knighted, and who acquired such immense riches as could not be counted. These companies advanced one day near to Paris and another day toward Orleans, another time to Chartres; and there was no town or fortress but what was taken and pillaged.... They rode over the country in parties of twenty, thirty, or forty, meeting with none to check their pillage....[7]

The importance of the Seine to the people who relied on it for their income is evident from a report dating from about 1345. This referred to the strong protests that arose when the French king wanted to raise taxes on the locals' use of the Seine and the neighboring rivers.

Prosperous Frenchmen in Paris attached great importance to their monopoly on their commercial use of the middle Seine and of the nearby Yonne and Oise rivers. They therefore stressed their desire to have more of a say in the tax structure, in large part because their earnings from river traffic might well enable them to buy landed fiefs of their own. These were the expensive properties that were valued both for financial income and, even more important, for the upward-social-mobility they made possible.

The bottom line of this dispute was that since the king was not willing to surrender any of his tax powers, the locals had no choice but to pay the higher tax bills he levied on them.

This they did, albeit unwillingly, because of the importance to them of the Seine river traffic, which was nicely summed up in about 1355 by the phrase *merchandise de l'eau* ("water-borne merchandise").

It referred to the high profits that the bourgeois (middle class) businessmen of Paris could expect to make from their Seine monopoly and their total control of all the river traffic going into and from the Paris region.

Other manmade restrictions on the use of French rivers for carrying cargo increased frequently. Tolls were the most burdensome of these. On the Seine, for example, tolls on commercial cargo had to be paid no less than eighteen times in the 80-mile-long stretch between the Mantes-la-Jolie region and Paris.

There was a considerable amount of passenger traffic, too, along this river, using large, specially designed river barges (known as "water coaches") that were pulled by teams of horses. In 1775, it was officially stated that these vessels offered "the greatest convenience for the transport of passengers and goods, thanks to their low fixed prices."[8]

One such vessel was nicknamed a *coche d'eau*, literally, a "water tick" or "water bug." More accurately, this type of boat was a shallow-draft passenger-carrying barge usually known as a *galiote*. Between 1775 and 1778, the administration of the *coches* d'eau, headquartered in Paris, passed to a new organization known as the *Diligences & Messageries* ("Stagecoach and Messages"), which provided good service to Rouen and to other cities along the Seine.

A *galiote* carried both passengers and goods and was very popular. With space for 89 passengers, it was drawn by four horses which were replaced with fresh horses at relay stations. A decree from a local official of 13 May 1809, for example, provided the following simple schedule over a distance of about 20 miles: Departure from Rolleboise at 8:00 p.m.; arriving in Poissy at 5:00 a.m. the next morning.

The upstream outbound journey took fully 9 hours to complete because of the river's current and the darkness, which made it very hard for the driver to see and to follow safely the poorly maintained towpath. The return trip downstream in daylight, however, took only 5 hours to complete. Similar vessels carried people and cargo to and from Paris, Mantes-la-Jolie, and Normandy.

A nineteenth-century description of such Seine travels runs along the following lightly edited lines[9]:

- The boat preferred by Parisians was the *galiote*, which went from Paris to Sèvres or to Saint-Cloud. This service was conducted between from Easter to All-Souls Day, using the port adjacent to the Pont-Royal bridge.
- The voyage was not expensive at all, so crowds of Parisians took this trip on Sundays and holidays, being carried downstream by the current in the morning and, in the evening, heading back upstream at the slow pace set by the horses hauling the boat. By 1864—and probably even earlier—steamboats had replaced horses on the trip to St. Cloud.[10]
- In 1784, Mrs. Cradock, an English lady, left us this account: "We walked to Sèvres, where we had to meet the *coche d'eau* for our return trip. We embarked on it at 6:00 AM. It is a big boat capable of carrying more than 100 passengers, with one long central room with windows and seats on both sides. The boat was navigated by

the helmsman and was pulled by six horses. It was very clean and is a very comfortable and safe way to travel. We disembarked in Paris, safe and sound, at 8:00 A.M."
- This trip proved to be so popular that there was not enough room aboard this big boat to accommodate all the people who wanted to be on it.
- The good news was that it was then very easy for such disappointed passengers to hire—and at lower cost—a water-taxi known as a *batelet,* which carried only 16 passengers and left at very convenient times. The very bad news was, it is claimed, that "the toughest sailor was more afraid of spending two hours in such a little boat on the Seine than of signing up on an ocean-going ship bound for the New World!"

In addition to the above vessels, there were also many salt-carrying cargo boats sailing up the Seine to Paris. They are said to have been required to pay about one twenty-seventh of the value of their cargo in river tolls, a stiff charge which was increased to one-twentieth in the 16th century. On the other hand, any cargoes destined for churches or other religious institutions were exempt from these tolls.[11]

On related fronts, in 1414 King Henry laid claim to the French throne and began preparations to invade France to seize claim what he believed was now his. The English therefore had their eyes on the Seine estuary as a valuable military and commercial prize during the Hundred Years War. In 1416, as a result, an English fleet landed on the right bank of the mouth of the Seine where it flows into the English Channel at Chef-de-Caux (now known as Cap de la Hève).

This English amphibious force, equipped with small oar-powered flat-bottomed boats to carry the troops ashore, consisted of 2,000 men-at-arms (lightly armored foot soldiers) with their swords, lances, and other hand weapons, plus 6,000 archers and support troops—perhaps 12,000 soldiers in all. They were landed successfully from their ships at Chef-de-Caux without facing any opposition from the French. They were so well-equipped that they looked much more like a well-organized army of conquest than a simple commando raid.[12]

Under the command of the King Henry V, who was the first English ruler who truly understood the use of ship-power as *a primary weapon of war* rather than simply relying on massed infantry attacks,[13] this impressive force besieged Harfleur, a charming small city located about one mile from the Seine at the head of a tributary valley of the Lézard river.

Harfleur was the principal seaport in north-western France for six centuries but was quite prone to siltation. For this reason, in the 16th century the deep-water port of Le Havre was built about three miles downstream to supplement it. Harfleur is now located on the eastern edge of Le Havre's large urban area but because of its silting problem, it serves only as an *adjunct* to Le Havre rather than as an important port in its own right.

Harfleur was established near a then-defunct French naval shipyard on the Seine known as the *clos-aux-galées*, where oared vessels (galleys) had been built, beginning in about 1293–1295. The shipyard had consisted of a massive wall, built around a loop in the Lézard river. To keep the water at bay, it was said to have been more than six and a half feet thick, stood fifty feet high above the ground, and was thirty-six feet deep.[14]

Harfleur later became, for a time, a nest of French pirates who attacked shipping in the Channel. Later, it again became strategically important as the key to safe navigation on the Seine. It was also essential for replenishing, chiefly by horse-drawn riverboats, the French food supplies stockpiled both in Rouen and Paris.

Lying on the north bank of the tidal Seine estuary, Harfleur controlled access to the Seine. If the English were able to capture Harfleur, they believed they would then have a stranglehold on all the commercial and military traffic on the river and could thus, if they chose to do so, shut down one of the most important inland waterways of France.

It was said that, for Henry V, Harfleur was "the key to the sea of all Normandy," a region that would be the scene of Anglo-French hostilities in the English Channel over many coming years. Harfleur was the also the French port which posed the most immediate threat to English nautical interests because it had become the favored base for French naval attacks on the south coast of England—by pirates, by privateers (a privateer is a private person or a ship that engages in maritime warfare under the legal protection of a commission of war), and by simple raiders.[15]

Supplying a large part of the Paris basin, the stocks of salt, which were essential for preserving fish and meat and which were held in Rouen, were still safe and secure. The port of Rouen itself was well-equipped. Indeed, it might well have become a second Calais, that is, another very successful medieval port. Henry V was well-aware of this fact but he lacked the sizeable land and naval forces that would be needed to capture Rouen, so he did not ever try to do so.

The English victory of 15 August 1416 in the Seine estuary near Harfleur was one of the biggest and most bloody naval clashes of the Hundred Years War. The floating corpses of sailors were visible for several days after this battle, being driven backwards and forwards with the tides. A sensitive observer—a monk of St. Denys—who remarked in sorrow that it "was deplorable that so many Christians should be sacrificed in the vain desire to acquire glory."[16]

5. The Seine in the Hundred Years War

The battle of 1416 erupted because although Henry V had wanted to transform Harfleur into as secure a base for him as Calais, the cross-English Channel distance to Harfleur was four times longer. It was thus beyond the easy reach of English naval power.

Thomas Beaufort, the commander of the English garrison at Harfleur, wrote very moving letters from Harfleur to England, describing the sufferings of his men. As a result, Henry V put his own brother, John, Duke of Bedford, in charge of attacking Harfleur.

Bedford spent the early summer of 1416 organizing his ships and seamen in Southampton in England, and by early August he had pulled together a fleet of about 100 ships. He set sail on 14 August and, helped by a fair wind, reached the Seine estuary that same evening.

The next morning, however, the rising sun revealed that a French fleet of about 150 ships that was already anchored off Harfleur—including eight Genoese carracks, which were bigger, taller, and more powerful than any ships in the English fleet. The Genoese were the best sailors in Europe, and from the high decks of their carracks they could rain arrows and other missiles down upon the English ships, which sat in the water lower than the carracks.

The good news, from the English point of view, was that when Bedford's fleet bore down on the French and Genoese ships under full sail, the sandbars and the confined spaces of the estuary allowed the much greater maneuverability of the English fleet to prevail during a hard-fought seven-hour-long battle. Bedford captured three carracks and forced one carrack to run aground. Both sides suffered heavy casualties, however, the English losing some 20 ships and their crews.

The battle broke the French blockade of Harfleur and thus helped Henry V to achieve English mastery of the local waters—a fact which turned out to be an important prelude to the later English conquest of Normandy itself.[17]

Over and above the details of the Hundred Years War, it was only the Seine that made possible the prosperous lives of the great local French merchants. These men were the charterers of river traffic in northern France who dealt at the same time not only in wine, wood, wheat, and salt, but also in the financial transactions which funded all this commerce. The active trade of such merchants also supported many people in the ports and in the ships, namely, the longshoremen, pilots, market women, rivermen, local officials, and even some of the courtiers in Paris who had a financial stake in this trade.

Seine river traffic was also extremely important to the riverine people making modest livings along the nearby Yonne, Marne, and Oise rivers. At the tolerable cost of some portages from one river drainage basin to another, the wines of Orleans and the Beaune region could be shipped from distant vineyards to the merchants and consumers of Paris.

Moreover, herring from Dieppe and Rouen could now be exported to more distant parts of France. The merchants of Arras, Amiens, Abbeville, and Lille were all major clients of the wine trade. Despite two portages, river transport was still the best way to get the fine wines of Beaune to the tables of the bourgeoisie of Flemish towns.

These favorable commercial considerations, however, must not blind us to the many reports of human suffering along the Seine during the Hundred Years War. For example, wolves dug up bodies from graveyards and even swam across the Seine and attacked people in Paris itself.[18] Perhaps the saddest and most enduring account, though, is the true story of Joan of Arc.[19]

Joan was a French peasant girl who, motivated by what she believed were explicit messages sent to her from Heaven, led a French army against the English in order to put King Charles VII on the throne of France. Jailed on the charge of being a "relapsed heretic," she was burned at the stake, aged about nineteen, at Rouen by the Roman Catholic church. Much later, in 1920, she would be canonized.

The executioner who had been called in to torture Joan when she was being held in a dungeon in Rouen was a man named Maugier Leparmentier. He described her death in these moving words:

> "Once in the fire, she cried out more than six times, 'Jesus!' and especially in her last breath, she cried with a strong voice, 'Jesus!' so that everyone present could hear it; almost all wept with pity."

Richard Beauchamp, the Earl of Warwick, who was in charge of the execution of Joan, ordered her ashes to be collected and then thrown into the nearby Seine so that no relics of her could be claimed and exploited later for religious or commercial purposes.

A local monk, Friar Isambart, who had gone into a nearby church to get a cross which he could hold up above Joan's eyes so that she could see it at the very moment of her death, later reported that the executioner himself had told him that

> although her body had been burned in the fire and reduced to ashes, her heart remained intact and full of blood ... despite the oil, the sulfur, and the carbon that he had applied to the entrails and the heart of Joan, he still could not make them burn in any way, nor could he reduce her entrails and her heart to ashes, at which he was as astonished as if by a confirmed miracle.[20]

On other fronts, during the Hundred Years War the fortress of Château-Gaillard in Normandy was built in 1197–1198 by Richard the Lionheart, who was both King of England and Duke of Normandy. The

5. The Seine in the Hundred Years War

total cost of this fortress, in English pounds sterling, was huge (£21,203) at a time when the total cost of any lesser castle never exceeded £2,893.[21]

Located on a limestone cliff overlooking a large meander of the Seine near the village of Les Andelys, this fortress figured in the struggle between the kings of France and the kings of England. It changed hands several times, and since 1862 its ruins have been classified as a French national monument.

Château-Galliard underwent several sieges during the Hundred Years War. When the French were in control, a bridge of boats, defended by ingenious floating towers mounted on boats, was set up to allow the French army to move freely back and forth between the fortress and the shore. Ultimately, the French were victorious in this campaign.

In 1203, King John of England ordered two of his best men—the famous knight William Marshal and the aggressive mercenary Lupescar—to lead a large expedition up the Seine to relieve Château-Galliard, which was then under siege. This effort, however, was decisively repulsed by the French knight William des Barres.

It is now not clear why Marshal and Lupescar failed in their assignment. One reason may have been that Marshal wanted to put all the blame on Lupescar alone for this debacle. Marshall therefore cast him in a very bad light, later writing as follows:

> But you should know first of all why it was that the king could not win the hearts of his men and draw them to him. Why? By my faith, he allowed Lupescar to treat them so harshly that he seized whatever he came across in the land, as if the land were at war. But that was nothing; for if he dishonoured the men's wives and daughters, not twopennyworth was paid in compensation.[22]

In 1599, Henry IV of France ordered the demolition of Château Gaillard. Although it was already in ruins then, he still felt it might somehow represent a threat to the security of the local French population.

One of the few bits of cheerful news to emerge from this grim fortress came in 1431, when a French army officer, Étienne de Vignobles, who was nicknamed by his enemies as "La Hire" ("the Hireling" or the mercenary) and who was a well-known companion of Joan of Arc, seized it by a surprise attack on behalf of a major French political faction known as the Armagnacs.

A contemporary and lightly annotated historical account by La Hire ran along the following lines:

> In this season, Étienne de Vignolles set out from Louviers with a large company of men-at-arms, who crossed the river of the Seine in boats, and came to take the fortress by climbing the limestone cliff of Château-Gaillard, which is seven leagues away from Rouen; [there], sitting on a rock near the said river of

the Seine, they found Sire Barbazen, who was a high-ranking prisoner of the King of England, and who had been captured in the city of Melun, of which he [Barbazen] was captain. And the victors brought the said Barbazen before the King [Charles VII], who was very joyful of his deliverance.[23]

6

A World Heritage Cultural Site and the Bridges (Ponts) Over the Seine in Paris

In 1991, UNESCO named, as a World Heritage Cultural Site in Paris, a 3½-mile-long central stretch of the Seine. It lies between the Pont de Sully in the east, on the one hand, and the Pont d'Iéna near the Eiffel Tower in the west, on the other.

In 2022, the City of Paris also honored this same stretch of the river by praising it in an official publication as a "Balade au fil de l'eau" ("A stroll along the waterway") and illustrating it with a colorful sketch map showing many places to see and things to do there.[1]

This chapter first describes the Cultural Site itself. It then goes on to introduce the present 37 Paris bridges and footbridges over the Seine, of which the most famous bridges are those of the Pont Alexandre III and the Pont Neuf.

All these crossing points connect the left bank and the right bank over an 8-mile-long stretch of the river in central Paris. A very notable bridge not in Paris and therefore not included above is the very impressive Pont de Normandie ("Normandy Bridge"), which links Le Havre and Honfleur and is the ninth-longest cable-stayed bridge in the world.

Many of the bridges of Paris have good stories to tell. The modern French writer Jean-Marc Larbodière, whose descriptions and photos of these bridges are exceptionally well done, summons the intrepid reader in these translated and lightly edited phrases:

> Dive into the tumultuous history of the 37 bridges of Paris—the wood bridges swept away by floods and ice; the bridges covered with houses that vanished in the waves or in the flames with their inhabitants still inside them; the suspended bridges which trembled with the passage of heavy convoys just before they collapsed....[2]

The Cultural Site

UNESCO has provided a brief but authoritative summary on its Cultural Site which is well-worth outlining here.[3] It begins with the observation that the evolution of Paris and its long history can most easily be seen and understood from the unique vantage points offered from the banks of the Seine.

Ever since its first human settlements were founded in prehistoric times, and notably during the later era of the Parisii tribes, the river has played two important roles for Paris. The first was simply to deter potential aggressors. The second was ultimately more important, however: the economic role which made possible the relatively seamless flow of people, goods, and services.

The Paris that arose in the 16th and the 20th centuries clearly shows its long-term relationship with the Seine.

The stretch of river between the Pont de Sully and the Pont d'Iéna was historically characterized by major differences in local functions. Upstream of this area, for example, was the major port of Paris with its accompanying shipping, labor, and administration.[4] Downstream were the elegant buildings of royal and aristocratic Paris. This latter site was where the structures, functions, and customs of the capital city gradually emerged and, ultimately, were preserved by the French government for future generations with much of their former glory still intact.

From the Île St-Louis to the Pont Neuf, from the Louvre to the Eiffel Tower, and from the Place de la Concorde to the Grand Palais and the Petit Palais, the evolution of Paris and its history can be best understood from the Seine. Many of the most important monuments of Paris have been built along either side of the river and thus profit from their perspectives overlooking it. As the UNESCO World Heritage Center notes,

> United by a grandiose river landscape, the monuments, the architecture, and the representative buildings along the banks of the Seine in Paris each illustrate with perfection most of the styles, decorative arts, and building methods employed over nearly eight centuries.[5]

For example, the Cathedral of Notre-Dame and the smaller but more radiant Sainte Chapelle are both architectural masterpieces of the Middle Ages. The Pont Neuf, constructed from 1578 to 1607, nicely illustrates the advanced abilities of France in bridge-building. The visual unity and the coherence of the Marais district and of the Île-Saint-Louis bear witness to the success of the new skill of French urban planning in the 17th and 18th centuries.

Last but by no means least, the banks of the Seine are adorned by fine examples of French style. These include:

- The Louvre, and the Hôtel des Invalides, the latter originally built as a big hospital but is now a museum commanding a splendid view of the Seine.
- The Cours-la-Reine, which was not only a carriageway and walkway for Queen Marie de Medici, but was also at that time the site of a major water pump for Seine water for Paris.
- This pump was the subject of a jolly and very busy painting by the artist Bizard in 1802. Entitled *La pompe marchande du Cours-la-Reine* ("The market pump of the Cours-la-Reine"), it highlights the pump itself drawing water from the Seine, pumped by hand by three men. It also depicts two horse-drawn carriages with big wooden barrels on them, waiting to hold the water thus pumped, and a wide range of people of various ages and different walks of life, who are passing by or who are flirting near the pump.[6]
- The Champs-Élysées, the École Militaire (the Military Academy), and the Monnaie (the Mint).

Many of the buildings that highlighted the Universal Exhibitions held in Paris in the 19th and 20th centuries have been well-preserved and today still ornament the banks of the Seine. At the top of almost everybody's list is the magnificent, soaring Eiffel Tower—an icon of the city of Paris and its then-state-of-the-art iron architecture. It is one of the wonders of *La Belle Époque* (French golden age of the late 19th century).

The Île Saint Louis, the Quai Malaquais, and the Quai Voltaire are also fine examples of the cohesion of the Parisian building skills honed during the 17th and 18th centuries. Finally, the huge squares and spacious avenues of Paris, conceived of and built by Baron Georges-Eugene Haussmann in the era of Napoleon III, have favorably impacted modern town planning in many other countries of the world.

Taken collectively, all the monuments and buildings of Paris now enjoy a very high level of legal and environmental protection. The government of France controls, directly or indirectly, all the public establishments of Paris; all the quays of the Seine, which are part of the country's fluvial public domain; the Hôtel de Ville, namely, the city hall of Paris, which was located on the Seine; all the parish churches; and numerous other historically significant buildings and plots of land in Paris.

In addition, since 2016 the permanent closure of the lower quays of the Seine to all automobile and truck traffic has greatly helped to preserve the authenticity and integrity of the river in Paris.

The 37 Bridges and Footbridges Over the Seine in Paris

Each of these crossing-points is interesting and historically significant today. Crude bridges, made of trimmed logs, were at first the only possible way for the earliest inhabitants both to defend Paris from external attacks and to keep their subsistence economy flowing along as smoothly as possible.

It is clear today that, without all its bridges (many of which have, in the past, repeatedly been swept away by the Seine, replaced, or significantly modified), Paris could never have risen to become one of the greatest cities on earth. Because of the significant histories and functions of these bridges, brief descriptions of all of them may be of some interest to newcomers to Paris who want to understand how the Seine and the city manage to work so well together.

The first two bridges in Paris were built by the early Parisii (the local inhabitants) in the 3rd century BC to connect the island of the Île-de-la-Cité with both the left and the right banks of the Seine. These log bridges were burned by the Parisii themselves in a failed effort to keep the city out of the hands of the invading Romans. Rebuilt by the Romans, they were then regularly destroyed and replaced over the coming centuries in the same locations.

Bridges over the Seine were increasingly important for the growing import-export economy of Paris but their numbers increased only slowly because of the cost and effort involved in building them. The following list of early bridges shows the trend:

1st century: 2 bridges
Year 900: 3 bridges
Year 1300: 4 bridges
Year 1420: 5 bridges
Year 1620: 7 bridges
Year 1320: 10 bridges[7]

There are now 37 bridges and footbridges in Paris across the Seine, of which five are for pedestrian use only and two are purely railroad bridges. Good stories are associated with many of them, and most of them also lend themselves to good photos.[8] Most scenically, some of them, and the waterways beneath them, define what is called in French *la traversée de Paris*, namely, "the crossing of, or the passage through, Paris."

They will all be introduced briefly in this chapter; many of them will also appear again in later pages. What is worth keeping in mind now that

6. A World Heritage Cultural Site and the Bridges (Ponts)   67

these bridges do offer us a remarkable mosaic of both the ever-changing social realities and the architecture of Paris.⁹

After 52 BC, for example, their prosperity and their more advanced technology permitted the imperial Romans to build much more durable bridges—made not of logs but of timber and stone. These helped protect the gradually-to-expand settlement that would eventually become known as Paris.

Located first on the left bank of the Seine, the town was set there because this area had a higher elevation which kept it out of reach of the flood waters. Later, the lower-lying right bank was settled, too. Initially, this had been bypassed for settlement because it collected water and was often simply a swamp. In fact, it was not until the Middle Ages, as Paris expanded very rapidly and needed more space in which to grow, that these right bank wetlands were filled in and would become prime real estate themselves.

In the 9th century, the Vikings appeared on the scene and attacked Paris several times. Unlike other invaders, however, they relied not on overland transport but on their own ships on the sea and on the rivers to move their ferocious and well-armed men quickly over considerable distances.

For example, during the last Viking attack on Paris, in 885, the fortified bridges that linked the Île de la Cité to both banks had prevented a Viking fleet of 700 "long ships" from rowing and sailing any further upriver.

In 886, however, after a flood had washed away the well-defended Petit Pont ("Little Bridge") at a very narrow part of the river, the Vikings were able to invade Paris. After a year of clashes with the Parisians, they permitted themselves to be bought off at a high price. They finally left Paris, reportedly only after receiving thousands of pounds of silver.

Today, five bridges link the Île Saint-Louis with the rest of Paris; eight bridges link the Île de la Cité to the rest of Paris; and one bridge links these two islands to each other. This chapter, variously drawn from more than 37 online articles and several books dealing with the Seine in Paris, describes all of them very briefly.

Our account must begin, upstream, at the river's entry into Paris at Pont Amont ("upstream bridge") and then proceeds downstream along the river to Pont Aval ("downstream bridge") at the river's exit from Paris.

1. Pont Amont carries the heavily used Boulevard Périphérique, which is the inner ring road of Paris, over the Seine. It does not have a formal official name but is currently known simply as "the upriver bridge." Because of the very intensive car and truck traffic, plus the

fumes from local factories, air quality here often leaves much to be desired.
2. Pont National, which was known as Pont Napoléon-III until 1870, is a road and rail bridge across the Seine in Paris. It was first built as a railway bridge in 1852–1853, and its width was then doubled in 1936.
3. Pont de Tolbiac was built during a wave of urbanization of eastern Paris in the second half of the 19th century. This bridge was hit by a downed British plane in 1943. In the 1990s it became the location for the popular dances known as "techno raves."
4. Passerelle (footbridge) Simone-de-Beauvoir was designed by a well-traveled Austrian architect as a "sweet" transport corridor, that is, one that is not polluting and is strictly limited to walkers, roller-skaters, and bicyclists crossing the Seine in Paris. Built in France and known for its simplicity and harmonious lines, it was transported to its final location by canal, by the North Sea, by the English Channel, and by French rivers, finally crossing Paris itself on a barge.
5. Pont de Bercy (Bridge of Bercy), now the site of the French Ministry of Finances, replaced an older bridge there in 1992 which was famous for a well-known French song, "Sous le ciel de Paris" ("Under the sky of Paris"). This song evokes a philosopher sitting on the bridge, while two musicians play tunes for a few visitors.

An illustration, made long before there was a modern bridge at Bercy, shows one of the banks of the Seine there in about 1716—already hyperactive with barges, pedestrians, local bigwigs, ladies of fashion, boatbuilders, and horsemen.[10]

6. Pont Charles-de-Gaulle is a one-way bridge carrying road traffic to another bridge further downstream (Pont Austerlitz), which in turn carries traffic in the opposite direction. The design of the first bridge was selected as being the one most likely to ease the very heavy bridge traffic of Paris; to connect the new national library of France with the right bank of the Seine; and to establish a direct link between two Paris railway stations (the Gare de Lyon and the Gare Austerlitz).
7. Viaduct d'Austerlitz is used only by Line 5 of the Paris Métro (subway). Because of the restrictions posed by river traffic on the Seine, a unique metal bridge was designed in 1903 that crossed the river in one very long (460-foot) single span. The steel arcs of this bridge were decorated with marine-themes reliefs such as dolphins, seashells, and seaweeds. In addition, parts of the steel footings of the

bridge were etched with figures from the Coat of Arms of the city of Paris, which symbolizes steadfastness in times of difficulty.

8. Pont d'Austerlitz, named after the battle of Austerlitz in 1805, was designed to link the Faubourg (neighborhood) Saint-Antoine on the right bank of the Seine to the Jardin des Plantes (the Garden of Plants) on the left bank.

The first bridge there, built in 1801, was later judged to be too narrow, so over the years its width was gradually increased to 98 feet in 1885. This expansion was necessary because it by then had to handle Paris traffic at a time when the city's population and its commercial and industrial might were all increasing very rapidly.

A pleasant illustration from about 1815 gives a colorful and patriotic look at the new *Halle aux Vins* (Wine Hall) located near the pont d'Austerlitz. It shows a nicely decked-out ship flying the tricolor blue, white, and red French flag, and towing two smaller boats, getting ready to land at the Wine Hall with a cargo of wines.[11]

9. Pont de Sully dates from 1876 and replaces two earlier suspension bridges. The first was destroyed during a revolution in 1848; the second collapsed in 1872 due to the corrosion of its cables. The south section of this bridge now offers a beautiful view of the Île de la Cité.

A painting, done in about 1900, of a yellow-overcast, cold, snowy January afternoon near the Pont de Sully, shows numerous cargo boats moored along the shore. None are underway due to the snowdrifts and freezing conditions. In short, no boating work on the Seine could be carried on then, and thus no money could be earned by the impoverished boatmen.[12]

10. Pont de la Tournelle (Tournelle Bridge) has been the site of successive bridges in 1620, 1637, 1651, 1918, and 1928. From 1627 to 1654, the bridges were made only of wood and therefore collapsed with depressing frequency: only later was stone used instead.

A large two-page portrait of the now-stone Pont de la Tournnelle shows a very busy scene indeed, with no end of bridges, people, swimmers, boats, animals, coaches, and carriages all competing for the viewer's attention.[13]

From 1674 to 1796 there was a mini-port, known as the port of Saint-Bernard, adjacent to the Pont de la Tournelle. This little port was in fact only a marginally wider stretch of the Seine itself. A contemporary two-page illustration, however, shows its shoreline as being quite busy with boats and people. Part of this mini-port, in any case, was so shallow that, at low water, a horse could have forded much of it without getting the rider's high-topped boots too wet.¹⁴

Since 1719, the water level on a scale at the Pont de la Tournelle has been used as an informal "zero mark" for the Seine at Paris, reflecting the ever-changing water levels of the river.

According to this scale and to other information, flood levels in western France could vary widely, ranging from exceptionally disastrous floods (the first record of which, historians tell us, was written by a cleric in Tours, France in 583); to high waters, during which horse-drawn haulage of boats was forbidden on the upper reaches of the Seine; to normal floods; to the prohibition of navigation downstream of Paris due to high waters; to "bonnes eaux" ("good waters," namely, average-level waters); and, finally, to low waters, which would have grounded all but the lightest and most shallow-draft boats.¹⁵ In practice, however, conditions for navigation on the Seine were usually not ideal for about six months of the year, although with care it could still be used then.

The name Pont de la Tournelle refers to a square turret, "La Tournelle," built in 1185 as part of a protective wall around medieval Paris. As will be mentioned later, there have been numerous walls built around Paris and the Seine over the passing years.

The turret was the departure point both for the chain used to close the Seine to shipping in time of war, and for the convicts in chains who were forced to walk from it all the way to the distant naval port of Toulon to serve in the galleys there.

Large amounts of hay as fodder for the many animals needed in Parisian life were shipped to and were stored at the nearby Port au Foin ("hay port") close to the Pont de la Tournelle. By 1900, for example, there were about 98,000 horses in Paris alone, requiring, every day, huge amounts of hay, straw, and oats in order to generate enough traction by horsepower to keep the city running smoothly. Until the advent of, first, the steam engine, and then, much later, the internal combustion engine, the horse-drawn barges of the Seine played the key roles in meeting these needs.

Bordered by old houses, the bridge itself and the Quai de la Tournelle now offer, along with the Pont de l'Archevêché, some of the most splendid views of the Île de la Cité, namely:

- In 1992 and 1998, numerous scenes in the movie *Highlander: The Series* were filmed along the Quai de la Tournelle underneath the Pont de la Tournelle.
- The Pont de la Tournelle is the location of a 1928 statue of Saint Geneviève, who is hailed as the patron saint of Paris.

11. Pont Marie is the oldest bridge in Paris after Pont Neuf, and in its simplicity is considered to be one of the most beautiful.

Pont Marie gets its name from the engineer Christophe Marie, who in 1605 proposed its construction as part of the urbanization of the Île Saint-Louis. It has been said by the modern French writer Guy Lambert that "Le pont Marie est né de l'urbanisation de L'île Saint-Louis." ("Pont Marie was born from the urban growth of the Île Saint-Louis.")[16]

In 1658, a flood destroyed two arches of the bridge. Twenty houses that had been built on top of the bridge were swept away then, along with 60 of their inhabitants. In 1740, the remaining houses atop Pont Marie were removed, and in 1769 it was forbidden to build any more houses on any bridges in Paris.

Two contemporary paintings give us insights into life on the Seine. One, done in the dawn hours of a day in 1758, shows a very placid, peaceful view of the bridge, highlighting its gently curved profile which, as a local expression had it, looked like "the arched back of a donkey."

Another painting, this time from about 1830, shows that while the river, its shores, and most of its arches were by then all jam-packed with boats, people, or horse-drawn wagons, the central arch of the bridge was left entirely unencumbered to permit river traffic to flow through it quickly and smoothly.

Excursion boat companies now operating in Paris on the Seine have sometimes claimed that Pont Marie is truly a "lovers' bridge," where an "old tradition," it is said, encourages you to kiss the person next to you and to make a wish. Charming as this notion may be, there is, alas, no historical basis for such an "old tradition."

12. Pont Louis-Philippe dates from 1833, when King Louis-Philippe celebrated his accession to the throne of France in the wake of the "Trois Glorieuses," that is, the "three glorious days" of a political uprising in July 1830, by laying the first stone for the bridge.

Although the bridge and its tollhouses were burnt down during the February revolution of 1848, the bridge itself was restored in 1862. An engraving from that latter year shows that the bridge under construction, with horse-drawn carriages, prosperous pedestrian families, and bridge-builders all much in evidence.

A remarkable but undated photograph taken for a publicity stunt, entitled "Le plongeon de la mort du haut de pont Louis-Philippe" ("The dive to death from the height of the Louis-Philippe bridge"), shows a daredevil bicyclist in mid-air, sitting on his bicycle. He is dressed in swimming trunks and has just ridden his bicycle at high speed off the bridge—planning to clear the edge of the bridge while still in the air and then to splash down safely in the Seine. It seems likely from the photo and from the title given to it, however, that instead he hit the edge of the bridge first and was killed.[17]

13. Pont Saint-Louis is the seventh bridge in the location, since 1630, to link the Île de la Cité with the Île Saint-Louis. An earlier bridge of 1717–1795 was nicknamed Pont Rouge (Red Bridge) because it was painted red. Much later, a footbridge of 1941 was said to been only an ugly "iron cage." The present bridge was inaugurated in 1970.
14. Pont de l'Archevêché (the Bridge of the Archbishop) is the narrowest road bridge in Paris. After the Pont des Arts was cleared in 2010 of the roughly 35 tons of "love padlocks" (the keys for which had been thrown into the Seine as a gesture of romantic devotion) that had been attached to it, lovers began to attach their padlocks to the Pont de l'Archevêché instead.
15. Pont au Double, so named for the "double" charge to use it (see below), was, in its first incarnation, a bridge used in the Middle Ages to transfer patients from the Hôtel-Dieu hospital to another hospital located on the nearby Île de la Cité. Some of these patients were housed in a two-story building on the bridge itself. Alas, their building and the patients within it, and the bridge itself, were all swept away several times by the flooding river.

Work on the present bridge began in 1626 and continued in in 1847 and 1882. The bridge gets its name from the higher toll fee that was charged there, known as a "double" denier, to pay for construction of the bridge. Its many arcades (vaulted spaces) had a picturesque quality that appealed very much to local artists, who did not want it replaced by a more modern and more sterile structure.

The local laundresses who used these arcades as very convenient and free places to wash both hospital linen and private clothing in the Seine, valued them, too. The very big "floating laundries," which were the big laundry boats moored not in the arcades but in the river itself, were eventually judged to be so unsightly, so unhygienic, and such a hindrance to safe navigation that they were gradually eliminated by 1898.

16. Pont d'Arcole is named for the battle of Arcole in Austria where Napoleon personally led a charge in 1796, waving the tricolor French flag, and defeated the Austrians. A related account is that a young member of Napoleon's army was killed in 1830 as he pushed the staff of the tricolor into the soil, crying out as he imitated Napoleon's action, "Remember that my name is Arcole!" In modern times, this

6. A World Heritage Cultural Site and the Bridges (Ponts)   73

Locks on a bridge over the Seine. This is the Pont de l'Archevêché (the Bridge of the Archbishop) festooned with "love padlocks," the keys to which were thrown into the Seine as a gesture of romantic devotion. In 2010 the Pont des Arts was cleared of the approximately 35 tons of padlocks that had been attached to it over the years, but lovers simply found other places in which to hang their padlocks.

bridge was also notable because it was over it that the first tanks of the French Army rolled during the Liberation of Paris in 1944.
17. Petit Pont (Little Bridge) is noteworthy because at least 13 of its predecessors have been destroyed by ice, storms, or other natural causes since the first bridge was built there in Gallo-Roman times. A modern expert on the bridges of Paris has joked that "up to the beginning of the 16th century, this bridge amused itself by experiencing, first-hand, all the possible variations of the word 'catastrophe.'"[18]

During the Middle Ages, the bridge was most famous for the loud and very lively banter of the market women who were selling food and goods there.

Much later, in 1718, two boats heavily laden with hay tried to pass beneath the bridge at about the same time. That night, a woman whose child had drowned in the Seine during the morning went out in a boat in search of the body. She carried a burning wooden taper to light her way. However, her boat collided with one of the barges loaded with hay, which caught fire. This fiery barge floated into the Petit Pont and burned it down. It was replaced with another bridge in 1719.

18. The present Pont Notre-Dame is the latest of a very long series of bridges that have existed here since at least the pre–Roman tribal era. It was the last of the Paris bridges over the Seine to be built during the Middle Ages. Very briefly, its story is as follows:

> In 886, during the siege of Paris and the Norman attacks, the Roman stone bridge of the time was destroyed and replaced, probably by a wooden plank bridge. Two later wooden bridges in the area were burned in 1111 and were replaced by two famous stone bridges, which in turn were destroyed in a flood of 1296. The wooden bridge that replaced them was destroyed by the floods of 1406. In 1412, King Charles VI of France ordered a new bridge to be built; it was the first version to be called "Notre-Dame."

Composed of solid wood, it took seven years to construct and had 60 houses perched on top of it, 30 on each side. This bridge collapsed in 1499 due to structural weaknesses caused by lack of repairs.

A contemporary account, summarized and edited here, tells the following story:

> During the winter of 1497–1498, floods had severely weakened this wooden bridge. As soon as the extent of the damage was fully understood, skilled carpenters warned both the *prévôt de marchands* [the chief merchant] and the local aldermen of the grave danger they faced, but these men did nothing at all.

Then, one dawn in 1499, a master carpenter rushed up to the most senior local official and warned him that the bridge would surely break up before noon on that very day. The official ordered all those living on the bridge to leave it at once, and he had archers posted to prevent anyone from going onto it.

Before noon on that day, a terrible crackling noise was heard as the bridge collapsed into a cloud of dust that made it impossible to see what was going on. The broken bridge fell into and blocked the Seine; despite the evacuation order, there were numerous casualties among those who were still living on the bridge. Prison sentences and stiff fines were later imposed on those officials responsible for this preventable disaster.[19]

A new bridge was built in 1507 and had 60 heavy houses built on it. They were the first dwellings in Paris to be given house numbers. They also reflected the growing gap between two coexisting but very different societies in Paris: *celle de la rue et celle de l'eau* ("that of the street and that of the river").[20] Both societies were well-represented on the Pont Neuf.

The "society of the street" referred to those living in the houses on the bridge that were occupied by rich merchants who sold expensive paintings there. In 1571, these houses were also elaborately decorated to celebrate a visit of King Charles IX. Remarkably, for this event, the sky itself was "masked"—it could not be seen at all because a highly decorated painted screen had been stretched over the tops of the narrow alleyways of the houses lining the bridge, thus blocking out the sky. The heavy houses would be demolished in 1786 for safety reasons.

The "society of the river" referred instead to the men and women involved in the "joust" described below. This activity involved physically fit young men and young women, who were watched very carefully and were applauded by the prosperous owners of homes on the bridge, who were viewing the "boating set in action" from their balconies.

An illustration of 1756, *La joute des mariniers* ("The joust of the mariners"), by the French artist Nicholas-Jean-Baptiste Raguenet (1715–1793), shows this unusual sport of "jousting" from rowing boats underway near the bridge pillars of the Pont Notre-Dame and the Pont-au-Change.

The Seine was the place where this artist, whose special skill was painting urban and river scenes very quickly to catch the changing light, got most of his inspiration. It was also the subject of some of his very best paintings, which invite the viewer to stand beside the artist as he deftly captures in paint the colorful people and river scenes.[21]

In the sport of boat-jousting, in each boat, an athletic young man or young woman, armed with a padded wooden "spear," stood erect in the stern of the boat and tried to knock his or her opponent off their own boat and into the Seine.[22]

A modern French writer has commented that "the 'people of the water' constituted a separate society which was complicated and diversified: this fact was indeed an essential component in the economic life of Paris."[23] A later and less stressful version of this sport continued on the river at least until 1922.

Another fine picture of the Seine by Raguenet shows the quai des Orfèvres (the wharf of the goldsmiths and jewelers) which was built between 1580 and 1643. Raguenet commented on this section of the river along the following lines in 1759:

> The quays of the Seine here and of the neighboring buildings must by law be conserved for the decoration of the city of Paris. One of the most beautiful ornaments of this neighborhood is that, as it now stands, the banks of the quays on both sides of the river cannot be filled up with houses but must be left in their present open state, from which one can enjoy the agreeable views of the Louvre.[24]

A new stone bridge was installed in Paris in 1853 with fewer arches (only five) than its predecessor. By 1860, a long and broad passageway under the river arches between the Pont Notre-Dame and the Pont-au-Change was closed off. It had contained many visually attractive but very damp and badly lit *cagnards* (vaulted galleries or open-ended grottos) located under the old Hôtel Dieu de la Cité hospital.[25]

Although very evocative and picturesque in the eyes of French artists, toward the end of their days these galleries came to be considered by most Parisians as being very unsightly and unhealthy. No tears were therefore shed when they were torn down when the hospital itself was leveled in 1877.

Though damp and cold, the galleries had long been relied on as totally rent-free working and living areas for impoverished boat-builders and their families. The men of these families were imagined by the French public as being totally idle during the day but then secretly becoming industrious robbers and cutthroats during the dark of the night. Their law-abiding women-folk, on the other hand, used the Seine to wash the clothes of their more prosperous neighbors, who were living in the houses or apartments built on the bridge directly above them.

The new stone bridge caused at least 35 water-traffic accidents between 1891 and 1910. Indeed, it posed such a navigational hazard that it became known to boatmen as the Pont du Diable (the Devil's Bridge). This led to the decision to replace it with a new metal bridge in 1919, which has stood there ever since.

19. Pont Saint-Michel was built in 1372 and has been rebuilt several
    times since then because, initially, it stood on wood pilings rather

6. A World Heritage Cultural Site and the Bridges (Ponts)

than on stone pilings. It and other early bridges were built *très étroits et en dos d'âne* ("very narrow, with a hump in the middle like a pack-saddle on a donkey"). They were covered with wooden houses which could easily catch fire or be swept away by floods and ice-flows.

Near this bridge is the Quai des Grands-Augustins, which was the first quay built (in 1312) and was named for the Augustinian monks who lived and worked there from 1293 until the French Revolution of 1789–1799. By the end of the 18th century, the banks of the Seine near this spot were attracting a wide variety of people: washerwomen, walkers, men digging for anything of value in the mud, and fishermen in small boats.

In 1811 a very lively and very colorful open-air market, *le marché à la Volaille et Pain* (the "Chicken and Bread Market"), was set up along this quay and quickly attracted many local painters. In a seventeenth-century picture of this market, the Seine and some of the bridges are clearly visible.[26]

The most modern and most recent version of the bridge was completed in 1857. Napoleon III used it to publicize his own master plan for Paris by placing an imperial capital "N" on the pilings supporting it. He also had an imperial eagle put on a piling of the Pont d'Iéna.

What this bridge is now most remembered for, however, is that, during the Algerian War of 1954–1962, a tragic and brutal attack there by French police in 1961 resulted in the murder of at least 40, and possibly as many as 300, Algerians.

Their deaths were due both to heavy-handed beatings by the police and because so many Algerians, alive or dead, were then simply thrown into the Seine by the police. Their bodies later washed ashore at many different points along the river.

20. Pont-au-Change, which is today, in river-related terms, treated as separating the upstream portion from the downstream portion of the Seine, owes its name to the goldsmiths and money changers who set up their shops on an earlier version of the bridge during the 12th century. These men played an essential financial role in the economic life in the Middle Ages. An engraving of about 1788 shows the demolition of the many heavy houses still lining this bridge.

During the 15th century, there were about thirty types of gold coins in circulation in the city, and about the same number of silver coins, too. Money changers had to know precisely how much, on any given day, each one was worth in terms of French currency, and could thereby earn small commissions by buying and selling them at the ever-changing market rates.

Pont-au-Change was rebuilt in stone between 1639 and 1647. An engraving dating from the end of the 17th century shows that the Seine downstream of the bridge was by then already chock-full of cargo boats, large and small, with their crews, officials, and onlookers.[27]

In addition, two elevated windmills, one on either end of the bridge, can be seen in the engraving. Their unusual height helped them to catch the wind better, while their excellent commercial location on the river itself made it easy for their employees to buy, process, and sell wheat and other ground grain to pedestrians and boatmen alike.

The present Pont-au-Change was rebuilt between 1858 and 1860 during the reign of Napoleon III. In the process, most of the many very picturesque old buildings there were torn down and were replaced by much more efficient but much less colorful nineteenth-century buildings.

This bridge figures prominently in Victor Hugo's famous 1831 novel *Les Misérables*. In Hugo's book, the senior police inspector on duty in Paris is unable to reconcile his sworn duty to surrender a wanted man to the police because, earlier, this same man had saved this inspector's life. The inspector cannot resolve this contradiction, and therefore concludes that he has no honorable choice but to commit suicide by throwing himself off the Pont-au-Change and into the Seine.

He was certainly not the only victim of suicide-on-the-Seine. For example, according to a 2007 account in the British newspaper *The Guardian*, 50 corpses were pulled out of the Seine's murky waters in 2006 alone, and 146 people were rescued alive. In 2021, Google reported that there were then credible accounts of up to 300 suicides in the Seine, with a few hundred more people still unaccounted for. About 90 people are now thought to attempt suicide in the Seine each year, of whom about 75 are saved.

21. Pont Neuf ("New Bridge") is the oldest standing bridge across the Seine. It was very popular spot in which to do business and in which to see-and-be seen. Because of its historical and social importance, it will be discussed at again later in this book.

An illustration from about 1800 shows its very busy boating scene, highlighted by numerous small skiffs used by passengers to get from one bank of the Seine to the other. These were colorfully known as *Barques à Charon* ("Charon boats"), named after the mythological Greek figure Charon, whose job it was to ferry the souls of the dead across the River Styx.

As late as 1830, the arches of Pont Neuf were still providing both living space for poor families and room for the laundry work by which the wives could help support large families.[28] Some of their colleagues undoubtedly found similar jobs on the great many *bateaux-lavoirs* ("laundry boats") moored in the Seine around Paris.

6. A World Heritage Cultural Site and the Bridges (Ponts) 79

22. Pont des Arts, demolished in 1981 because of its fragility, was rebuilt in the same style in 1984 but with fewer arches—only seven.

By 2014 there were more than 700,000 love-padlocks attached to this bridge, which constituted both a safety concern for the bridge because of their great weight and an eyesore for Parisians. In 2015, city council workmen from Paris began to cut off the locks after years of complaints from the inhabitants of Paris. It is now illegal to attach locks to this bridge.

The Pont des Arts has long had a humorous connotation. In his 1954 song about this bridge, Georges Brassens, for example, warned young women: "If by chance when you are on the Pont des Arts and plan to cross it in a high wind, the naughty wind requires that you take good care to manage your skirt properly!"[29]

23. Pont du Carrousel has been rebuilt several times since 1831 but is most prominently and sadly remembered today for the Brahim Bouarram Affair, in which the Moroccan immigrant Brahim Bouarram and many of his co-religionists drowned after violently being pushed into the Seine by members of a right-wing National Front procession. On a more positive note, however, this bridge is the one closest to the artistic treasures of the Louvre.
24. Pont Royal, built between 1685 and 1689 to replace an earlier bridge built of wood, was a great success. Paintings of c. 1684 and of 1738 show it surrounded by boats in the Seine and being heavily used by merchants and travelers along its banks. Because navigation could be so difficult between Pont-Royal and Pont-au-Change, in 1745, two newly developed winches were installed there replace the horses previously used to help navigators move the boats upstream against the strong current.[30]

Together with the Pont-Neuf, the Louvre, and the college of Four Nations, Pont Royal also became a key part of *le basin du Louvre* ("the Louvre basin")—a dramatic and large reach of the Seine dedicated to such popular public events as holiday celebrations and theatrical spectacles, which were very much appreciated by the rank-and-file Parisians.

On the eve of the French Revolution in 1789, a colorful painting of the Louvre basin shows a heavily laden cargo boat slowly making its way *upstream against the strong current of the Seine*. What is noteworthy is that this boat has no engine, no sails, no oars, no poles, and no horses pulling it. How, then, could it make any headway against the current?

The answer lies in what was known as an "aquamotor." This was a clever machine that was moored upstream under a bridge which had a strong flow of water under it. The running water drove paddle wheels inside the machine which in turn powered a winch that, thanks to a long and strong rope attached to the bow of the boat, slowly towed the boat upstream to the bridge.[31]

Today this bridge has a hydrographic ladder which shows the water level and the year of Seine floods in Paris.

25. Passerelle Léopold-Sédar-Senghor is architecturally unique. Completed in 1999, it is covered in exotic wood and is named in honor of Léopold-Sédar-Senghor, the first President of Senegal from 1960 to 1980.
26. Pont de la Concorde was initially built from 1786 to 1791 during the turmoil of the French Revolution using stone taken from the Bastille—the fortress and prison captured by the revolutionaries in 1789. The Seine still flows along smoothly under the bridge's five very broad arches, which were designed to be big enough to drain off as much water and as quickly as possible during the river's floods. Today the bridge carries much of Paris's very heavy road traffic.
27. Pont Alexandre III, built between 1896 and 1900, is a marvel of nineteenth-century engineering and is known for its exuberant use of Art Nouveau lamps, cherubs, nymphs, and winged horses. It has appeared frequently in modern films and videos of Paris. To make sure it did not become a bottleneck that impeded navigation on the Seine, however, it was designed and built with only one very broad (bank-to-bank) arch over the river.

This majestic bridge was erected for the World Fair of 1900. Its first stone was laid by Tsar Nicolas II in 1896 and, ever since then, the bridge has symbolized the traditional political and economic bonds between France and Russia. The bridge was a technical and dramatic achievement in its own time. The two golden Pegasus statues on the left bank of the Seine represent war, while the two statues on the right bank represent peace.

28. Pont des Invalides is today the lowest (the most downstream) bridge crossing the Seine in Paris. Its predecessor dated from 1821, and the only modification to the present bridge was to expand its pavement in 1956.
29. Pont de l'Alma commemorates the battle of Alma during the Crimean War, in which a Turkish-French-British alliance defeated the Russian army in 1854. This bridge was constructed extremely rapidly—in just over three months—by 600 men working on it at the same time.

As mentioned earlier, the general public in Paris has long used the statue of a soldier, known as *The Zouave*, installed on one side of this bridge to measure the rising level of the Seine in times of flood.

6. A World Heritage Cultural Site and the Bridges (Ponts)

30. Passerelle Debilly is named after a French general who was killed during the battle of Jena in 1806. This footbridge was used as a clandestine gathering place for the secret service agents of East Germany during the Cold War. In 1989, a German diplomat working for the Secret Service of the Democratic Republic of Germany was found dead on this footbridge several days after the fall of the Berlin Wall.
31. Pont d'Iéna ("Jena Bridge") dates from 1807, when Napoleon, I ordered it built to commemorate his victory in 1806 at the battle of Jena. When France faced a military setback in 1815, a victorious Prussian general wanted to blow up this bridge and had mines placed on it for this purpose. Louis XVIII, however, intervened and saved the bridge, which later, from 1848 to 1853, was decorated by fine sculptures.

At least until 1945, this bridge was also a favored spot for swimmers and divers. In more recent times, it is best known for the "Renault stairs"— the stairs down which the actor James Bond drove a hijacked Renault 11 taxi while chasing an assassin.

32. Pont de Bir-Hakeim was named to commemorate the battle of Bir Hakeim, fought by Free French forces against the German Afrika Korps in 1942. It has featured in many movies, e.g., *Last Tango in Paris*, and is still a very popular venue for weddings, when the billowing white dress of a bride always highlights the handsome but stern supports of the bridge itself.
33. Pont Rouelle is now used only for railway service.
34. Pont de Grenelle was renamed in 2016 to honor the students of the French Cavalry School who defended the Loire region in the 1940 battle of Saumur. In the middle of this bridge, dating from the 1960s, is a copy of the Statue of Liberty by the sculptor Auguste Bartholdi.
35. Pont Mirabeau, listed as an historical monument in 1975, was celebrated in a 1912 poem by Guillaume Apollinaire that was later set to music. Entitled *Sous le pont Mirabeau coule la Seine* ("Under the bridge of Mirabeau flows the Seine"), it tells us that "we must always remember the loves that we have had. Joy always comes after sorrow."[32]

The original wooden structure with six arches was replaced in 1874 by an iron bridge, which was in turn replaced by the present structure in 1966. It is now decorated with four large statutes of lovely female figures which make its pylons unusually photogenic.

36. Pont de Garigliano is the tallest river bridge in Paris, being 33 feet above the level of the Seine. It attracts, alas, a number of people bent on suicide.
37. Pont Aval was opened in 1968 and owes its name to its position on the Seine. "Aval" means "downstream" in French: it is the last bridge over the Seine in Paris before it leaves the city and continues its journey to the English Channel.

7

Île Saint-Louis

This chapter and the chapters immediately following it discuss some of the most noteworthy historical monuments and buildings located along the 3½-mile-long stretch of the Seine in central Paris. We have found this distance to be an easy and very pleasant stroll, beginning at Pont Sully in the east and then following the Seine downstream to the Eiffel Tower in the west.

Taken collectively, the structures on this walk constitute the UNESCO World Heritage Site. They include: the Île Saint-Louis; Notre Dame, which is truly the cradle of Paris, located in the very heart of the city; La Sainte-Chapelle; the Pont Neuf; the Louvre; the Musée d'Orsay; the Place de la Concorde; the Grand Palais and the Petit Palais; and, last but by no means least, the sky-scraping Eiffel Tower.

An illustration of the Île Saint-Louis, seen from the Place de Grève between 1753 and 1756, gives a dramatic view of the Seine and of the big buildings, bridges, boats, horse-drawn wagons, and pedestrians there at that time.[1]

Another illustration from about 1840 shows two rivermen plying their trade by navigating a heavy and cumbersome "train" of logs around a bend in the Seine near the Île Saint-Louis. In this same picture, two or three boatloads of prosperous and well-dressed city men and city women are in the process of enjoying a relaxing day out on the water.[2]

We will begin here with the Île Saint-Louis, which offers some early and excellent examples of Parisian architecture, construction, and town planning during the 17th and 18th centuries. Because of its stellar location on the Seine, if we ourselves had huge sums of money at our disposal and if a suitable property was for sale there, the Île Saint-Louis is where we would want to live in Paris because of its elegance and its central location.

Although there now seems to be no official French government mandatory management plan or management authority focused exclusively on Île Saint-Louis, thanks to broader but very stiff legal and regulatory protections all significant management decisions by owners or tenants there are in fact controlled by the French government.

For example, the "Cahier des prescriptions urbaines et paysagères pour la mise en valeur des Berges de la Seine dans Paris" ("Urban and Landscape Requirements for the Enhancement of the Banks of the Seine in Paris") is the basic reference document for all activities and installations along the river's banks there.

Île Saint-Louis itself is quite small—only 27 acres in size and with a population of only about 4,453 inhabitants—and it is one of the only two natural (non-man-made) islands in the Seine near Paris. The other island is the nearby Île de la Cité, which is the location of the great cathedral of Notre-Dame de Paris and other impressive sights. Five bridges connect the Île Saint-Louis to both banks of the Seine and to the Île de la Cité, the latter by the Pont Saint-Louis.

First known as the Île Notre-Dame, the Île Saint-Louis was initially used only for grazing cattle, fishing, drying laundry, and as a good place to fight a duel. In 1360, it was bisected by a canal designed to bring it within the protection of a new wall around Paris being built by King Charles V. The smaller segment of the island that was left outside the wall was renamed the Île des Vaches (Island of Cows) and was used to graze cattle, build boats, and store wood.

One of the first real estate developers of the Île Saint-Louis was Christophe Marie who, starting in 1614, became the chief builder for Marie de Medici, the widow of King Henry IV of France and the regent of the young King Louis XIII.

Marie de Medici instructed Christophe Marie as her builder to fill in the canal which divided the island and then to build solid stone banks around the island to keep it dry and thus turn it into a very desirable building site. She promised to provide a long list of benefits, ranging from tennis courts to laundry boats,[3] to prospective buyers. She did in fact sell some lots, but most of her aristocratic customers preferred to settle in the Marais quarter instead because, unlike the Île Saint-Louis, it had enough room for the big gardens they valued.

Moreover, the canons of the cathedral of Notre-Dame, who were the clerics who lived there under a religious rule of life known as a "canon" and who collectively owned a good bit of the island, strongly resisted the Queen's development efforts. In the end, Christophe Marie was driven into bankruptcy. The best lots (the waterfront properties) were bought by rich investors; the poorer merchants and the artisans fared as well as they could by living in the interior of the island. In 1725 the island was named in memory of Louis because it was believed that he had sometimes held court and rendered justice there.

7. Île Saint-Louis

In 17th and 18th-century Paris, the Île Saint-Louis was one of the richest neighborhoods of the city. Today many large, very elegant, and quite private townhouses can still be found along the Quai d'Anjou and elsewhere.

The Quai de Bourbon, for example, is named for the French royal family. It is quite unusual because all its houses *faced the Seine*, contrary to local tradition, which held that houses should *face away from it*, presumably so that the rich men and their delicate wives who lived there would not be forced to gaze upon dirty water and dirty river-families.

In addition, the Quai d'Orleans was the site of the first urban master plan ever drawn up for Paris. Another interesting street is the main commercial street of the island. Known as the Rue Saint-Louis en l'Île, it runs down the center of the town from one end of the island to the other.

Its most famous residential building is the palatial privately owned mansion known as Hôtel Lambert. This magisterial townhouse has a rotunda overlooking the adjacent Seine and was built in 1640 by the royal architect Louis Le Vau.[4]

Over the years, Hôtel Lambert had many remarkable residents. In the 18th century, for example, the owner was the Marquis de Chatelet, whose wife, Émilie de Breteuil, was for fifteen years the mistress of the French Enlightenment writer, historian, and philosopher Voltaire (1694–1778). Voltaire was very famous for his biting wit, for his telling criticisms of the Roman Catholic Church, and for his calls for freedom of speech, freedom of religion, and the separation of church and state.

In addition, this stately dwelling was also the home of a Polish prince in 1843, who entertained many famous writers and musicians. Later, it became the home of the French actress Michèle Morgan; the art collector Baron Guy de Rothschild; and Abdallah Al Thani, brother of the immensely wealthy Emir of Qatar. It was seriously damaged by a fire in 2013 but has now been fully restored.

Today, however, the Île Saint-Louis is probably best known to the general public for the products of Glaces Berthillon, a French manufacturer and retailer of luxury ice cream and fine sorbet. The company's primary store is located on the Île Saint-Louis and attracts many French and foreign visitors. There are often long lines of customers in front of the store.

8

The Glory of Notre-Dame de Paris

This great medieval cathedral by the Seine, whose name in French means "Our Lady of Paris" (the Virgin Mary), is one of the finest and largest examples of French Gothic architecture in the world. It can be appreciated from the Seine itself by boat, as well as by land from its shore. Because of limitations of space here, this chapter can touch on only a few of its many key points.

Visually, the façade of the cathedral is highlighted by an immense "parvis," a forecourt, constructed in the 19th century, whose name comes from the Greek word for "paradise." The modern French scholar Alain Erlande-Brandenburg adds that "the sober grandeur of the façade comes from the visual interplay between the vertical and horizontal lines of the church, on the one hand, and the variations in the façade caused by its huge doorways, bays, and stained glass windows, on the other."[1]

Construction began in 1163 under the leadership of Bishop Maurice de Sully, who wanted to build this church in the new Gothic style. Hallmarks of this style include the use of pointed arches, ribbed vaults, and buttresses to support the master vault. These innovations led to the virtual disappearance of very heavy and cumbersome stone walls, and to their replacement by the large but light stained glass of "radiant architecture" (see below).

The cathedral was largely completed by 1345, although modifications went on for many subsequent years. The high walls around it were built as part of a construction plan to transform the soft marshy edges of the Île de la Cité into the firm herb gardens so much valued by the canons who lived there. During the Middle Ages, the island was also used as an archery and crossbow range, and by washerwomen as a good place to dry the clothes they had just washed in the Seine.

Today, the cathedral is most famous for its dramatic use of ribbed

8. The Glory of Notre-Dame de Paris

Notre-Dame and the Seine. Having survived a huge and nearly terminal fire in 2019, Notre-Dame is arguably one of the finest and largest examples of French Gothic architecture in the world. Its name in French means "Our Lady of Paris," referring to the Virgin Mary. Located on the banks of the Seine, it can be appreciated from the Seine by boat and from the shore.

vaults; flying buttresses; huge and exceptionally colorful stained glass rose windows; numerous sculptural adornments, illustrating Biblical stories for those who could not read, so that the church became a *liber pauperum* (a "poor people's book"); monstrous, sonorous church bells; gargoyles that divert rainwater from the roof and project it a far away from the foundations of the building; and, last but never least, some highly valued relics of the Christian faith.

Badly damaged by neglect and by vandalism during the French Revolution, Norte-Dame was saved from total destruction only beginning in 1831, when Victor Hugo published his famous novel, *Notre-Dame de Paris* (known in English as *The Hunchback of Notre-Dame*). In our own times, the cathedral was badly damaged by a great fire in 2019, which will be discussed here in later pages.

This cathedral, located on the Île de la Cité in the middle of the Seine, is the one of the most visited monuments in Paris, with about 12 million people coming to see it every year. The best single description we have ever read of it is also the shortest. It consists of only three French words, namely: *La Cathédrale Rayonnante* ("The Radiant Cathedral").[2]

Outstanding medieval architects, working on the cathedral from about 1250 to 1270, achieved the amazing result of *éclairement* ("illumination")—chiefly by doubling the height of the big windows to let in much more light. This off-set the major defect in the cathedral: the very feeble lighting of its somber interior.

For all these reasons, Notre-Dame merits a description here. Our comments are inspired by two excellent sources in French. These are (1) Alain Erlande-Brandenburgh's magisterial, lavishly illustrated 2015 book, *Notre-Dame de Paris*, and (2) Jean-Marie Pérouse de Monclos's scholarly commentary on the cathedral, which appears in his 1994 study of the great monuments of Paris. Both these works are listed in the bibliography of the present book.

The history of the Notre-Dame area goes back to at least to 14 BC to 37 BC, to the reign of the Roman Emperor Tiberias. This is shown by the discovery of the Pillar of the Boatmen, known in French as *le pilier de Nautes*, which was found buried under the choir of the cathedral of Notre-Dame during repair-work in 1711.

It was a remarkable tribute to the Seine itself and to the hardy boatmen who worked along it and lived near it. Both were so important that, as the French medievalist Jean Favier tells us, from the earliest recorded times on, "the major commercial thoroughfare, and the foundation of the prosperity of Paris, was always the Seine."[3]

Paris, founded at an ideally located junction of river and road, was the key city in which local boatmen, longshoremen, clerics, merchants, and scholars all wanted to live and work. Fundamentally, it owed its prosperity to domestic and foreign trade, and to the resulting easy transport and transshipment of all kinds of merchandise and foodstuffs.

Its early Roman-built and principal road axis linked the left bank of the Seine, where the forum was the key feature, to the right bank, which was dotted with simple dwellings. Because of the importance of the river, however, in this setting the boatmen clearly played a key role in local affairs and were among the town's leading citizens, not just manual workers on the river.

The carved stone pillar—an offering from the boatmen of the Seine to Tiberius—shows the great importance of the river even at that early time. Now on display in Paris at the Cluny museum, the Musée national du Moyen Age ("National museum of the Middle Ages"), it features images from both the Celtic pantheon and from that of the Roman era (the deity Jupiter). As such, it is a rare but good example of syncretism in France—the amalgamation of two very different religions or cultures.[4]

Much later, because of its strategic location on the Île de la Cité, the cathedral of Notre-Dame was most often painted or illustrated as being surrounded by large numbers of both cargo and passenger boats. One of the biggest and best contemporary illustrations dates from the end of the 17th century: it shows the Seine at the eastern tip of the Île de la Cité, chock-full of boats.

This is the view that contemporary boatmen would have seen every day as they navigated their vessels along the Seine.[5] Because of the dangers involved in river navigation and the high value of some of the goods they transported, these men were very carefully selected. River merchants chose only the most able men and then presented them to the *prévot* (the senior government official) to receive a formal letter of commission as a *maître de pont* ("master of the bridge").[6]

A great deal has been written about Notre-Dame over the years, perhaps most famously in Victor Hugo's 1831 novel *Norte-Dame de Paris*. Hugo was quite appalled that because the cathedral had not been maintained for many years that it was in very bad shape indeed when he wrote the novel. Because of his anger at this state of affairs, he was single-handedly responsible for saving this then-very-down-at-heel cathedral from total ruin.

He summed up his strong personal feelings in 1831 along these translated lines:

> Without doubt, the cathedral of Notre-Dame de Paris is still a majestic and sublime edifice. Nevertheless, no matter how well her beauty has been preserved in her old age, it is still hard not to object to the numberless degradations and mutilations that both time and mankind have inflicted on this venerable monument, without showing any respect for two great leaders—Charlemagne, who laid its first stone, and Philippe Augustus, who laid the last.
>
> On the face of this old queen of our cathedrals, alongside a wrinkle [some small defect], one also always finds a scar [some more serious damage to the building caused lack of proper maintenance].[7]

Hugo's book inspired so much popular interest in Notre-Dame that the result was a major restoration project undertaken between 1844 and 1864, led by the French architect Eugène Viollet-le-Duc. In a nice touch, the latter's real-life facial features were reproduced on the statue of Saint Thomas, which was located at the base of the cathedral's spire, built in 1859, but which was, alas, destroyed by the great fire of 2019. France has now decided to replace this spire.

Hugo's novel also contained a much deeper message embedded in its long and very dramatic plot. As he stressed in a Note to the 1832 edition of the book, *it is the cathedral itself that becomes the focal point of the inevitable and recurrent cycles of human development*, namely, first due to the stern repression by religious and secular authorities, which then eventually gives way to more human freedom as the day of the common man finally begins to dawn. *Notre-Dame de Paris is* thus, in Hugo's view, not just a literary drama but in fact a monument to Romanticism in its most vigorous form.[8]

The cathedral of Norte-Dame has always inspired legions of artists and photographers. The best modern photographs we know of are those in Alain Erlande-Brandenburgh's excellent 2015 French-text book, *Notre-Dame de Paris*, which is listed in the bibliography.

One of the most colorful early descriptions of Notre-Dame comes from the medieval French philosopher, theologian, and political writer Jean de Jandun (c. 1285–1328). He describes it in these ringing words, as translated from his 1323 *Treatise on the Praises of Paris*. The extract given below has been shortened and lightly edited.

Jean de Jandan tells us:

> The most glorious church of the most glorious Virgin Mary, mother of God, deservedly shines out, like the sun among stars. And although some speakers, by their own free judgment, because [they are] able to see only a few things easily, may say that some other [church] is more beautiful, I believe, respectfully, that if they attend more diligently to the whole and the parts [of Notre-Dame], they will quickly retract this opinion.
>
> Where indeed, I ask, would they find two towers of such magnificence and perfection, so high, so large, so strong, clothed roundabout with such multiple varieties of ornaments?
>
> Where, I ask, would they find such a multipartite arrangement of so many lateral vaults, above and below? Where, I ask, would they find such light-filled amenities as the many surrounding chapels? Furthermore, let them tell me in what church I may see such a large cross, of which one arm separates the choir from the nave.
>
> Finally I would willingly learn where [there are] two such circles, situated opposite each other in a straight line, which on account of their appearance are given the name of the fourth vowel [namely, "O"]; among which [are] smaller orbs and circles, with wondrous artifice, so that some arranged circularly, others angularly, surround windows ruddy with precious colours and beautiful with the most subtle figures of the pictures.
>
> In fact, I believe that this church offers the carefully discriminating such cause for admiration that its inspection can scarcely sate the soul.[9]

One of the special qualities of Notre-Dame is its generous use of the "flying buttress" (in French "*arc-boutant*"). These were buttresses used in large-scale construction projects. They consisted of two basic parts: (1) a massive vertical pier of masonry, located *well away from the wall* of a given building, and (2) a masonry arch—the "flyer" of the flying buttress, which bridged the gap between the pier and the wall.

The purpose of this arrangement was to transfer to the ground, by

8. The Glory of Notre-Dame de Paris

both means of the flying buttress and by the massive pillar of masonry, the enormous lateral forces generated by a heavy vaulted ceiling of stone and by the great pressure of any strong wind on a big roof. The flying buttresses of Notre-Dame were among the first to be used in a Gothic cathedral.

Gradually, later architects were able to make the arches quite long, e.g., up to 50 feet in length, quite strong, and quite thin. In fact, some of the arches used in Amiens Cathedral, Le Mans Cathedral, and Beauvais Cathedral (all located in France) were built with only one thickness of wedge-brick, with a capping stone atop. Another practical use of the flying buttress was to reinforce an old load-bearing wall that was in danger of collapsing.

From an aesthetic point of view, the flying buttress also made the interior of cathedrals much less leaden, much brighter, and therefore more comfortable places for people to sit, stand, or kneel. It was now possible, for example, for architects to use many large stained glass windows, which gave the impression of more open space with fewer visual boundaries. Since these windows usually depicted Biblical themes, they were also, in effect, easily understood picture-books for the many illiterate men, women, and children who were attending religious services.

We are indeed very lucky that Notre-Dame is still with us. As mentioned earlier, on 15 April 2019, while the cathedral was being renovated and restored, its roof caught fire and burned for nearly 15 hours before the flames could be put out by huge amounts of water pumped up from the Seine.

The 800-ton timber and lead-coated spire of the cathedral and the entire lead-covered wooden roof covering the nave, the choir, and the transept were entirely destroyed. Molten lead contaminated the site and the nearby environment. After the fire, many ideas were put forward for restoring Notre-Dame, but the French National Assembly finally decided that restoration must preserve the cathedral's traditional historic, artistic, and architectural qualities.

Reconstruction began only after the cathedral had been finally stabilized against any possible collapse caused by the fire, with the ambitious goal of completing all the work by the opening of the 2024 Summer Olympics in Paris.

Until then, Notre-Dame is closed to the public. The first post-fire mass will be held in the cathedral nave in 2024 when Notre-Dame will formally be returned to control of the Roman Catholic Church, even if all the reconstruction work has not been finished by then. In the meantime, an upgrading of the area around the cathedral will open it up towards the Seine and will help the 12 million or so visitors who come each year move through this monumental area more smoothly.

Plans now call for the square in front of the cathedral to be treated as a kind of "physical clearing" in this very populous urban landscape. It will be surrounded by trees which will give some shade to the visitors lining up during the summer and which will also provide more open and more expansive views of the Seine itself. This new and more pedestrian-friendly open space will be in place by 2027.[10]

In the meantime, an unexpected treasure was found during a search of the burned area. This is an ancient sarcophagus made of lead which is believed to have contained the remains of a high-ranking person, probably an official of the cathedral. It dates from about the 14th century.

With it, fragments of a rood screen were found, too. A common feature in late medieval church architecture, a rood screen was an ornate partition installed between the chancel and nave. It was typically an open tracery made of wood, stone, or wrought iron.

The world-famous rose windows of Notre-Dame are still among the greatest artistic and technical achievements of the entire Middle Ages. A rose window is a circular window, especially one that has ornamental tracery radiating out from the center to form a symmetrical rose-like pattern which supports the many pieces of stained glass.

In Notre-Dame there are three rose windows—the West Rose (built c. 1225), the North Rose (built in 1250), and the South Rose (built in 1260)—all of them are magnificent works of art. Taken collectively, they constitute a trio of immense round stained-glass windows installed over the three main portals of the cathedral. Seemingly miraculously, none of the rose windows suffered any serious damage during the great fire.

One of the best descriptions of how these windows were made comes from Georgetown University's Repository Library, which makes the following points (lightly edited here):

- The remarkable fact that *glass* could be involved in piercing a wall supporting many tons of stone is a quintessentially Gothic architectural feat.
- It was accomplished by crossing apertures with visually delicate but structurally strong webs of stone. These divide the glass into smaller shapes in a symmetrical way, thus distributing weight equally across the perforated wall and creating the impression of a curtain of light.
- Norte Dame's north transept wall, consisting of a rose window surmounting 18 lancet windows, was built ca. 1250–1260 while Jean de Chelles was the architect. Most of the original thirteenth-century glasswork is still intact, filtering light into a rainbow of blues, reds, greens, browns, and yellows.

8. The Glory of Notre-Dame de Paris

- The wide spectrum of colors achieved in Medieval France's stained glass windows was produced by varying both the proportion of metal added to molten glass and the temperature to which the mixture was heated. Impurities in the metals, bubbles in the cooled glass, and variations in the thickness of the cut would ultimately contribute to the jewel-like quality of the finished windows.
- The colored glass was cut to size by using heat or a diamond. Precise details, such as facial features, drapery, and foliage, were first painted on the glass with a mixture of scrap glass, copper, and blue sapphire dissolved in wine or in urine. The resulting "glass painting" was then baked again, thus generating chemical reactions that produced visually striking results.[11]

9

The Sainte-Chapelle

Two historic illustrations of this outstanding building (arguably one of the most glorious buildings in the whole world) show us, in 1754 and in 1818 respectively, its location on the Île de la Cité itself and its position near the Seine bridges of the Pont-au-Change and the Pont Notre-Dame.[1]

In 1242–1248, King Louis IX of France ordered the Sainte-Chapelle (Holy Chapel) to be built in the heart of his fine residence in Paris—the Palais de la Cité (Palace of the City). Today the Sainte Chapelle is no longer a church. It was secularized after the French Revolution and is now operated by the French Centre of National Monuments, along with the nearby Conciergerie, which is the other remaining part of the original palace. During the French Revolution, a total of about 4,000 prisoners were housed here at one time or another.

Completed in the record time of only six years, the Sainte-Chapelle was both a monument and a reliquary to house what was believed to be the Crown of Thorns worn by Christ when he was crucified. It is said that King Louis paid more for the Crown of Thorns that he did for the entire chapel. Possession of these holy relics was believed by many of the people of the time to be conclusive proof that Louis IX was in fact the legitimate and the most powerful monarch of Western Christianity and therefore its secular leader.

The Sainte-Chapelle is adorned with a unique set of 15 stained glass windows 49 feet high, which depict 1,113 scenes from the Old and the New Testament, telling the story of the world from its beginning up to the arrival of the relics in Paris. There is also a large rose window, 29 feet in diameter, which is technically described, thanks to its flame-like curling designs, as being "flamboyant." It was installed in the 15th century.

All these windows bath the inner walls with an ever-changing flood of light. This remarkable building is therefore widely considered to be the crown jewel of French Rayonnant (Radiant) Gothic architecture and was listed as a historic monument in 1862.

9. The Sainte-Chapelle

There are two chapels in the Sainte-Chapelle. The lower chapel, now used as a souvenir shop for the National Center for Historic Monuments, is low, dark, and somber because it is overshadowed by the adjoining buildings. In sharp contrast, however, the height, elegance, magnificence, and intensity of the colors of the upper chapel itself are all justifiably world-famous.

These latter are the qualities that the French poet, dramatist, and diplomat Paul Claudel (1868–1955) must have had in mind when, in *L'oeil écoute* ("The eye listens"), he wrote a moving description of the stained glass windows of the upper chapel.

Because his account was written in a very concise and highly stylized "artistic" French which is not easy to translate into standard English, we will simply paraphrase its essence, using his own here-translated terms as much as possible.

- Claudel tells the reader that this curtain of stained glass is "an ardent confession of pulverized colors and luminous points."
- Because of the religious scenes it depicts, it has value not so much as a continuing story, but rather as "a hymn to the simultaneous and permanent flowering of the colorful glass panels around us."
- This abstract artistic approach can also be understood in purely intellectual terms. Here, indeed, Claudel believes, we can understand that this approach also represents "paradise rediscovered."[2]

10

Pont Neuf

Pont Neuf ("New Bridge"), now the oldest bridge across the Seine, was the brainchild of Henri III in 1577 and was financed by his royal treasury. It is located on the downstream end of the Île de la Cité, the small island which was the historic birthplace of the city of Paris.

Built in 1578–1607, this bridge has been listed since 1889 by the French Ministry of Culture as a historical monument. It was the first bridge in Paris to cross both sections of the Seine, the first bridge not to have any houses built on it, and the first bridge to have pavements for carts and pedestrians installed on it.

In the 17th century, there were very few bridges in Paris and the residents wanted very much to be able to cross the Seine at a convenient point downstream of the tip of the narrow Île de la Cité. Construction of a new bridge there first got underway in 1578 but technical problems delayed the work until 1602. The Pont Neuf we see today was finally opened to the public in 1606.

Exceptionally, in order to preserve the impressive views of Paris that could be seen from the bridge, no houses were allowed to be built on it. That said, a very active commercial life was nevertheless encouraged or at least tolerated for many years: clothes dealers, food stalls, and many other business enterprises soon set up their shops near the bridge along the nearby footpaths bordering the Seine.

Remarkably, a photo taken in around 1900 shows mattress makers hard at work on the Quai du Louvre, just downstream from the Pont-Neuf. The raw materials they needed (wool, hair, and feathers) were all delivered to them by barges plying the Seine.[1]

In addition, many ambitious singers, actors, and other entertainers eagerly came forward to cater to the crowds that always formed around and on the bridge. These people were celebrated in a song of the times under Louis XIII (1601–1643), entitled "Les Filouteries du Pont-Neuf" ("Frauds of the Pont-Neuf"), which ran along the following lines:

10. Pont Neuf

> You, meeting-place of charlatans,
> Tricksters, tarts,
> Oh Pont-Neuf, theater of the street!
> Sellers of unguents and suppositories,
> Home of teeth-pullers, rag merchants, booksellers, show-offs,
> Singers of new songs,
> Panderers, purse-cutters,
> Smart-asses and masters of filthy trades.[2]

Named "New Bridge" to distinguish it from earlier bridges, Pont Neuf is now composed of two separate spans. One of them has five arches and extends to the left bank of the Île de la Cité; the other has seven arches and links the island to the right bank.

Old engraved maps of Paris show Pont Neuf as lightly touching the downstream tip of the Île de la Cité. During the many years that have passed since then a natural sandbar in the river, coupled with the building of the big stone-faced embankments (known as *quais*) along the Seine which slowed its flow there, have extended the island a bit further downstream.

The result is that there is a now small public park at its very tip, known as the Square du Vert-Galant—named in honor of King Henry IV, who was jokingly referred to as the *vert galant* (the contemporary translation of this was "gay blade") because of his roving eye for the ladies, even in his old age.

In the Middle Ages, a tiny island—known as the Île aux Juifs ("the Island of the Jews")—was at that time separate from the Île de la Cité, though it was later united with it. It was valued by French rulers as a very fine place for public executions. It had plenty of logs to use when burning criminals alive in big, very visible, fires, and plenty of river water to use to put out the fires safely.

These fires were stacked high so that they could easily be seen from the Île de la Cité and from both banks of the Seine. Thereby showing that royal justice was actively at work, they were also far enough away, however, from all the wooden houses and buildings of Paris itself not to risk setting them alight.

As we will see in the final chapter of this book, Jacques de Molay, the last Grand Master of the Order of the Temple, and two of his surviving companions, were burned alive at the stake there in 1314.

Another historical footnote here is the 381 stone masks known as *mascarons*, each of them different, which decorate the sides of the bridge. They depict the heads of forest and field divinities and of satyrs and other mythical woods-dwellers. Some modern commentators have joked that what they really symbolize are all the pretty young women who were seduced by the royal and still-randy Green Gallant!

Pont Neuf was completed in 1387. As soon as it was finished, the banks near it were quickly filled with houses. The first bridge-occupants were dyers and tapestry-weavers. Later, in the 17th century, perfume makers and booksellers set up their own shops on the bridge.

A medley of historical sources gives us accurate snapshots of life and love along the Pont Neuf from about 1701 to 1909. Lightly edited, annotated, and listed in chronological order, the following citations have been chosen for local color and for their chatty "heard on the street" qualities. They cannot be end-noted but, in overview, this is what they tell us:

- During and long after the 16th century, the Pont Neuf was a favorite rendezvous of news vendors, jugglers, showmen, loungers, and thieves. Indeed, any popular witticism in verse was known as *un Pont-Neuf*—as a joking remark heard on the bridge.
- A letter of 1701, purportedly from a Sicilian tourist, runs along these lines:

    One finds on the Pont-Neuf an infinity of people who give tickets to special events; some put fallen teeth back in; and others make crystal eyes. There are those who cure incurable illnesses; those who claim to have discovered the virtues of some powdered stones to whiten and to beautify the face. This one claims to make old men young and virile again; there are those who remove wrinkles from the forehead and the eyes; those who make wooden legs to repair those lost by explosions; finally, everybody is so strongly and continually focused only on his or her own work that the Devil himself can find no one to tempt—except on holidays and Sundays, when there are so many idle people on the bridge.

- In 1862, criminal gangs hid out in and around the bridge, making it a very dangerous place in which to loiter. Indeed, for a long time the bridge even had its own gallows!
- The English traveler J.C. Hare (1834–1903) mentioned that the Pont Neuf was such a heavily traveled thoroughfare that the Paris police would conclude, if they did not see a wanted man on the bridge after they had waited and watched it for three consecutive days, that this was conclusive proof that he had already left Paris.

Today one of the less-traveled parts of the Île de la Cité is the small square known as Place Dauphine. It occupies a triangular space in the western part of the Île de la Cité near the Palais de Justice, with the tip of its triangle serving as a key part of the Pont Neuf over the Seine.

Place Dauphine is named after the Dauphin (the future King Louis XIII of France) and was gradually developed between 1380 and 1620. In 1607, Henri IV changed what was then only a muddy marsh into a lovely formal triangular square surrounded by elegant townhouses. At first, it attracted upmarket traders, especially goldsmiths and silversmiths, but in the 17th and 18th centuries the judicial police force replaced all these traders with its own large headquarters.

Writing in the 17th century, a French historian said of the varied architecture of the Place Dauphine, "This mixture of stone, brick, and tile creates a union of colors which are pleasing to see and which on all sides form a perspective no less playful than extraordinary."[3] Although many changes have been made to Place Dauphine over all the intervening years, it is still a small but very attractive part of the Seine-scene.

It has even been claimed that Place Dauphine is one of the most romantic squares in Paris, being described as "intimate" and "secret." The walls of the buildings around it, plus its many trees, help to maintain an atmosphere of calm, which is an asset for the many small art galleries, cafes, and restaurants now located there.

To get there, one can begin at the Place du Pont-Neuf, which is located at the bridge itself, and then take a small side street named Rue Henri-Robert.

It has also been claimed, jokingly, that because its triangular shape can be imagined as evoking a female pubis, Place Dauphine is really "the sex of Paris." Whether this is true or not, Place Dauphine has in fact often been a filming location in modern times.

11

The Louvre

Located on the banks of the Seine and serving as the residence of the kings of France from the time of Philippe Auguste at the end of the 12th century until 1682, when Louis XIV moved his court to Versailles, the Louvre has been an enduring symbol of eight centuries of royal history and over the years it has had a variety of names.

The Port of the Louvre, for example, was previously known both as the Port du Musée ("the Port of the Museum") and as the Port Saint-Nicolas. Although the Louvre is most famous today for its artistic objects and displays, its port, located at the foot of the Grande Galerie of the Louvre, was by the late 19th century the business crossroads of France, handling large amounts of both commercial goods and consumer goods.

The Port of the Louvre was built in 1804 and was designed to have enough deep water at its moorings to float the biggest boats used in river trade at that time.[1] We therefore need to say a word about it here.

At these moorings, one could admire ships that had come from far beyond the Paris basin, e.g., from Dieppe, Le Havre, Bordeaux, Nantes, Rouen, and Provence. Moreover, there were also big three-masted schooners trading with London and carrying English sandstone in return for French sugar from the Caribbean.

The cargoes for sale at the Port of the Louvre offered a remarkable range of items for sale. These included waxes from Russia, oils from the Mediterranean, salts from the Atlantic, soap from Toulon and Marseille, oranges from Saint-Domingo and Algiers, Indian peppers, and Turkish coffee.

Along the Seine in Paris, all kinds of building materials were offered for sale, both for urban mega-projects and for smaller business and family needs. As mentioned before, a good supply of firewood, stacked in the holds and on the decks of cargo boats, or floated down the Seine as big rafts of wood, was essential for business and family warmth and cooking, but it was not always available.

11. The Louvre

The nineteenth-century French writer, Sébastien Mercier, who will be discussed later, complains that in his era the demand for firewood was so great, and the fireplaces waiting for it were so numerous, that the wood had no time to dry properly. He complained that "This float of wood is delivered to you muddy and damp: it gives off a lot of smoke and almost no fire!"[2]

Fruit and vegetables, meat and seafood, wines and other drinks— all these were transported by the Seine. Taverns set up along the banks of the river did a booming business as Parisians turned up in droves on weekday evenings or on Sundays to dance, flirt, drink inexpensive wines, and eat fish chowder and fried fish. The Seine itself was the main drinking water source for most Parisians, either drunk strait from the main drinking-water fountain at Notre-Dame, or filtered and delivered to houses.

The only important person who was not enchanted by all this untidy gaiety and mirth was the Emperor Napoleon himself. He did not appreciate, for example, seeing big piles of firewood slowly drying near some of the most elegant official and family buildings in Paris.

To regulate the river and to promote more trade upon it, he introduced plans to upgrade the Seine at Paris. This involved building bridges; installing more than a mile of high embankments along the river to keep the floods away from built-up areas; organizing the maintenance of navigable channels in the Seine; and creating a police force for the river.

High embankments were gradually built in order to transform the Seine near Paris into a big canal. This process was so thorough that the Emperor's architect, Pierre-François Fontaine, could boast as early as 1816 that "Of all these improvements that have been made to Paris over the last years, the clearing of bridges and banks is no doubt one of the most striking."[3] With high walls and big buildings dominating the banks of the river, however, there was very little room left on the shores of the Seine for any leisure-time activities by Parisians.

To turn now to the Louvre itself, this fine museum owns more than 615,000 objects and some 38,000 works of art are on display here, dating from prehistory to the 21st century. Moreover, hundreds of windows in the Louvre provide excellent views of the Seine, the Pont Neuf, and many famous buildings in this part of Paris.

The collections of the Louvre span several thousand years and are divided into eight curatorial departments:

- Egyptian Antiquities
- Near Eastern Antiquities
- Greek, Etruscan and Roman Antiquities

- Paintings
- Sculptures
- Decorative Arts
- Prints and Drawings
- Islamic Art

So much has already been written about the holdings of this great museum, however, that it may be more useful here to touch on some key points of its history. First, however, we must mention the importance that the Louvre can have to visitors on a personal family level.

An excellent example here is Louise Janin (1893–1997), the aunt and great-aunt of the coauthors. She was an American artist from San Francisco who lived in and painted in Paris since 1926 and who was, as a result, probably more French than American.

When she took one of the coauthors to the Louvre for the first time, she asked the guard at the front desk only one very simple and very direct question, in French, namely: "Où est-elle?" ("Where is she?").

The guard instantly understood that Louise was asking where we could find Leonardo da Vinci's most famous work, the Mona Lisa (painted c. 1503), and kindly told us how to find it. See Appendix 2 for a brief history of this world-renown portrait.

The Louvre also had a very important social aspect in addition to its artistic aspects. In the 18th century, for example, Louis Sébastien Mercier, a young but very able French novelist, playwright, and intellectual who we have mentioned earlier, wrote a good deal about life in Paris, such as his 1781 book, *Tableau de Paris* (*Portrait of Paris*).

He comments happily that the Louvre was by then already such a major pole of French life that

> I have run so far to make this portrait of Paris that I can honestly say that I have made it with my legs. I have also learned to walk on the stones of the capital in a nimble fashion, quick and lively. This is the secret that one must acquire in order to see everything....
>
> [In Paris], in order to find someone you are looking for all you need to do is to stroll around in the Louvre for one hour every day. Just as the heart of a human being is the center of movement and circulation of the blood, so, too, is the Louvre central to the life of Paris.[4]

Today the Louvre's Pyramid evokes strong feelings among its viewers, not all of them positive. The Pyramid is a big and very controversial glass and metal structure 71 feet high, with a square base having sides 112 feet long and a base surface area of 11,000 square feet. It was designed by the Chinese American architect I.M. Pei (whose last name in English is pronounced as "Pay") and is located in the main courtyard of the Louvre.

11. The Louvre

Completed in 1988, it has become a landmark of the city of Paris and has generated no end of comments—both pro and con—over the years.

The pyramid and the large underground lobby beneath it were designed and built because the Louvre's previous layout could no longer handle the ever-increasing flood of visitors who wanted to go there. Now, after entering the pyramid, visitors can descend into a spacious lobby beneath it and then can easily make their way into to the main buildings of the Louvre.

That said, however, the many critics of the Louvre Pyramid had one or more strong complaints about it. They asserted, for example, that:

1. The unusually modern design of this building clashed with the classic French Renaissance style and with the long history of the Louvre itself.
2. Since in ancient Egypt the pyramid was inextricably associated with death, it was not suitable for a vibrant "living museum" in Paris.
3. The pyramid was the egotistical folly of the then–French President François Mitterrand.

The Louvre and its Pyramid. The Louvre is an enduring symbol of eight centuries of royal French history. Located on the right bank of the Seine, it is probably the finest museum in the world. The Louvre's Pyramid—a large and controversial glass and metal structure—was designed in 1987 by the Chinese American architect I.M. Pei and has become a landmark of the city of Paris.

4. Chinese American architect I.M. Pei did not know enough about French culture to be given this sensitive assignment.
5. Some also felt that Pei charged far too much for his services. They therefore joked that "With I. M., you must pay, and pay, and pay."

This museum is housed in the Louvre Palace, originally built as a medieval fortress from the late 12th to 13th century for King Philip II. As the city of Paris grew, however, it gradually lost its defensive function and, in 1546, King Francis I, who was a keen art collector, turned it into the primary residence of the French kings.[5]

Both these kings greatly expanded the artistic holdings of the crown, and Louis XIV acquired the art collection of Charles I of England after the latter's execution during the English Civil War. This collection would be extended many times over the years to become the Louvre as we know it today.

As mentioned earlier, in 1682 Louis XIV decided to move his royal household from the Louvre to the Palace of Versailles, located about 12 miles southwest of the Louvre.

A huge water-pumping apparatus on the Seine, known as the Machine de Marly, had 14 big paddle wheels nearly 40 feet in diameter. These lifted the waters of the Seine by three stages in order to provide a reliable water supply for court at Versailles via a long aqueduct built between 1681 and 1685. It was this very feat that freed the Louvre itself and enabled it to become the site of the royal collection, which after 1692 also included ancient Greek and Roman sculpture.

During the French Revolution, which began in 1789, the National Assembly decreed that the Louvre should be used as a permanent museum to house the masterpieces of French and other art. In 1793, the revolutionary French government opened the Musée Central des Arts in the Grande Galerie of the Louvre, with an exhibition of 537 paintings, most of them being royal property or confiscated church property.

Because of structural problem with the building itself, the museum was closed from 1796 to 1801. The museum's collections grew very rapidly as the French army seized art and archeological items from the territories and nations conquered in the Revolutionary and Napoleonic Wars. Much of this plundered art was eventually returned to the rightful owners after Napoleon was defeated in 1815, but the Louvre's Egyptian antiquities collection and other departments still owe much to his conquests.

Two new wings were added in the 19th century. This new multi-building Louvre complex was completed in 1857 during the reign of Napoleon III. Known as the New Louvre, it was basically an amalgamation into a single unified and palatial complex of both the Louvre and the nearby Palais des Tuileries.

This accomplishment led to Napoleon III being hailed as one of the great builders of his time. The Palace des Tuileries no longer exits but in its place is the Tuileries Garden, the largest and oldest French garden, which has been classified as a historical monument since 1914 and is worth visiting.

In the 1980s and 1990s, the museum was officially known as the Grand Louvre and underwent major remodeling and improvements. In 1993, on the 200th anniversary of the museum, a rebuilt wing previously occupied by the French ministry of finance was opened to the public. This was the first time that the entire Louvre was devoted solely to museum activities.[6]

The Louvre was closed for 150 days in 2020 due to the COVID-19 pandemic and attendance plunged by 72 percent to 2.7 million. Even so, the Louvre still topped the list of the most-visited art museums in the world thereafter.

The holdings of the Louvre are so vast and so varied that the visitor must choose his or her "favorite" items with some care. Because of their focus near the banks of the Seine, the coauthors of this book are partial to a lovely painting which is folio 10 of the *Très Riches Heures du duc de Berry* ("the Very Rich Hours of the Duke of Berry") series of 1413–1416. The duke was one of the powerful uncles of Charles VI and is remembered today chiefly for the *Très Riches Heures*.

Entitled *le mois d'octobre* ("the month of October"), folio 10 shows two men broadcasting seeds and harrowing a small plot of land on the left bank of the Seine. It also depicts three small fishing or passenger boats drawn up on the riverbank, which is nearly overshadowed by a towering castle on the other side of the river. Finally, a nice human touch here is a life-like scarecrow, dressed as an archer and holding a bow; it is set up in an adjacent field to scare away the magpies and crows which would otherwise eat the newly sown seeds.

12

The Musée d'Orsay

This museum, located in Paris on the left bank of the Seine, was previously the Gare d'Orsay, a large railway station built in the Beaux-Arts style between 1898 and 1900. Its fine and perfectly symmetrical northern façade is one of the chief landmarks on the Seine between the Île de la Cité and the Eiffel Tower.

The museum is largely devoted to French art from 1848 to 1914, including paintings, sculptures, furniture, and photography. Perhaps most significantly, it houses the biggest grouping in the world of Impressionist and post–Impressionist masterpieces. Some of the most famous works are by such artistic luminaries as Monet, Manet, Degas, Renoir, Cézanne, Gaugin, Millet, and Van Gogh.

It is the second most-visited museum in France, after the Louvre, and now welcomes more than one million visitors per year. At any given time, about 3,000 works of art are on display here. Two of the most interesting of its holdings are described below.

The first is a 1:100 scale model of an aerial view of the Paris Opera and its surrounding region. The model is installed beneath glass flooring, which visitors can walk on and thus, by looking down, can learn a good deal about the city planning of Paris at that time. This installation is one of the most popular exhibits in the entire museum.

The second unique exhibit is the outstanding art collection entitled "A Passion for France: The Marlene and Spencer Hays Collection." Given to the museum by the Hays in 2016, it is the most significant donation that any French museum has received from a foreign donor since 1945. Moreover, the personal story of the Hays themselves is so full of human interest that it simply must be mentioned here.[1]

This American couple came from the dusty streets of small towns in Oklahoma and Texas. The day after they were married in 1956, they were given a $40 loan from Granny Mary, Spencer's grandmother, and used it to

12. The Musée d'Orsay

The Musée d'Orsay. Set on the left bank of the Seine, this former railway station was built in the Beaux-Arts style between 1898 and 1900. It is the second most-visited museum in Paris after the Louvre and houses the biggest collection in the world of Impressionist and post–Impressionist masterpieces. Some 3,000 works of art are usually on display here.

travel from Texas to Nashville, Tennessee. This small loan would become the basis of the rags-to-riches story of this couple.

Spencer first got a very modest job in Nashville selling books door-to-door for the Southwestern Company. This began simply as a summer job for him to earn money for college, but Spencer was so hardworking and so very able that it eventually expanded into a 60-year-long career with the company. This remarkable career benefited not only the Hays themselves but also the many thousands of employees and their families who would work for them.

In addition, it gave the couple the financial resources they needed in order to build up an art collection over a period of nearly 50 years. It now includes almost 600 paintings, drawings, and sculptures. The heart of their collection is the work of the "Nabi" artists led by Bonnard and Vuillard.

Les Nabis were a group of young French artists active in Paris from 1888 to 1900 who played a large part in the transition from Impressionism to the early manifestations of Modernism. The Nabis took their name from a Hebrew term meaning "prophets." They wanted to revitalize modern painting in much the same way that the ancient prophets had revitalized Israel.

13

The Place de la Concorde and Louis XVI

Dating from 1722, this is the biggest public square in Paris, covering about 19 acres. Because it was a central stage for the tumultuous events of the French Revolution, it was the site of many public executions of commoners and nobles alike. During the course of the revolution, the square was temporarily named as the Place de la Révolution.

The first executions by guillotine in this square were of two thieves who had stolen the royal crown diamonds from the Hotel de la Marine, the headquarters of the French navy, which were then located there. These men were beheaded in 1792. The guillotine was also used in January 1793 to execute King Louis XVI—an event that because of its historical importance will be discussed in the following pages.

In the meantime, as what became known as the Reign of Terror began, the guillotine was set up again in May 1793 and remained there for thirteen months. Of the 2,498 persons executed by the guillotine in Paris during the French Revolution, 1,119 were executed on the Place de la Concorde, 73 on Place de la Bastille, and 1,306 on Place de la Nation. The last executions were carried out in May 1795.

It should be noted in passing that the guillotine was considered at the time to be a new and far more humane form of execution.

Before it was invented, members of the nobility condemned to death were beheaded by the stroke of a sword or an axe. If the executioner misjudged his aim, the victim would not die instantly. It often took two or more blows to kill the condemned person. This person or their relatives would sometimes first pay the executioner to sharpen his blade carefully in order to assure a quick and relatively painless death.

Commoners, on the other hand, were often hanged from lamp posts during the revolution—a process which could take many minutes for them to strangle to death slowly. In an early phase of the revolution (before the

13. The Place de la Concorde and Louis XVI

guillotine was adopted), revolutionaries often shouted this slogan: *À la lanterne!* ("To the lamp post! String them up!") King Louis XVI was executed by guillotine in 1793 in what is now the Place de la Concorde, and his story is sufficiently interesting to be summarized here.

As a boy, Louis-Auguste, to give him his proper name, was intelligent, strong, and healthy, but very shy. This latter quality, which led to timidity and indecisiveness in his adult life, was encouraged by two of his tutors, who taught him that timidity was a virtue in strong monarchs and that he should never let people read his mind.

Louis became King of France in 1774 and held this position until the monarchy itself was abolished in 1792. The story of his reign was not, alas, a happy one. Some of its most notable events were, very briefly, as follows:

He first tried to reform the French government by following the new teachings of the Enlightenment. These included efforts to end serfdom, to remove the land tax and the labor tax, to increase tolerance for non–Catholics, and to abolish the death penalty for military deserters. The French nobility, however, was very hostile to these proposals. The elite class successfully prevented all of them from being put into practice.

Following the advice of his liberal economic minister, Louis deregulated the grain market but this drove up the price of bread, which was the most important part of the French diet. The scarcity of food after an especially bad harvest in 1775 prompted the masses to revolt.

From 1776 on, Louis actively supported the colonists of North America, who were fighting for their freedom from British rule. They finally achieved this in 1783 but the ensuing debt and financial crisis in France contributed to the unpopularity of the French government.

Discontent among the middle and lower classes of France led to growing public opposition to the French aristocracy and to the absolute monarchy of which Louis and his wife Queen Marie Antoinette were the most flagrant examples. Rising tensions and riots forced Louis to accept the legislative authority of the National Assembly (the Parliament) of France.

As his popularity plunged even further, in 1791 Louis fled from Paris to Varennes near the French border with Austria (the home-country of Queen Marie Antoinette)—a move which justified rumors that he hoped foreign intervention would save him.

Louis was arrested at the time of an insurrection in August 1792. The First French Republic was proclaimed the next month. Tried by the National Convention, he was found guilty of high treason and was executed by guillotine on 21 January 1793.

Louis was the only king of France to be executed, and his death brought to an end more than one thousand years of continuous French monarchy. Nine months after his death, the former Queen of France, Marie Antoinette, was also guillotined at the same location in Paris.

14

The Petit Palais

This building, whose name means "Small Palace" in English, is now an art museum near the Seine that was originally built for France's Exposition Universelle ("Universal Exposition") of 1900. An interesting historical footnote here is that by the time of this Exposition, the Seine and its many bridges had already become part of the "eternal" (but, in fact, ever-changing) Paris beloved by tourists.[1]

Charles Girault, the architect, drew heavily on late seventeenth-century and early eighteenth-century French building styles for the Petit Palais. His design was creative, original, and fitted perfectly into its given

Tourist-oriented boats on the Seine. A range of commercial boats offered by several companies gives visitors to Paris an excellent introduction to the Seine and to river-views of some of its most famous buildings.

location. Built around a central courtyard and a garden similar to that of the adjacent Grand Palais ("Large Palace"), which will be discussed in the next chapter, it was constructed to serve as a permanent fine arts museum for many years into the future.

Taken as a whole, the 1900 Exhibition was very popular; a drawing made of it then shows packed passenger boats and large crowds of spectators. Public reaction to the Petit Palais itself was generally positive. This building has also served as the model for later museums in Belgium and Chile. Echoing its location in Paris so close to the Seine, the Petit Palais contains some French works of art drawing attention to the Seine. One of them is a statute by Désiré-Maurice Ferray entitled "The Seine and its tributaries."

15

The Grand Palais

Opened in 1900, this huge monument, whose name means "Large Palace" in French, is located on the Champs-Élyées opposite the Petit Palais and is also quite close to the Seine.

Serving as the major trade fair and convention center of Paris, it hosted a great many events over the years but suddenly showed its advanced age in 1993 when a riveted portion of it fell from the ceiling 114 feet to the floor during an exhibition devoted to design. This "red warning light," as it were, eventually led to the Grand Palais being closed in 2021 for very extensive repairs and renovation, with a reopening slated for the spring of 2025.

A brief review of some of its past high points runs along the following chronological lines:

- Built in Paris beginning in 1897 for the Universal Exhibition of 1900, the Grand Palais replaced the vast but unattractive Palais de l'Industrie (Palace of Industry) of 1855. The new building was to be a "Monument consecrated by the Republic to the glory of French art."
- It was joked that it was as "one of the last milestones of an era before the coming of the electricity fairy." In other words, as was the case for all other earlier public structures, a generous supply of natural light was essential for any building designed to hold large crowds of people.
- Beginning in 1901, the Grand Palais hosted a very large number and a very wide range of events. These include art fairs, technical exhibitions, trade fairs, horse shows, concerts, circus or music-hall shows, flower shows, congresses, and fashion shows. Two of the best-attended shows in recent years focused, respectively, on Picasso in 2008, with more than 783,000 visitors, and on Monet in 2010, with more than 911,000 visitors.

16

The Eiffel Tower

This magnificent wrought-iron, 1062-foot-high, lattice-work tower in Paris, standing near the Seine, is named for the engineer Gustave Eiffel. His company designed and built it from 1887 to 1889 essentially as a temporary "pop-up" monument—the literal high point of the 1889 World Fair. From 1889 to 1930 it was the tallest structure in the world. Thanks to a new antenna 19 feet long, it is now 1,082 feet high.

More than 250 million people have visited the tower since it was completed in 1889; today, about 25,000 people go it every day. Nicknamed in French *la dame de fer* ("the Iron Lady"), it is now the most visited monument in the world which charges an entrance fee. It is also the tallest structure in Paris and in 1991 was named to be part of the UNESCO World Heritage Site entitled "Paris, Banks of the Seine."

It has three levels for visitors, with restaurants on the first and second levels. The climb from the ground floor to the first level is 300 steps, as is the climb from the first to the second level. A top level is usually accessible only by an elevator.

Emile Goudeau, a French journalist, visited the construction site of the tower at the beginning of 1889 and described the scene there in the following translation:

> A thick cloud of tar and coal smoke seized the throat, and we were deafened by the din of metal screaming beneath the hammer. Over there, they were still working on the bolts [the rivets] that held the structure together: workmen with their iron bludgeons, perched on a ledge just a few centimetres wide, took turns at striking the rivets.
>
> One could have taken them for blacksmiths contentedly beating out a rhythm on an anvil in some village forge, except that these smiths were not striking down vertically, but horizontally, and as with each blow came a shower of sparks [because the rivets were red-hot], these black figures, appearing larger than life against the background of the open sky, looked as if they were reaping lightning bolts in the clouds.[1]

16. The Eiffel Tower

The Eiffel Tower and Pont Alexandre III. Named for its designer and builder, the French engineer Gustave Eiffel, the splendid wrought-iron, 1062-foot high, lattice-work Eiffel Towe stands on the left bank of the Seine. From 1889 to 1930 it was the tallest structure in the world. In French, it bears the apt name of *la dame de fer* ("the Iron Lady") and is now part of UNESCO's "Paris, Banks of the Seine" World Heritage Site. Pont Alexandre III is famous for its exuberant use of Art Nouveau lamps, cherubs, nymphs, and winged horses.

In modern times, the Eiffel Tower has appeared very frequently in works of fiction because of its iconic nature as representing Paris. It has even been joked, for example, that no matter where in Paris a film scene is set, the producers are likely to make sure that the tower is somehow visible in the background.

From its very beginning, the tower has had a very strong public attraction, but by the 1920s this had evolved into it becoming a symbol of modernity. Little by little, the tower's image became totally associated with Paris itself, until it reached its present peak of being the worldwide and instantly recognizable symbol of the capital.

Nothing lasts forever, however, if it not properly maintained. This is indeed the case with the Eiffel Tower. Experts say that the Tower is now riddled with rust and desperately needs very extensive repairs, at an estimated cost of about $72.4 million.

Critics tell us that it is being given only a cosmetic makeover in preparation for the 2024 Olympic Games in Paris. They claim that, at best, this makeover will either be entirely useless or will simply lead to more corrosion, which is caused by the oxidization of iron when exposed to air and water.[2]

17

Bateau Mouche Excursion Boats

One of the classic and favorite activities for visitors to Paris is to spend time on an excursion or party boat known in French as a *Bateau Mouche*.

Bateau Mouche (singular) is the name of this type of tourist boat; *Bateaux Mouches* (plural) is the name of the company that pioneered the use of these vessels (la Compagnie des Beaux-Mouches) and continues to do so, with great success, today.

Singular or plural, the name translates literally as "fly boat(s)"—"fly" meaning the insect of this name. In historical terms, however, it derives from the fact that these boats were originally built in boatyards located in the La Mouche area in the city of Lyon.

The French entrepreneur Jean Bruel (1917–2003) was the entrepreneur who first had the idea developing a fleet of these boats which give tourists a unique sight-seeing experience on the Seine. In 1949, he bought one of the last steamboats, which had been used in the Universal Exhibition of 1900, and introduced a novel activity on the Seine: well-run guided tours, departing from a fixed port and returning to the same place.

Bruel had an excellent feel for public relations, introducing an entirely fictional character—"Jean-Sébastien Mouche"—at a 1953 inauguration ceremony of a new boat with the same named, and hailing him as the creator of the famous Bateaux-Mouches company.

The earliest appearance of similar boats, however, was when steamers were used at the Paris Exhibition in 1867. Their popularity was heightened in the Franco-Prussian War of 1870, when the French Red Cross had medals struck honoring the Bateau-Mouche boats used to transport wounded soldiers.

Today, the modern versions of these early boats are exceptionally popular tourist attractions in Paris. This "tourist fleet" is composed of 15 ships that navigate an annual distance equal to traveling around the world five times. Since its beginning, the fleet has welcomed over 150,000,000 passengers on board.

Many of these ships can seat several hundred people on their open upper deck and on their enclosed lower deck. Some of them have sliding canopies that can be closed to protect travelers during bad weather. Most of these boats also have a live or recorded commentary describing, in a range of languages, the sights along the Seine that the boat is then passing. A number of cruises on the Seine are always on offer in Paris and can easily be found online or in a guidebook.

A typical cruise lasts about an hour. Many companies offer more elaborate lunch, dinner, and dinner-show cruises, too, and are equipped with searchlights to illuminate historic landmarks passed after dark.

These boats also navigate some of the Paris canals, such as the now-industrialized Canal Saint-Martin, which was ordered by Napoleon I in 1802 to join the River Ourcq to the Seine, but the Seine itself is usually the first choice of the first-time tourist. In shipping terms, however, the Canal Saint-Martin was a great success: a postcard dating from 1908 shows that by then it had already become an industrial port in its own right.[1]

Named after 16th to 19th century that used to stand there, today's Port de l'Arsenal (the Port of the Arsenal) connects the Canal Saint-Martin to the Seine and now hosts up to 177 yachts. In 2017, it was integrated into the newly created Rives-de-Seine (Banks of the Seine) park. Two photos described below will show just far this area has come in terms of environmental quality.

A photo of the Port de l'Arsenal taken at the end of the 1970s shows shipping containers and other heavy construction-related materials lined up there, cheek-by-jowl, all along the quay of the Seine, with no room at all between them and the residential and office buildings rising a bit further inland. This was then, in short, a purely industrial enclave dedicated only to economic activity, with no relationship whatsoever to the adjacent river itself.

Fast-forward now to the early 1980s: a marina has been built and is lined with moored yachts; a broad walkway invites pedestrians to stroll along it and admire the boats and the nearby Seine lock; and, finally, a green curtain of trees and shrubs soften the sight of the buildings.

A similar transformation has taken place at the *port de la Tournelle*, which was formerly a big and rather ugly parking lot on the bank of the Seine in the 1980s. It now offers walkers a broad tree-lined walkway with an unimpeded view of the cathedral of Notre-Dame. An underground tunnel there has been filled in and has been replaced with a pedestrian path and improvements for bicycle travel.[2]

17. Bateau Mouche *Excursion Boats*

 Because the Seine is so centrally located, passengers on a boat tour get to see a great deal of Paris in relative comfort. Both banks of the Seine are clearly visible from the boat and a number of significant sites can easily be seen from it. These include, for example, the Eiffel Tower; Notre-Dame Cathedral; the Conciergerie; the Alexander III Bridge; the Pont Neuf; the Orsay Museum; the Louvre Museum; and Les Invalides, Napoleon's burial site.

 Boat tours in Paris have flourished since after World War II. Every year, about 2,500 passengers now embark on these boats, making them the fourth most-visited paying attraction in Paris (after the Eiffel Tower, the Louvre Museum, and the Georges Pompidou Centre of Arts and Culture). Efforts are underway to build 100 percent recyclable boats that run on cleaner energy and have fewer emissions.

18

Illustrations and Descriptions of the River Seine

When she lived in Paris, Queen Marie de Medici (1575–1642) fondly remembered her evening strolls along the Arno River in Florence and wanted to duplicate this pleasant experience in Paris along the Seine.

As a result, in 1628 the impressive Cours-la-Reine (the "Course of the Queen") pathway was laid out to the west of the Tuileries palace and along the same path leading to Versailles. It ran parallel to the Seine and was 5,948 feet long and 124 feet wide.

In the same era, the French also decided to link King Louis XIV's chateau of Saint-Germain with the Tuileries via an extension of the avenue of the Champs-Élysées. Paralleling the Seine, this magnificent wooded area, as seen in an illustration of 1738, served the purpose very well.

The net result was that contemporary artists, having now mastered the new art of using perspective in their illustrations, could show the viewer just how the Course of the Queen, the garden of the Tuilleries, and the Champs-Élysées all worked together, visually, to form an elegant border highlighting the Seine itself.

In addition, about ten green "alleyways of trees" were planted along parts of the Seine in central Paris so that the public could use and enjoy them without any charge.

Memorable paintings by the artists known as the Impressionists also captured French life on the Seine during the 19th century.[1] These artists used a bold new approach to their subjects by setting up their easels outdoors—in the open air (*en plein-air* in French)—and by then recording on their canvases the ever-changing light and the colorful reflections on the flowing river.

This *plein-air* approach broke all the traditional academic and artistic rules of the time. Impressionism arose in France in the 19th century and was based on painting out-of-doors and, equally importantly,

18. Illustrations and Descriptions of the River Seine

painting spontaneously "on the spot," rather that working in an indoor studio using previously drawn and carefully arranged sketches.[2] This new approach helped artists capture the momentary but striking effects of the always-changing sunlight on local objects and their patterns of color.

The long, iconic, Seine flows slowly through the heart of Paris before eventually emptying into the English Channel. The river was always a favorite subject of the Impressionists and other artists. Their artistic brushwork, however, had to become much quicker and had to be broken into small separate dots of color in order to capture the fleeting light over the Seine.

Listed in random order, these artists include Vincent van Gogh; Claude Monet; Pierre Bonnard; Berthe Morisot; Gustave Caillebotte; Pierre-Auguste Renoir; Georges Seurat; Édouard Manet; Paul Signac; Camille Pissarro (who, remarkably, between 1900 and 1903 produced about 30 paintings of the Seine from the same second-story window of a house on the Place Dauphine in Paris); Edgar Degas; Alfred Sisley; Albert Lebourg; and Robert-Antoine Pinchon.

Many other artists who focused on the Seine are discussed in French in the book by Bennetot et al entitled *La Seine: une vallée, des imaginaires* ("*The Seine: a valley and a world of imagination*"), which is listed here in the bibliography.

On a personal level, of the work of all these accomplished artists, we have a warm spot in our hearts for the paintings of the remarkable Dutch painter Vincent van Gogh.

During his time in Paris, he often carried his outdoor easel, paints, and brushes with him while he looked for interesting subjects to paint. The Seine was one of his favorites, and some of his many pictures of the river are listed below. They all date from 1886 to 1887 and many of them were painted in the northwestern suburbs of Paris in Clichy and Asnières along the Seine:

"Fishing in Spring, the Pont de Clichy"
"Pont du Carrousel with Louvre"
"Bridge of Asnières"
"Banks of the Seine with the Pont de Clichy"
"Riverbank in Springtime"
"The Seine with the Pont de la Grande Jatte"
"The Banks of the Seine"
"Bridges across the Seine at Asnières"
"Walk Along the Banks of the Seine near Asnières"
"View of a River with Rowing Boats"

There are so many excellent literary descriptions of the Seine that we must content ourselves here with the one by the French novelist Guy de Maupassant (1850–1892).

For eight years, from 1872 to 1880, he combined his two main hobbies—boating and admiring women—on the Seine during Sundays and holidays. On his walks with his "docile girls," as he called them, he introduced himself as "Master Joseph Plum, rower on the waters of Bezon and surrounding places."

Guy de Maupassant puts the following words into the mouth of one his literary characters:

> My greatest and my only absorbing passion over a ten year period was the Seine. Ah! This beautiful, calm, varying, and stinking river full of mirages and debris! I loved it so much, I believe, because it gave me, it seems to me, the sense of life.
>
> Like others who also have memories of tender nights, I have memories of sunrises in the morning fogs; of floating erratic vapors, as white as dead people before the dawn; of the first heartbreakingly beautiful rays of rosy sunlight slipping over the fields; and of a silvery moon on trembling and flowing water, whose light generates dreams.[3]

19

The Latin Quarter and Peter Abelard

The Latin Quarter of Paris is located on the left bank of the Seine. It is where the still-world-famous university of the Sorbonne was founded in 1257 and which would become one of the most important centers for learning in Europe for several hundred years. In addition, this part of Paris (the 5th *arrondissement*) now houses, among other items, the *Jardin des Plantes* (Garden of Plants), the *Museum National d'Histoire Naturelle* (Museum of Natural History), and a menagerie.

The Latin Quarter is so named because, during the Middle Ages, virtually all academic matters were discussed only in Latin, which was the scholarly language of the day. Indeed, students could be penalized if their teachers overheard them using any other language.

Today the narrow winding cobblestone streets of the Latin Quarter remind the visitor of what Paris must have looked like when so many young clerics, that is the students themselves, roamed its streets, chiefly speaking Latin.

It must be understood here these young clerics *were not ordained priests* but were instead only students who occupied the very first, entry-level, step into the very complicated hierarchy of the medieval Roman Catholic Church.

For this reason alone, they were legally considered to be "clerics." Such a religious status was extremely important to them because it gave them *legal immunity from arrest for any secular offensives they might commit*. (Religious offenses were adjudicated by the Church.) They also sometimes received a small annual income. As such, it was very valuable and much-desired position.

In the end, most of these young men never graduated from their colleges or became ordained priests. Instead, it was much more common for them to drop out of their studies after a year or two and take up secular jobs instead.

This was easy enough to do because the excellent intellectual and social skills they had learned in the Latin Quarter were now highly valued by employers, who had to deal with an increasingly complicated domestic and sometimes international economy. Once they were no longer clerics, these young men were of course free to marry and to have children.

In the Middle Ages there were at least six notable colleges in the Latin Quarter, known, respectively, as the *collèges* of the Ecossois, of Navarre, of Montaigu, of Sante-Barbe, of France, and of the Bernadins. Of these, the last one is probably the most interesting today.

Part of the historic University of Paris, the Collège des Bernadins (College of the Bernadins) was founded in 1246 for the Cistercian monks who were the elite of their Order and who were assigned to study theology and philosophy in such colleges. Fully restored in 2008, the Collège des Bernadins is now a site for religious research, conferences, concerts, and activities for young people. Since 2009 it has also housed the Académie Catholique de France (the Catholic Academy of France).

One of the most famous scholars and arguably the most interesting figure of the Latin Quarter was the twelfth-century philosopher Peter (Pierre in French) Abelard (1079–1142). At two points in his stormy academic career, he taught at a school he had founded near Paris on a hilltop overlooking the left bank of the Seine. This school was known as the Montagne Sainte-Geneviève (the Mountain of Sainte-Geneviève).

Thanks to his brilliant lectures, Abelard attracted a great many students. One report claimed that he had taught a total of "5,000" students in Paris, but this figure must be seen in light of the medieval habit of greatly exaggerating numbers in order to make a dramatic point.

Because of Abelard's historical importance and the remarkable human interest of his story, we must begin here with a short summary of his life—especially his torrid but disastrous love affair with Heloise, a brilliant young student—and will then look at some of his major philosophical and theological works.

Abelard was born into a family of the lesser French nobility in about 1079. He was an outstanding student from a very early age and was so attracted to the life of the mind that he renounced knighthood, the usual calling for a young man from a good family, in order to be free to study philosophy with famous experts.

A polymath, he would also become a gifted poet, a musician, and a monk. His genius was visible in everything he did. Both his supporters and his many opponents agreed that his quick wit, perfect memory, sharp tongue, and unbridled arrogance made him quite unbeatable in debate. Indeed, it was said of him that he had *never once* lost an argument!

Abelard was the greatest logician on the Middle Ages; the founder of

19. The Latin Quarter and Peter Abelard

scholastic theology; the intellectual progenitor of the University of Paris; and the first great nominalist philosopher. (Nominalism is a philosophical doctrine holding that *concepts* are merely human constructions and that the names given to them are only language conventions.) He was also a very moving author.

Let us now hear what he has to say about his love affair with the student Heloise, which began in about 1116. He tells us that

> Now there dwelt in that same city of Paris a certain young girl named Heloise, the niece of a canon [Canon Fulbert, an influential cathedral cleric] … Of no mean beauty, she stood out above all by reason of her abundant knowledge of letters [namely her linguistic and literary skills]….
>
> Under the pretense of study, we spent our hours in the happiness of love … our kisses far outnumbered our reasoned words … our inexperience in such delights [both of them had been virgins when their affair began] made us all the more ardent in our pursuit of them, so that our thirst for one another was still unquenched.[1]
>
> Heloise herself strongly underlined what Abelard says above. "Which queen, which princess," she wrote, "would not have envied my joys and my bed?"[2]

The couple's great happiness, however, soon led to their great sorrow. Abelard explains to the reader that Canon Fulbert and his kinsmen had come to believe—quite incorrectly, in fact—that Abelard was secretly trying to get rid of Heloise by forcing her to become a nun.

The enemies of Abelard therefore punished him by violently seizing him when he was asleep in his lodgings and by castrating him there. Two his assailants, one of whom was his servant who had taken a bribe to help attack him, were later captured and were punished not only by being castrated themselves but also by being blinded, too.

Today, Abelard's strongest claim to fame rests not on his sexual activities but on his philosophical work. This work is, however, much too detailed to be presented here. Suffice it to say now only that it involved seven very difficult and interrelated fields of study, namely, dialectics, metaphysics, logic, the philosophy of language, the philosophy of mind, ethics, and theology.

20

The Riverbanks (*Berges*) of the Seine in Paris

The Seine flows through Paris, from east to west, for about eight miles. As mentioned earlier, there it has a maximum width of about 656 feet and an average depth of about 31 feet. Its riverbanks and, most dramatically, the steep stone embankments in central Paris which were built in 1910 to prevent the city from being flooded at times of high water, have been mentioned in earlier pages but they merit more attention here.

In 2010, writing of the riverbanks and of the Seine in general, Bertrand Delanoë, who was the mayor of Paris at that time, believed that

> Paris is born of the Seine, and is built as part of it and as surrounding it. It is the life-line of our capital. Our river is, in addition, a unifying element which is of fundamental importance to the Paris region as a whole. It is in a spirit of consultation with the public that we have opened up to our future the riverbanks of the Seine.[1]

The earliest centralized urban planning or any other organized efforts to improve these riverbanks for health or cosmetic reasons date from before the 14th century. Later, however, in addition to their obvious nautical value, it was found that they could also be used either for punishment or for picnic delights.

Regarding punishment, on 21 July 1768, for example, an apprentice cobbler—young Firmin Boidin by name—was punished in the pillory on the Pont Neuf between noon and 2:00 p.m. Perhaps his head and his arms were placed in a wooden stock; if not, he must have been tied up in some way so that he could not escape. Two signs were pinned to his clothing—one on his chest, the other on his back, both reading "For Begging." Such a public shaming was indeed a stiff penalty at that time.[2]

On the more positive "delight" side, we can keep in mind two very well-done American works on the joys of Paris. These are (1) Ernest Hemingway's book *Paris is a Moveable Feast* (1964), and (2) Woody Allen's film

20. The Riverbanks (Berges) of the Seine in Paris

Two girls eating lunch by the Seine. A picnic lunch on the banks of the Seine is always pleasant.

Midnight in Paris (2011). Any readers who have the opportunity to wander along these riverbanks will almost certainly encounter some visual delights on their own. The evocative French verb *flâner* ("to stroll") can ideally be used here to connote a very pleasant but aimless wandering without any clearly defined purpose or fixed timetable.

There were seven different possible "faces" of a Seine riverbank—the places where the land meets the water.

These faces ranged from a very gradual unpaved slope (*grève* in French), either straight or curved, in the latter case possibly forming a semi-protected cove, on the one hand, to a very sturdy wooden dock built high above the waterline, on the other. Such a dock would have been tall enough, and with enough deep water in front of it, to permit boats to moor there in order to load and to discharge their cargo.

Today, since the banks of the Seine are now reinforced with heavy rocks to avoid erosion, they are not suitable mooring-sites for boats. On the plus side, however, not only do the banks of the Seine contain some of the most memorable monuments of Paris but they also are home to its memorable bridges and footbridges.

Before the first quays along the Seine were built at the start of the 14th century, the riverbanks remained in their natural low-level sandy or muddy states. Often being quite broad, however, they could be used at will

Another shot of these two girls eating a picnic lunch by the Seine. This old Seine boat is still in use, now carrying visitors rather than cargo.

for boat repairs, horseback riding, walking, socializing, and even swimming or wading—in addition, of course, to the constant on-loading and off-loading of river boats themselves. Over time, and especially near the bridges of Paris, they became very crowded by boats, small businesses, workers, shoppers looking for bargains, and idle spectators.

The earliest quay to be built was the Quai des Grands-Augustins in 1313, followed by the Quai de la Mégisserie in 1369. Pont Neuf itself dates from 1607. Although a customer could usually find what he was looking for on the quays, he sometimes had to deal with the insolent men who were part of the king's household and who therefore categorically refused to wait patiently in line to be served in their turn.

These men, regardless of whether they were lackeys or princes, were so sure of their own places in society that they always pushed their way up to the front of the queue since this was a normal part of their lifestyle.

The problem became sufficiently tiresome for Louis XIV to led him try to reimpose some discipline on the quays by issuing a decree in 1625. It ran along the following lines:

> His majesty has expressly forbidden his and the queen's officers, archers, pages, lackeys, stablemen, princes, princesses, and gentlemen, no matter who they are, under pain of severe punishment, to stop their disorderly behavior in ports and public places so that the merchants can sell goods to the public as they have long been doing under well-established regulations.[3]

20. The Riverbanks (Berges) of the Seine in Paris

One of the most dramatic cultural events in the history of the quays is what is known as the *monumentalisation de la Seine*—(the process of viewing and treating the Seine as *a cultural monument* of France, not just as a body of water).

This event was the magnificent fireworks display arranged in 1722 by the City of Paris to celebrate the royal wedding of Princess Louise Élisabeth of France and Prince Philippe of Spain. In addition, at the same time it publicly reflected the growing international nautical power of both countries.

As depicted in a very colorful painting by François Blondel which is now in the Rothschild collection of the Louvre, this event took place on the Seine near the half-mile of royal and aristocratic mansions overlooking the river. It was highlighted by theatrical performances; by nautical "jousts" on the river between rival boat crews; by boats carrying historical displays; and, of course, by world-class fireworks.[4]

In 1753, the Place Louis-XV, now known as the Place de la Concorde, was built along the quay on the right bank of the river. In this process, the numerous houses that lined the riverbanks there at that time were all destroyed, with no attention being paid by the authorities to the bitter complaints of the homeowners.

The open spaces thus created by the destruction were quickly filled by new and much higher quays and by new bridges: fifteen of the latter had spanned the Seine by 1870. At about the same time, new and lower quays for smaller boats were also designed to service the ever-expanding river traffic.

Towpaths were developed along the river so that horses, and sometimes men alone, known in English as "haulers," could tug the heavy cargo boats through the shallowest stretches of the river.

The economic importance of such *haulage* ("hauling") was so great that when the French Revolution ended the stiff duties imposed by the French government on merchandise imported into France, this event was vividly celebrated in an illustration of 1791. It shows deliriously happy teamsters waving flags in the wind while standing on top of small urban monuments, surrounded by the many different kinds of the draft animals, carts, carriages, and boats that were so essential in their river-borne trade.[5]

Indeed, the banks of the Seine saw such heavy use that they later became the sites of the Universal Exhibitions held in Paris from 1855 to 1900. Trees that were planted on the banks to provide shade for the crowds and for scenic reasons included plane trees, Italian poplars, aspens, and willows.

In the 20th century, motor vehicle traffic increasingly expanded onto the paved banks of the Seine. The first expressway, built on the right bank between 1961 and 1967, was named for French President Georges-Pompidou in 1977. At one point, this expressway was said to be carrying up to 40,000 vehicles per day. On the left bank, a much shorter expressway segment was opened between the quay Anatole-France and the quay Branly.

This latter was designed to be the first segment of a major new Seine-bank expressway project, but the idea was scrapped in 1974 after the election of President Giscard-d'Estaing and in the wake of very strong opposition from French environmentalists.

In later years, some of the motor vehicle traffic, which was exceptionally heavy along the river, would be increasingly restricted, ultimately culminating in the creation of a *new motor vehicle-free park* known as the Parc Rives-de-Seine ("Park on the banks of the Seine") in 2017.

This park, which has been called "the green lung of Paris," consists of 24 acres of open land along the riverbanks, stretching over a total of four miles.

On the left bank of the Seine, strollers and sports enthusiasts can get some fresh air and exercise from the Pont des Arts to the Eiffel Tower, via the Musée d'Orsay and the Pont de l'Alma. On the right bank, the area from the Senghor footbridge to the Place de la Bastille is theirs to use and enjoy.

There is also an extensive *Grande Randonnée* (long-distance foot trail) along the Seine in Paris which covers even more of this scenic region.

No discussion of the banks of the Seine in Paris, however, would be complete with some mention of the colorful booksellers (*bouquinistes*) there. They first appeared on the Quai Voltaire in 1891. Today their little green booths, none of which can be more than about nine yards long, still offer an interesting selection of old and sometimes rare books. There are about 245 Seine booksellers now. A few of them have been recruited from other professions. At this writing, for example, one of these newcomers was a former seaman.

An old story about the Seine book trade runs as follows:

> When said by an older and prosperous Paris husband to his wife on a pleasant Sunday afternoon many years ago, the phrase "I think I'll visit the *bouquinistes* this afternoon" might well mean that he planned to visit his mistress then.

The French poet and essayist Léon-Paul Fargue sets this historic scene for us:

> Elderly Parisian men of no particular importance, dressed to the nines, gray trousers and spats, sideburns carefully brushed, imposing collar, flashy or delicate necktie under a well-proportioned collar, a flower in the buttonhole, a smile always in place on happy lips.

20. *The Riverbanks* (Berges) *of the Seine in Paris* 131

They were well-cared for, spoiled old gentlemen with private incomes; and while waiting to go off to their *rendezvous gallants* [trysts] they would move in a trance of pleasure among astronomical maps, postage stamps, erotic prints, and first editions.[6]

Any account of the banks of the Seine in Paris must also mention the *guinguettes*. These were the extremely popular bars, with restaurants and

A bookseller (*bouquiniste*) along the Seine near Notre-Dame. Booksellers first appeared along the Seine in 1891. There about 245 of them now, working out of little green booths about nine yards long and offering a colorful selection of used and sometimes rare books. Some of these booksellers are recruited from other professions: indeed, one was formerly in the French Navy.

dance halls often attached, that were located during the 18th century and 19th century in the suburbs of Paris along the Seine, and in some other cities of France as well.

Their name comes from the word *guinguet*, which meant, according to a French dictionary of 1750, "a sour light local green wine, such as found around Paris." Rowing was a major pastime at these establishments. It attracted crowds of eager onlookers, some of whom were dressed like make-believe pirates and who bellowed conflicting and ignorant advice to the few real oarsmen who were already out on the water or who were preparing to go out on it. Some of the men of these crowds also danced gaily along the banks, to the tune of inexpensive flutes.[7]

Often built along on the rivers and just outside a city's limits in order to escape the stiff customs barriers and taxes that would have made it too expensive for them to do business there, *guinguettes* attracted many working class families. They were excellent places, especially on Sundays and holidays, for these men and women to see and be seen; to meet old friends and make new ones; (usually for men only) to get drunk; and sometimes to swim.

The famous French caricaturist Honoré Daumier (1808–1879) has left us an amusing drawing set on the Seine in this era.[8] It shows two men in a skiff who are ostensibly trying to "save" a swimmer by using a boat hook to snag his swimming trunks. They are working very energetically, despite the swimmer's vigorous protests, to haul him firmly alongside their skiff.

The name of the boatman with the book hook is Gaspard; his companion, who rows the skiff and who is the captain and the speaker, is not named.

The caption of the illustration runs along these (translated) lines: "Haul hard, Gaspard! Don't let him get away: he must drown!"

The swimmer, now quite angry, shouts at the two men: "Please leave me alone! You can see perfectly well that I'm a very good swimmer and I just want you to leave me in peace so I can enjoy my swim!"

The captain says: "Pull harder, Gaspard! If we listen to such swimmers we won't be able to 'save' a single one—we must take this guy to the Police Chief at the nearby quay of Bercy. He will give us the standard award of 25 francs for saving this man ... and that's not counting the very generous tip the Chief will surely give us!"

Another cartoon of 1880 also captures very nicely the ambiance of such a place—in this case, a well-known *guinguette* called the *Grenouillère* ("the Froggery"). It especially appealed to male patrons because of all the attractive female swimmers who disported themselves there.

Located on the Seine at the town of Bougival, it shows a large and very happy crowd of people of various ages and social classes, eating, drinking,

20. The Riverbanks (Berges) of the Seine in Paris

swimming, sailing, dancing, flirting, and generally thoroughly enjoying themselves.[9]

The expansion of the railways in the 1880s, with their many trains serving the eastern suburbs of Paris, contributed to the flourishing of the *guinguettes*. Renoir, Van Gogh, and other artists loved the atmosphere in them and often captured it on canvas.

The bad news was that, beginning in the 1960s, television and a ban on swimming in the Seine and some other rivers (due to increasing levels of pollution and more barge traffic) caused a sharp decline in the number of *guinguettes*. Since the 1980s, however, there has been a modest revival of this form of public entertainment, particularly along the Marne river.

As writers, we owe special debts to libraries and all other places where books are stored and treasured. For this reason it is appropriate for us here to "tip our hats" (the French word for this polite old-fashioned gesture is *chapeau!*, meaning "hats off!") to the National Library of France (the Bibliothèque nationale de France).

This famous library is located on the banks of the Seine, just east of the Île de la Cité and downtown Paris. Its four glittering towers are the modern architect's response to the age-old Paris tradition of erecting stunning monumental public architecture.

The motivating idea behind the library dates from a royal collection of the 14th century, but the first legislation regarding the required Legal Deposit of books there was enforced by King Francis I in 1537.

It was not until 1994, however, that it became the Bibliothèque nationale de France and one of the largest heritage, public, and research libraries in the world. Throughout its history, it has always discharged its responsibilities of collecting and preserving all the national and global collections in its care.

We would also like to say "hats off!" to the nameless and numberless longshoremen of the Seine who risked their lives every day just to earn enough money to stay alive. A nineteenth-century illustration, for example, shows us that the Seine did support these men, but only in a very miserable lifestyle based only on occasional part-time and badly paid jobs.

They crewed the cargo-carrying river boats; cut, assembled, and navigated the big "trains" of floating logs; sawed and stacked up firewood; and hunted for scrap metal of any value along the banks of the river and in the adjoining streets of Paris. One of the greatest dangers they faced was that the big drains along the canals of the river, which they searched by hand looking for any small items of value, could easily become subterranean death-traps for any careless longshoremen.

The illustration mentioned above explains that the longshoremen did not wear shirts when working because their hard labor made them sweat very profusely. Although going shirtless when working outdoors may not be uncommon in our own times, in the era being discussed here it would have been considered the equivalent of a man going out in public stark-naked.

This illustration, very lightly annotated, makes the following points:

> The longshoremen go naked (this means "stripped to the waist"), and every day they often have to stand, hip-deep, in the cold river, their foreheads dripping with sweat. The paleness of their faces announces to us that they will not be able to continue their terrible labor for any great length of time [because they will be too tired, too sick, or too injured to continue to work]. Their bodies are disfigured by the thick mud which clings to them and which weakens their nerves.[10]

In addition, we read that the longshoremen

> drank great quantities of alcohol, which destroyed even the most robust constitutions, they soon fell prey to high fevers, pneumonia, pleurisy, stomach and chest problems, and horrible ulcers on their legs which they called the "frog disease."[11]

On a more positive note, we must also remember that the banks of the Seine in Paris were indeed very good places in which to buy and to sell many of the items needed for daily life in the city.

Illustrations from 1670, 1830, and 1860, for example, show that up to 300 women would queue up at moored boats at 5:00 a.m. each day to buy fresh fish. In the 19th century, 48 boats that sold fish were moored in the Seine, some of the catch coming by canal from the Loire basin.

Other boats selling charcoal; firewood, some of it in piles "as high as riverside workers' houses"; sand and gravel for construction purposes; and water-borne transportation of both heavy merchandise and of passengers could readily be arranged along the Seine's, banks, too.[12]

21

The *Brigade Fluviale* (River Police) of Paris

Most foreign visitors to Paris and, indeed, most of the Parisians themselves, are not likely to have any direct contact with the French river and nautical brigades. These are the official armed units of the French police and gendarmes who patrol Paris' and other waterways. Nevertheless, their story is interesting, important, and worth reviewing briefly here.[1]

Policing the rivers of France is the job of both the national police and the national gendarmerie, each of which has similar administrative and judicial assignments. They share a commitment to ensuring the safety of people and goods along the French waterways and river banks. They are also trained in the effective and safe use of the 9 mm semiautomatic pistols they carry every day, and of heavier weapons, too.

In 1900, the first river brigade of Paris was created by Louis Lépine, the Paris prefect (senior officer) of police. Originally, 40 divers were recruited from among the ranks of Paris police. They had to pass very demanding tests (swimming, diving, navigation, and rescue) and training before being able to join the brigade.

This new brigade was such a success during the Paris Exhibition of 1901 that the next year, possibly for public relations reasons, Lépine decided to give it the catchier shorthand title of the "Fluv" (from the word "Fluviale"). So that his officers could monitor the riverbanks, too, he equipped them with bicycles and with two Newfoundland dogs.

In the many years since then, the river brigade of Paris has flourished, thanks in part to the development of tourism and the arrival of the famous Bateau-Mouche tourist boat in the 1950s. The Fluv, although today without its dogs (the last dog died in 2009 and has never been replaced) patrols 2,112 miles of waterways in the Île-de-France region.

In recent years, 14 river brigades and 4 interior nautical brigades have safeguarded the inland waterways of France. The Paris river brigade now consists of about 100 police officers, including 12 well-trained women. For both economic and environmental reasons, river transport has increased very rapidly in France—leading to ever-greater demands on the country's waterways and on the Fluv.

In 2010, the Command of the Gendarmerie des Voies Navigables (the central police unit in charge of navigable waterways) was created at Conflans-Sainte-Honorine in the Paris region. This is the point at which the River Oise joins the Seine and is also the location of the well-organized Inland Waterways Museum.

The Seine is the main waterway-artery of Paris, carrying 20 per cent of its transported goods. The planned construction of a major new canal linking the major ports of the Seine, e.g., Le Havre, Rouen, and Paris, to the rivers of Northern Europe will further stimulate the transport of goods by river and further complicate the duties of the river police.

The Paris River Police work very closely with the Paris Fire Service (Sapeurs Pompiers de Paris) during any emergency where both the river and the shoreline are involved. The Paris Fire Service is not a civilian force but is part of the French armed forces. It has boats of its own so that it can take to the water whenever necessary.

Perhaps the best most recent example of their close cooperation was on 15 April 2019, the day of the great Notre-Dame fire in Paris.

During this fire, the biggest firefighting boat, the *Île-de-France*, was moored along the riverbank directly beneath the cathedral and used its powerful engines to pump high volumes of water from the Seine into mobile fire stations set up ashore.

Pumping continued non-stop until the flames were finally extinguished in the early hours of the next morning. About 500 firefighters slaved away at this ultimately successful effort to save Notre-Dame from certain destruction. None of them died; only one of them was slightly injured. General Jean-Claude Gallet, commander of the firefighting brigade of Paris, nicely summed up the situation in one short sentence: "The water of the Seine saved Notre-Dame."[2]

Today the Fluv offers services as varied as a multi-bladed Swiss Army knife: it can handle a very wide variety of assignments. These include:

- Towing boats which have lost power or are otherwise in distress.
- Putting out any fires aboard ships, both vessels large or small.
- Maintaining good order on waterways and riverbanks by monitoring both commercial ports and pleasure ports.
- Intervening to keep damaged barges from sinking, e.g., by repairing any holes in their hulls and by pumping out incoming water.

21. The Brigade Fluviale *(River Police) of Paris*

- Rescuing people who are about to drown—getting them out of the water, either by diving into the water to rescue them by hand, or approaching them safely by boat. Fluv men and women are trained to provide first aid until medical help can arrive.
- Using SONAR and other means, search for and if possible recover corpses from the waterways. (In one recent year, the Fluv rescued 107 living people and recovered 50 corpses.)
- Controlling boats on the waterways by making sure they are not going too fast and are abiding by the rules of navigation; have the proper safety equipment; and are not carrying illegal goods. The Flu wants to reduce river pollution by trying to catch any polluters red-handed. It also must provide security for high-profile political or other public events; report and identify submerged vehicles; and, last not but not least, try to prevent the burglary of houseboats.

22

The Bloody Seine

"Kill them all," the French king, Charles IX, ordered his staff in 1572, "so that none shall reproach me for it," and his order for a massacre of Protestants was quickly carried out.[1] The corpses from this event were dumped into the Seine: proof that the river has had a bloody past as well as a peaceful present.

Our story begins with a wedding. On 18 August 1572, Marguerite de Valois, a Catholic who was the king's sister, married Henry de Navarre, the Protestant aristocrat of the Bourbon family who would later become King Henri IV of France and, eventually, the first town planner of Paris itself.

This was a marriage carefully arranged by Catherine de Medici (1575–1642), Queen of France and Navarre as the second wife of King Henry IV, and as regent of France between 1610 and 1617. She has long been associated with the wars of religion between Catholics and Protestants. Her role in the St. Bartholomew's Day massacre has always made her a controversial figure in the history of France.

Catherine thought that the marriage would bring these two hostile religious factions into a happy union that would support the French monarchy. In fact, she also had a secret and much more ambitious plan: to get rid of Admiral de Coligny, an important military and political leader who favored the Protestant policies of countering corruption in France itself and of reducing France's strong ties to Catholic Italy and Spain.

On Catherine's orders, a marksman was assigned to ambush Coligny as he was on his way to a meeting at the Louvre. Two shots were fired at him; he was wounded in his left shoulder but survived. Although Catherine and her Catholic pro-royal followers were quick to visit him at his residence and to offer their "most sincere" condolences, his Protestant supporters did not believe their lamentations for a moment and argued instead for retaliation against the Catholic royal government.

To prevent what he feared would be a Protestant insurrection to overthrow him, the king ordered that the city of Paris be closed to all outsiders.

22. The Bloody Seine

On 23 August 1572, he wrote to the Queen of England promising that those who had attacked Coligny would be captured and punished. However, he quickly decided that he had to act immediately if he wanted to be sure of keeping his throne. For this reason, at 2 a.m. on 24 August 1572 he gave the famous "Kill them all" order mentioned above, and the massacre began.

As a first step, he wanted to make sure that Coligny himself was truly out of the way. The Duke de Guise, a strong supporter of the king, and his henchmen therefore cut off Coligny's head and, using a rope, then dangled it from a window of an apartment. The duke told his men that this was a very good start but that much more now had to be done in order to carry out the king's order.

The duke's men accordingly dragged Coligny's corpse through the streets of Paris, calling on the population to rise and to murder the Protestants, who were the king's enemies. Coligny's testicles were torn off and tossed into the Seine, after which his headless body was dumped into the river, too. Finally, his corpse was dragged out of the Seine and hung up by its feet for several days at Montfaucon, the site of the huge gallows in Paris which were used to execute notorious criminals.

Andrew Hussey, a modern historian, has described what happened next:

> From the Louvre to the backstreets of the Île de la Cité and the Latin Quarter, a madness swept the city. The ordinary people of Paris were overwhelmingly Catholics and the Protestants were [their] aristocratic overseers.... It was now time to settle accounts.
>
> Most of the important murders, at least from a political point of view, took place in the opening hours of the massacre. But the blind killing, driven by blood-lust and ancient hatreds, went on through the day and night until the streets looked like a battlefield....
>
> Pezou, a butcher by profession and a captain faithful to the Duke, prided himself on slitting the throats of more than 120 Protestants in a few hours, and throwing the bodies into the Seine with his own hands....
>
> There was so much blood that it ran in torrents.... Within days, the Seine was so swollen with bodies that they floated back onto the banks of the river almost as soon as they had been thrown in.... The king merely laughed when his captains reported that Paris could not swallow all these Protestants.[2]

About 3,000 Protestants were killed in Paris during this massacre.

23

The Unknown Woman of the Seine

One of the bits of local color about the Seine which is probably not familiar to most readers of this book is "L'Inconnue de la Seine" ("The Unknown Woman of the Seine"). She is worth introducing here.

This woman's name will never be known but she was probably French and was about 20 years old. She merits our attention because her plaster death mask became a very popular ornament on the walls of bohemian artists' homes in Paris after 1900.[1]

She is estimated to have been born in about 1865 and to have died in Paris in about 1885. Her pretty young face—calm, happy, apparently quite satisfied with her life, and illuminated by a gentle Mona Lisa-like smile—has long been a source of inspiration for literary works, both in French and in other languages.

Legend has it that the corpse of this woman was pulled out of the Seine in Paris, and that an employee of the local morgue was so struck by the beauty of her face that the employee had a plaster cast made of it. Over the years, many copies of this cast were made and it quickly became a fashionable if macabre ornament in the apartments of bohemian Paris.

The remarkable, unique, and carefree style of life these men and women—poets, artists, writers, architects, and musicians—was captured very nicely in a song by the drinker and philosopher Fernand Desnoyer (1862–1869). It ran along these (translated) lines:

> When the bourgeois slumbers at night
> We are thirsty, still;
> Let's drink the night through!
> It's quite dark outside;
> But the windows on the streets area
> Ablaze like people's glances.
> Burning atmosphere,
> Girls in the smoke,

> Brandy and noise.
> This is our night!
> Drink is the real pleasure!
> There's nothing after!
> Nothing but to drink again,
> While we wait for the dawn to rise![2]

In point of fact, however, the Paris painter Jules Lefebvre told his draftsman Georges Villa that this death mask was made from the face of a young model who had died of tuberculosis around 1875. Viewers are often moved to speculate on the happy expression on her face and on her likely life, death, and social standing.

Moreover, writers rose to this challenge, too. In 1972, one author claimed that a whole generation of German girls had modeled their looks on the "Unknown." Another writer said that this mask had become an erotic ideal for French and German actresses. The famous French writer Albert Camus wrote in French that it was "a cast of the touching face of the Unknown of the Seine, with the smile of a drowned Mona Lisa."

Perhaps most remarkably, since 1960 a Norwegian company has used the face of the "Unknown" on its first-aid training dummy. Known in English as "Resuscitate Anne," this dummy is used for mouth-to-mouth ventilation; this "womanly dummy" has therefore earned the nickname of being "the most kissed woman in the world."

24

The "Thirty Glorious Years"

In French history, the expression "Les Trente Gloriouses" ("The Thirty Glorious Years") refers to the rapid economic and demographic growth of France between 1945 to 1975, especially in the Seine valley, following the end of World War II.

Setting the stage, as it were, by the end of the 19th century the development of heavy industry along the Seine valley downstream of Paris had already speeded up considerably—to the extent that French writers have called this process "the second industrial revolution." The enterprises most affected included the factories handling metals, minerals, wood products, textiles, paper, cereals, rubber, and energy, e.g., electricity, coal, and petroleum products.

A chart of the increase in ship traffic at the port of Rouen, the major port then closest to Paris itself, shows a sharp rise beginning in about 1900 and, after the fall caused by World War II, and then a rapid increase continuing into our own times. A related chart, this time with the heavy industrial sites highlighted in different colors, shows them sprinkled very thickly along the banks of the Seine, both downstream and upstream of Paris.[1]

The "Thirty Glorious Years" along the Seine valley came about because of the valley's strategic position during World War II. Bombing raids during the battle for Normandy had caused massive damage: many cities (Le Havre, Caen, Saint-Lô, Caudebec-en-Caux, etc.) were hit very hard.

On 25 August 1944, even though he knew that he had already lost the war, Hitler ordered German General von Choltitz to burn Paris, and is said to have asked him, "Is Paris burning?" Fortunately, the General ignored this maniacal question. It is said that a Swedish diplomat had convinced the General that it would be much, much better for him to be remembered as the *savior* of Paris rather than as its destroyer!

After the war, all the bridges downstream of Paris had to be rebuilt.

24. The "Thirty Glorious Years"

The railway line between Paris and Le Havre had to be rebuilt entirely, too, in 1948. In the Paris area, the destruction was less severe, but some places (Boulogne-Billancourt and Mantes-la-Jolie) suffered damage. A map of Le Havre shows that the reconstruction of this major port lasted from 1947 to 1960.

On the plus side, the ports benefited greatly from the new and more modern facilities built there. Le Havre profited from the import of petroleum products. Rouen, for its part, began to handle cereal exports in 1958 after the first silos were built there.

Very ambitious plans were drawn up to improve the flow of goods and services in the Seine valley as a whole. However, since no single new national authority was ever created and empowered to make all the complicated and, indeed, virtually endless national and international decisions such plans would involve, in practice this admirable concept seems to have been left, for better or worse, chiefly in the hands of the local authorities.

This may not have been such a bad result, however, because ever since the heyday of the "Trente Glorieuses," the Seine valley has experienced what one French commentator said was "a certain stagnation of the population and a feeble attractiveness" for potential investors.[2]

These problems are due chiefly to the rise of very high-technology, low-cost production elsewhere in the world and to the ever-growing importance of Paris itself as a major financial, cultural, and managerial center. Bold new large-scale projects will probably not be needed in the Seine valley for the immediate future.

25

Paris and the Man-Made Evolution of the Seine Basin

From the headwaters of the Seine near Dijon to its estuary in the English Channel, this famous river has, over many years, been extensively modified in order to meet different and ever-changing human needs.[1] This chapter focuses chiefly on Paris but has something to say about other parts of the Seine basin, too.

The Seine has captivated writers for a long time. In 1790, for example, a 28-year-old Russian visitor, Nicola Karamzine, recorded his impressions in a book on his travels in France.

When he first arrived at a promontory overlooking Paris, he was lost in admiration and wrote that he was almost light-headed with the remarkable view laid out before him. This moment was, as he later wrote to his friends, one of the most charming moments of his trip, and he eagerly looked forward to his descent into the streets of Paris itself.

He was initially disappointed by what he saw: straight streets that were badly designed, muddy, and with ugly houses and badly dressed people in them. However, this depressing scene changed completely when he reached the banks of the Seine itself.

There he found magnificent houses six stories high and many expensive shops. He wrote of his arrival:

> What a huge crowd of people was there! What excitement and what noise! Fine carriages passed one after another! People bellowed "Take me to the station! To the station!" and they moved like the wave of the sea!
>
> This indescribable noise, this marvelous assortment of objects for sale, this extraordinary richness, this exceptional vivacity of the people certainly surprised me. It seemed to me that I was like a single grain of sand that had fallen into a gulf in the sea and was now being rolled around by a torrent of water![2]

Impressive as the river may still be today, another writer tells us how much it had changed by the 1920s. Writing in 1927, the French scholar

25. Paris and the Man-Made Evolution of the Seine Basin

Henri Lemoine, an expert on the waterways of Paris, studied the Seine then with a deep feeling of nostalgia and regret. He quoted an earlier French author along these lines:

> Our ancestors were much better neighbors of the Seine than we are today. We do not know it as thoroughly as they did and, as has been explained elsewhere, the reasons are that "The quays along the river are too high, and the river itself is too far away" for us to appreciate it fully.[3]

French perceptions of the Seine have had to change because keeping the river in safe operating condition has always required a great deal of hard work and a willingness to accept new technology. Major efforts to improve navigation there have been going on at least since 1830. The river has variously been called upon to meet the challenging tasks of supplying drinking water to Paris and other growing cities; irrigating crops and transporting them to market; and, in the past, as we have seen, rafting downstream large shipments of logs for firewood and construction purposes.

Watermills on the Seine constantly ground grain to make bread, always the staple of French life. In the Middle Ages, when Paris alone consumed more than 100,000 tons of bread per year, these mills were exceptionally important.

They were often set up on the Seine under a bridge where the current was strongest; were mounted on pylons in the middle of the river for the same purpose; or, perhaps less commonly, were built into boats that would be moored near one edge of the current.

Supervised by mill-mechanics who worked from small open boats anchored near the mills, these artisans had to be on excellent terms with the local watermen to keep the mills working safely and the river traffic flowing smoothly.

In the 1800s, Paris was already a large metropolis located in the middle of the Seine basin and had 11 percent of the region's total population of 4.5 million people. It relied very heavily on the basin and on distant hinterlands for almost all its food and its energy needs. In that era, the Seine basin had several environmental characteristics[4]:

- The streams of the basin's plateau had not been dammed or regulated in any significant way.
- There were many fish ponds located on the plateau, and many water-storage ponds that were used to help raft timber downstream.
- Water mills were no longer temporary structures on the banks of the Seine but were fixed in place in the river.
- Water on the alluvial plain still meandered freely: no canals controlled its flow.

- Since the Seine within Paris itself was not regulated, its banks consisted chiefly of gently sloping sandy or muddy slopes which were often used as temporary moorings for on-loading and off-loading riverboat cargo.

During the Napoleonic era, France first began to build navigation facilities on the Seine in Paris, with a range of harbors, artificial banks, and docks. From 1830 to the present day, most of the Seine and its tributaries have gradually been physically modified, from the headwaters all the way down to the estuary. Ship traffic is now very heavy: each year, for example, more than 4,000 cargo vessels loaded with a total of 20 million tons of freight make the voyage between Le Havre and Rouen.

By the 2000s, a number of major water-related changes were evident:

- Tiled drains, irrigation programs, and drainage ditches were commonly used to conserve water and to improve the yields of croplands near the Seine.
- Some urban and suburban rivers were deepened or were covered over entirely.
- The abandoned sandpits in flood plains naturally filled with standing water and have become excellent havens for birds and other wildlife.
- Artificial navigation channels and locks were installed across floodplains.
- Navigated sections of rivers were kept at stable levels between the locks.
- In urban sectors, high artificial banks were built and river levels were carefully regulated.
- Overall, agriculture is still important in the Seine basin but excessive fertilizer is one of the causes of nitrogen in the ground- and surface-water. Remedial measures will not have any immediate effects on groundwater because of the long retention time of nitrates in the groundwater systems of the basin.

Today, the Seine and other waterways of the region must be dredged to keep navigation safe; the locks and weirs must be maintained; sand and gravel must be supplied on demand for the extensive construction projects in Paris and elsewhere in the Seine basin; hydropower facilities must be operated safely; and careful attention must be given to flood-control to pollution-control as well.

It is indeed an irony that in "proud Paris" the historically severe pollution of the Seine itself was officially ignored before the introduction of a primitive drainage system in the city in 1833. Long before then,

25. Paris and the Man-Made Evolution of the Seine Basin

wastewater and everything that it could possibly transport usually did not flow directly into the river itself but instead simply came to rest much earlier—in the form of a dark, sticky, filthy sludge—on the streets, the gardens, and the roads of Paris.

Early environmental conditions were in fact so bad that the French publication *Géographe parisien* ("Geography of Paris") could complain in 1769:

> Every year, Paris spends a very large amount of money to transport sludge out of the city. This black sludge stinks and its smell really offends foreign visitors. If it touches any piece of clothing, it leaves the equivalent of a permanent burn mark on it. This fact gives rise to the old saying that something "sticks like the sludge of Paris."[5]

In the 1830s, French river engineers working for the Ponts et Chaussées (Bridges and Roads) Department began to design and build a huge new waterway network, which had to be—and was in fact—charted with enormous precision and accuracy.

Retrieved from various archives, these waterway measurements have now been checked, selectively geo-referenced, and digitalized within an open-access database known as ArchiSeine, begun in 2013. This has allowed modern researchers to quantify the state of French rivers in terms of in their lateral, longitudinal, and vertical dimensions.

Measurements include both long-term, slowly developing natural dynamics, such as meander movements, and the much more abrupt modifications caused by man-made river works that are all closely connected to the always-growing demands of Paris. The net result of these demands has been that, from its headwaters to its estuary, the physical characteristics of the Seine River system have been substantially changed by human activities.

It is hard to overestimate the importance of Paris itself on the Seine. It has caused many immediate, many close, and many distant changes to the river. Outlined below in simple form, they include the following:

- The "artificialization" of the course of the river: its course is now dredged, and its banks in Paris, built up over many years and then faced with stone, are not allowed to change like natural riverbanks that are always subject to the weather.
- The flow of the Seine at Paris and the water level there is tightly regulated.
- The flows of some suburban rivers have been diverted and do not reach the Seine itself.
- Upstream, since 1950 France has been able to regulate, both on the Seine and on its tributaries the Yonne, the Marne, and the

Aube, four large storage reservoirs which are designed both for flood control and to prevent water levels from falling too low and thus impeding river navigation. These help in maintaining a constant level for the river through Paris, but they cannot prevent significant increases in river levels during periods of extreme runoff.
- River sections as far away as 155 miles from Paris are now maintained by dredging to the levels best suited for safe navigation.
- On the Seine, there is only one large commercial port, Gennevilliers, which is 5 miles from Paris. It handles heavy petroleum products and building materials and is one of the biggest port complexes in Europe. It was built in the 1930s by Fulgence Bienvenüe, the creator of the Paris subway. This exceptional engineer even used the rubble from the subway to build the quays of the big port.
- There are also about 23 tiny ports along the middle reaches of the Seine near Paris, which are used by private or small-scale commercial navigators and are only moorings, not well-equipped anchorages.

An authoritative summary on the Seine basin, written by Josette A. Garnier of the French National Center for Scientific Research and by two of her colleagues, makes the following points, which have been lightly annotated here[6]:

- The Seine receives the effluents of both the 17 million people living in the Greater Paris region and of the many industries supporting these people. Intensive agriculture based on agrochemicals is a cause of water quality degradation. Physical modifications to the river, such as canalization and the building of reservoirs, have had negative impacts, too.
- From the 1970s to the 1990s, Seine water quality was very poor downstream of Paris. Environmental problems included: lack of oxygen during the summer months; nutrient excesses and eutrophication (the process by which bodies of water are enriched by nitrogen and phosphorus, causing algal blooms); and severe contamination by metals, persistent organic compounds and emergent pollutants, including plastic debris. All of these were very detrimental to aquatic life, as proven by the very low numbers and very few varieties of fish in the river at that time.
- From the 1990s to the present day, water quality in the Seine has improved significantly due to urban and industrial wastewater

25. Paris and the Man-Made Evolution of the Seine Basin 149

treatment but still needs more work. The Seine's ecosystem remains quite fragile, due in part to the continuing and heavy impact of agricultural pollution. The good news is that, in the late 2010s, specialists counted more than 30 species of fish (a surprisingly large number for the Seine at that time) living within the city limits of Paris.

26

The Old Ports of Paris

As noted earlier, Paris drew a good part of its prosperity from trading along the Seine, which was made possible only by numerous small ports and by a large number of full-time and part-time workers, both of which had to handle a wide range of imports and exports.

During the Middle Ages, Paris became the chief port of France in terms of the number of its river-borne shipments and its physical size. The port covered most of the right bank of the Seine and significant parts of the left bank and of the Île de la Cité.

In the process, the city of Paris successfully limited the physical and legal size of the Seine in Paris itself by means of an impressive system of restrictive quays, walls, and shorelines, rather than trying to continue to handle cargo only on the broad muddy or sandy banks of the river. These changes were supported by the large river-and-land-based workforce which was needed to keep cargo shipments, boat traffic, and all river repairs working smoothly.[1]

In 1760, the high point of river-borne commerce in pre–Revolutionary France, about 20 small ports along the right and left banks of the Seine and on the Île de la Cité were already flourishing. Contemporary French authors wrote about some of them in detail, and it is worth while looking at a few of their accounts in 1763 and 1799 for the local color they provide.

We will first touch on those on the right bank of the Seine and then those on the left bank.[2] The biggest, most active, and most important port on the right bank was the *port de Grève*, located where the Hôtel-de-Ville (the town hall) of Paris stands today. It served as the beating heart of the Seine river traffic and was always crowded with people and with long, strong cargo boats of a type mentioned here earlier and known as *marnois* ("Marne boats").

Heavily used by many different types of cargo and passenger boats, this port was quite large by medieval standards, being about 546 yards

26. The Old Ports of Paris

long and 43 yards wide. A seventeenth-century illustration shows that it then took up nearly half of the width of the Seine there, with large numbers of cargo boats moored side-to-side at and near the port.[3]

On the right bank of the river, the *port de la Rapée*, named after a French general, was the main harbor for boats carrying wine, where they were documented, measured, and judged for their river-worthiness. Once all the paperwork was in good order, their skippers could then designate which Parisian ports of call they were bound for.

At the nearby *port au plâtre* (the port for plaster), chalky stones were loaded aboard and, when later discharged, were replaced by firewood for heating and by lumber for construction. A neighboring port dealt in fruit and wood; stacks of good-quality lumber on a little island there covered it completely.

The *port au charbon* (the port for coal) offloaded coal into boats, while the *port Saint-Paul* (Saint Paul port) dealt chiefly in wheat, but also welcomed passenger boats carrying travelers bound for French towns. An engraving from 1775 shows the joyous atmosphere of travelers and their friends when meeting and greeting each other at the port of Saint-Paul, while an engraving of about 1830 shows this port as being packed with boats in the Seine, plus many horses, carriages, and carts on the quay.[4]

Alongside this port were also places on the river where various merchandise could be offloaded, e.g., metalwork from Champagne, and wines from Bourgogne and other regions. A mid–eighteenth-century painting of this port shows it to have spread out over both sides of the river, with passenger boats much in evidence.

Other ports dealt in many kinds of freshwater fish; in bales of hay; and in wheat and other grains. The port named for Saint-Nicolas was said to have so many different kinds of goods for sale that it was referred to as *la caverne d'Ali Baba* (named after the mythical magic cave of Ali Baba). There one could find many wonderful foodstuffs imported from places such as Rouen, Le Havre, Provence, Dieppe, and Holland.

Moreover, a picture painted at the end of the 17th century depicts Port Saint-Nicolas and the riverside of the Louvre. This area often handled cargo from the lower reaches of the Seine, e.g., oysters. Many washerwomen are also shown, both ashore and afloat in their laundry boats, showing that this was a fine place to have your laundry done, too.[5]

There were many longshoremen working at Port Saint-Nicolas over the years. A nice touch of humor was recorded there, as satire, by a French artist at the end of 19th century and can amuse us here.

At that time, many service industries had been set up on boats permanently moored in the Seine, e.g., public baths offering swimming in both warm and cold water, and laundry service. All of these became such a navigation hazard, however, that gradually they were removed by the river authorities.

In a humorous vein, the French artist portrays two longshoremen, dressed in rough working clothes, who are chatting idly and passing time while standing among the old cannons and cannonballs stored at Port Saint-Nicolas on the Seine. The first longshoreman says to his companion, "Do you think that all this weaponry here is to protect us from attacks by the Cossacks [fierce Russian soldiers]?" His companion replies, "You really aren't a true Parisian after all! If you were, you would understand that all these cannons and cannonballs are here *only to be used on us* if we don't support the government's new policy of closing down all the floating service industries and jobs on the Seine!"[6]

The most down-river port along the right bank was *Port-Royal* (Royal Port), where one could find a seat in a *galiotte* (a passenger boat powered both by oars and sails). Once underway, this boat would let the traveler pass the day very peacefully, admiring the slowly passing and totally charming rural countryside.

On the left bank of the Seine, the most upriver port was the *Salt-pêtrière* (the Saltpeter Port: saltpeter was a key component of gunpowder). In reality, however, it dealt not in military matters but only in good wood for carpentry, which was off-loaded there.

Other ports included:

- *Port Saint-Bernard*, which was the best place to buy wines from Champagne, Burgundy, and Orleans, and, in the 19th century, was also the site of a new *halle aux vins* (major wine market) in Paris.
- More recently, the *Quai Saint-Bernard* demonstrates, in front of the steel railings that set it off from the neighboring *Jardin des Plantes* ("Plant Garden"), the four different transportation routes that, in this very restricted space, are now simultaneously in use there today, namely, a major road, a pedestrian walkway, the railroad, and the Seine.
- The *port de la Tournelle*, which specialized in "aristocratic" (best quality) wines for the upper classes.
- The *port de Miramiones*, which handled construction materials, tiles, bricks, hay, charcoal, and autumn fruits such as apples and chestnuts.
- The *port des Théatins*, where there were boats loaded with firewood and charcoal, and offered other goods for sale in the town square.
- The *port de la Grenouillère* ("froggy region"), a section of the Seine in which there were many experts skilled at handling the long heavy "trains" of floating logs.

- The last port, on the *Île Macquerelle*, where ancient cargo boats which were no longer safe to use on the waterways were *déchirées* ("shredded"), i.e., broken up for firewood.
- Eloquent "criers of wine," that is to say, wine salesmen, accompanied by some of their most expert customers, were sent out in small boats to meet the incoming ships carrying barrels of wine to taste the wine itself and to make sure it was of good quality before being landed and paid for ashore.[7]

Commercial standards for most items in the Middle Ages, however, were usually left in the hands of the trade guilds to set and to enforce. The results probably varied a great deal and may often have left something to be desired. Contemporary accounts give us an idea about the most common abuses in the markets[8]:

- An artisan "bends time" to his own liking. A saying of the day was that "At 9:00 AM, the worker says it is really 3:00 PM, and that at 3:00 PM he says it is really night, and thus time for him to leave his job."
- Innkeepers and wine dealers secretly mix water with their wine, or mix bad wine with good wine.
- The innkeeper, knowing how much his customers need to have light in the evening, bills a customer for six times the real price for a sputtering candle, and demands extra payment if he also uses the innkeeper's dice.
- Old women dilute with water the milk they sell, and soak their cheeses in broth to make them plumper and more attractive.
- Flax which is marketed by weight is left out all night on the wet grass so that it will be heavier when sold the next day.
- Before selling a pig carcass, butchers use its blood to redden the gills of stale and discolored fish.
- Drapers use measuring tapes of different lengths on cloth which they are buying and on cloth which they are selling.
- One customer asked his local butcher to give him a discount on sausages because, the customer explained, he had bought all his meat from that same butcher for the past seven years. The butcher then exclaimed in amazement: "Seven years! And you are still alive!"

The old ports of the Seine were very colorful places indeed. Two modern scholars, drawing on information from the 18th century, have made points along the following lines for us:

> Although there is no historical paper trail on this, a reasonable guess is that the Seine and its banks were among the most fascinating places in all of Paris.

The reason was that this very constricted area contained a multitude of very different people, united only in their own need or wish to be along the Seine. They included, among other folks, smugglers, washerwomen, men carrying drinking water, carpenters, longshoremen, crews tending log drives on the river, prostitutes, customs agents, and masons. Many of these people could be seen in the different ports for hay, wheat, and wines, or on the quays of the river.[9]

To take but one case, the Port au Blé (the Wheat Port), according to a picture of it painted at the high point of its activity in 1782, crowds of shoppers afoot or in carriages jostle each other along a bank of the Seine, with rows of handsome houses and with cargo boats drawn up on the shore serving as a backdrop.[10]

With such a diverse but generally impoverished population, however, frictions could never be avoided. For example, after about 1721, five senior inspectors reported that the problems they faced included the following:

- Frauds, clandestine deposits of goods, poor working conditions at the port of Paris, and problems of navigation there.
- The chief corrective measure available to the inspectors was imposing fines on lawbreakers. A fisherman who was discovered illegally fishing on an arm of the Seine near the Hôtel-Dieu was subjected to a stiff fine of 100 French *livres*. (In France during this era, several currencies were in use at the same time—for example, *livres tournois* and *livres parisis*. Their value fluctuated due to government devaluations.) A cart-driver had to pay 10 *livres* for insulting an officer in charge of grain shipments at the port.
- Other sentences could be much harsher. Three men who stole lead and carpentry lumber at the ports were sentenced first to be confined on public display in the pillory for two hours beneath a sign stating their offenses. They were then branded with a red-hot iron to show that they were thieves and were sentenced to serve in the galleys—for three years for the two lead-thieves, and for nine years for the lumber-thief. It is unlikely that the latter would have survived such a long sentence in the galleys.[11]

Because of the importance of river traffic to the economy of Paris and other ports and quays in France, it was subject to strict controls. An official listing of 1771, for example, shows that a total of 942 men were directly involved in manual or supervisory positions involving the transport of wood, coal and charcoal, grains, salt, wines and liquors, navigation and port services, and the port administration.

The eventual canalization of the Seine; the evolution of land-based traction, e.g., the spread of the railroads; and the great flood of 1910 all contributed to the disappearance of some of the smallest industrial ports around Paris. What was most remarkable, however, was not the inevitable evolution and change of the port scene there, but rather the flowering of the concept of *Paris-port-de-mer*, that is to say, of *"Paris as a seaport."*[12]

Although this now seems to us only a will-o-the-wisp, this idea did attract some high-level attention, first in the 18th century, and then more concretely in 1824. In that year, a French engineer put forward a proposal to link Le Havre to Paris by means of a canal following the bed of the Seine. In 1863, two French engineers suggested a way to build a huge new canal to create a "Port Maritime de Gennevilliers" very close to Paris. Many other similar "creative" proposals would surface over the coming years.

The high point of this fantasy came in about 1900, when four French postcards depicted some hypothetical scenes showing "Paris as a seaport." They offered the public the following mythical and joking glimpses into the future:

- A big ocean-going freighter steams past the former palace of Chaillot in Paris itself.
- Bathing in the sea attracts hardy swimmers off the now-surf-filled Place de la Concorde in Paris.
- A dike of big boulders in the sea protects a large monument in Lille, France.
- At sea off the former Paris train station known as *la gare d'Orsay*, a big steamer equipped with sails welcomes liners which have come directly to Paris from Antwerp or London via a mythical new canal.

27

Haropa Port
The Combined Ports of Le Havre, Rouen, and Paris

"Haropa Port" is an acronym coined from the names of the three key French ports—Le Havre, Rouen, and Paris—which were officially merged into a single mega-port in 2022.[1]

Because earlier in this book we have already discussed much of the historical Seine-related and maritime background of Paris, this chapter will focus chiefly on Le Havre and Rouen, which so far have been mentioned only in passing. We can then say something more about the modern port of Paris.

Le Havre

Le Havre is a city in the Seine France-Maritime department of the Normandy region of northern France. Located on the right bank of the Seine estuary on the English Channel, it is the second port in France (after Marseille) for total ship traffic and the first French port for containers. Because of its vital ties to the Seine, it can profitably be discussed here in some depth.

This historic port has had a variety of names. Originally known as Franciscopolis after the French King Françôis I, who founded it in 1517 to replace the silted-up harbors of Harfleur and Honfleur, it was later renamed Le Havre-de-Grace ("Harbor of Grace") after an existing chapel of a similar name.

Its earliest incarnation was as a rudimentary port for the Neolithic-age people who first settled down there and prospered. Later, during the Iron Age, Celtics lived there, too, and Le Havre began to host the river traffic along the Seine which supported the cities located at the mouth of the Seine estuary. In fact, a Roman road linked a town at the mouth of the Seine with Le Harve.

The oldest building in Le Havre today is the ninth-century Graville Abbey. In the 11th century, the village and commercial port of Leure appeared, this little port serving chiefly as a shelter for ships anchored there and waiting until the turn of the tide permitted them to enter the port of Honfleur itself.

This made it possible for pirates who knew the area well to prey on ships lying at anchor in the Seine estuary close to Leure. In 1308, for example, a ship that was anchored there, laden with cargo from Rouen for sale England (canvas for sails, heavy ropes, and a sizeable amount of gold and silver), was attacked by Norman pirates. They ordered the ship to set sail and to go far out into the English Channel. There the pirates stole everything they could—including even the clothes of the crew![2]

Hamlets of fishermen, farmers, and ship-artisans, plus the parishes of local churches, all flourished in this region during the latter part of the Middle Ages. During the Hundred Years War, the fortified ports of Leure and Harfleur were destroyed. By the start of the 16th century, three new developments—the growth of the English Channel and the Seine trade; the further silting-up of Harfleur; and the well-founded French fear of an English assault near the mouth of the Seine—all combined to persuade François I to establish a new port and a new town at Le Havre.

In 1517, the king signed a founding charter for Le Havre and gave responsibility for its construction to his Vice Admiral. A tall tower would defend the entrance to the port and, despite problems with the local marshlands and storms, Le Havre welcomed its first ship the following year. It was thereafter used as an assembly point for French warships and as a harbor for the cod fishery in Newfoundland in what is now eastern Canada.

At this time, the New World was attracting many European adventurers, some of whom sailed out of Le Havre to found a colony in Brazil in 1555. Trade with the New World expanded briskly and classic New World products such as sugar, deer hides, and tobacco were arriving in Le Havre before the end of the 16th century.

In 1564, Le Havre was the port of departure for the French expedition which had established the first French colony in what is now the United States at Fort Caroline, near present-day Jacksonville, Florida. A French artist on this expedition painted the first known depictions by a European of the Indian tribes living in northeastern Florida and southeastern Georgia. Today a dock in Le Havre still bears the name of one of these early French explorers and cartographers: Guillaume Le Testu (1500–1573).

Le Havre was very much affected by the "wars of religion" between the French Catholics and the French Protestants. In 1562, for example, Protestants took over Le Havre, looted Catholic churches, and expelled the Catholics. Fearing a counterattack by the armies of the French king, the Protestants called on the English Protestants for help, who replied by sending in English troops.

French forces, however, nevertheless attacked Le Havre and in 1563 drove out the English soldiers stationed there. The fort built by the English was destroyed; new fortifications were built by the French between 1594 and 1610; and, in 1581, work was begun on a canal linking Harfleur with the estuary of the Seine.

The defense responsibilities of Le Havre were reaffirmed and upgraded in the 16th century when an arsenal was created there, a naval basin was developed, the walls of the city were strengthened, and a fortress was built in the city. During the 17th century, Le Havre also upgraded its maritime duties by becoming the headquarters of the Company of the Orient in 1643. As such, it encouraged the importation of exotic products from America, such as sugar, cotton, tobacco, coffee, and spices.

The slave trade greatly enriched local traders during the 18th century. There were 399 slave-trade expeditions in the 17th and 18th centuries, and Le Havre became the third-largest slave trade port in France (after Nantes and La Rochelle). However, the wars of Louis XIV and Louis XV momentarily slowed the development of Le Havre, which Anglo-Dutch ships bombarded in 1694 and 1696.

On other watery fronts, in 1707, Michel Dubocage, a ship captain, explored the Pacific Ocean aboard his vessel *Discovery* and discovered the atoll of Clipperton Island in the far northeastern reaches of the Pacific Ocean. After he got back to Le Havre, he made a fortune by setting up a trading company and bought a magnificent house in Le Havre.

Another captain from Le Havre, Jean-Baptiste d'Après de Mannevillette (1707–1780), worked for the British East India Company and mapped the coasts of India and China.

From the middle of the 18th century, wealthy traders were building handsome houses on the coast near Le Havre. This building-boom may have been chiefly due to Madame de Pompadour, mistress of King Louis XV, who wanted to see and to live by the sea. The king chose Le Havre to satisfy her extravagant desires. It was claimed by some of her many enemies that these desires had quite ruined Le Havre's finances.

Le Havre was, during 1759, the staging point for a planned French invasion of England during the Seven Years' War: thousands of men, horses, and ships were assembled at Le Havre. The French plan failed, however, due to a two-day naval bombardment of Le Havre by the ships of the Royal Navy, which destroyed many of the invasion barges (we would now call them "landing craft") which had been stockpiled at there for use in the planned invasion. The French therefore had to cancel their attack.

Between 1789 and 1793, the port of Le Havre was the second biggest in France, after that of Nantes. It was important to France both because of the vital grain trade (Le Havre supplied grain needed for bread in Paris) and because it was strategically important, being so close (only 92 miles) to the coast of England, the greatest enemy of France.

The dramatic events of the French Revolution in Paris and elsewhere affected Le Havre as well. The city had to cope with riots, warfare, insurrections, and economic stagnation. A Chamber of Commerce was founded in 1800 but because of a war against the British and due to a blockade, port activity in Le Havre fell off very sharply, piracy bloomed, and the population of Le Havre declined. It was not until after the end of the Revolutionary and the Napoleonic wars that Le Havre's shipping trade began to recover.

The presence of peace, security, and economic growth encouraged a large increase in the population of Le Havre. Because of a crisis in the cloth-weaving industry in France, many unemployed cloth and other workers flocked to Le Havre, looking for new jobs and cheap housing. On the docks and in the factories of the city, visitors could see a wide range of Italian, Poles, North African, and English, Nordic, and Alsatian businessmen.

The city and its port were later reinvigorated by major development projects, partly funded by the French government. The years from 1850 to 1914 have been called a "golden age": trade expanded, and Le Havre was graced with new construction projects, e.g., boulevards, a city hall, courthouse, and a stock exchange.

Its commerce, too, benefited from the improved propellors for ships and from the new docks and warehouses which appeared there in the wake of the arrival of the railroad in 1848. Factories related to port traffic, e.g., shipyards, sugar refineries, and rope factories did well, too. Le Havre even became a fashionable seaside resort for Parisians. Transatlantic steamer travel flourished, beginning in the 1830s.

During times of war, Le Havre suffered, however. World War I killed about 6,000 people, mainly soldiers who were sent away from the city to distant battlefields. The only positive news was that Le Havre also served as a base for British warships, and 1.9 million British soldiers passed through the port, considerably boosting the income of the city in the process.

After the war, the travel industry did well: the liner *Normandie* began sailing to New York in 1935. During World War II, however, German forces occupied Le Havre and turned it into a naval base in preparation for their planned invasion of Britain, which, fortunately, never occurred.

Le Havre suffered 132 bombings by the Allies during the war, and the Nazis destroyed the port's infrastructure and sank ships there before leaving the city. The greatest destruction of Le Havre occurred on 5 and 6 September 1944 when the British Air Force bombed the city center and the port to weaken the Germans' grip. Despite the heavy damage it sustained, however, Le Havre became the location of large-scale Replacement Depots and a key part of the U.S. Army's Communications Zone.

Much later, in the 1970s, economic problems in Le Havre led to the closure of some of the ship-building facilities; the end of ocean liner service to New York; the gradual restructuring of the city away from heavy industry and towards academic and tourism development; and the modernization of the port itself.

Most currently, in the spring of 2023, efforts were underway to make ethanol and other environmentally friendly products more easily available to ships on the Seine.

Rouen

Located near the tidal limit of the Seine (the highest point the tide naturally reaches), the city of Rouen has been an active river port since Roman times. Small craft were by then already braving the challenges of the maritime Seine to ship all kinds of goods to and from France and England.

The Vikings invaded the lower valley of the Seine in 841; overran what is now Rouen; and, as mentioned earlier in this book, after the approval in 911 by King Charles of their leader Rollo, they settled down as peaceful farmers, not as piratical raiders. In the 10th century, Rouen became the capital of the Duchy of Normandy and remained the seat of power there until William the Conqueror built a castle for himself in Caen.

Before 1142, not far from Rouen there existed a priory of canons, e.g., clergy, on the banks of the Seine in what is now the French department of Eure in Normandy. Known to folklore as the Prieuré des Deux Amants (the Priory of the Two Lovers), its romantic story is this:

- A Norman lord had a very pretty niece who was madly in love with a very handsome young man of the neighborhood. He was ardently in love with her, too.
- The lord, however, wanted convincing proof that this young man was in fact strong and virile enough to be a real asset to his noble household. He therefore told the young man that he would give him his niece only if the young man could carry her—without

stopping or resting at all!—all the way from the lord's castle up to the top of a distant mountain that could be seen from the windows of the castle.
- The strong young man—confident that his great love would make his burden very light—set off at once, carrying his beloved in his arms. He did manage to carry her to the mountaintop but, alas, he collapsed and died there within an hour due to exhaustion.
- She made her way back to the castle safely but, a few days later, she, too died there of sorrow. The lord, to atone for his fatal order, then founded on the mountaintop a priory in their joint honor.[3]

In 1204, King Philippe Augustus entered Rouen and annexed it to his other holdings in what is now France, replacing the Norman castle there with his own Château Bouvreuil. Rouen depended on the international river traffic of the Seine for its prosperity: French wine and wheat, for example, were exported to England, with tin and wool being received in return.

When urban strife threatened Rouen in the 13th century (the mayor was assassinated and the houses of the local aristocracy were looted), in 1291 Philip IV restored order by suppressing the city's lucrative monopoly on river traffic and forcing the residents to repurchase their former river-rights. When another urban revolt broke out in 1389, it was suppressed by the withdrawal of the city charter of Rouen and by preventing the locals from trading via the Seine.

In 1419, during the Hundred Years War, Rouen surrendered to Henry V of England, who annexed Normandy to his domains. But the city did not escape English attack very easily because Alain Blanchard, the captain of the French crossbowmen defending Rouen, had murdered English prisoners by hanging them from the city's walls.

In retaliation, when the English victors demanded that three of the city's most respected residents be surrendered to them to be beheaded, two of these men (the vicar general of the archbishop and the master of artillery) were rich and were able to pay a stiff ransom to the King of England. Their lives were spared. Blanchard, however, was too poor to pay anything and, as a result, he was beheaded.

Rouen became the chief city of English power in English-occupied France. When the Duke of Bedford bought Joan of Arc her liberty from the Duke of Burgundy, who had been keeping her in jail since May 1430, she was sent to Rouen to be tried there during Christmas 1430.

After a long and well-documented trial by a church court, Joan was sentenced to be burned at the stake in Rouen—a sentence which, as noted earlier, was carried out on 30 May 1431.

That same year, in Paris, the young Henry VI was crowned King of England and of France before visiting Rouen, where he was acclaimed by the crowds. The king of France, Charles VII, recaptured Rouen in 1449–18 years after Joan's death and after 30 years of English occupation.

During the Renaissance period, the naval dockyards at Rouen, where new orders for ships and repairs had been greatly reduced by the Hundred Years War, became busy again. Rouen became the fourth most populous city in the country (after Paris, Marseille, and Lyon); a cradle of the Renaissance in Normandy; and, quite prosperous, too, thanks to the cloth and silk industries and to metallurgy.

In addition, fishermen from Rouen sailed long distances, e.g., to the Baltic, to catch herring, which was salted to preserve it. The Medici family made Rouen their main port for the resale of alum, which was used in dyeing and tanning. Moreover, by the beginning of the 16th century, Rouen became the chief French port through which was trade with conducted with Brazil, principally for the import of cloth dyes.

On the religious front, severe tensions arose from 1560 on between the Protestants and Catholics of Rouen, to such an extent that the Protestants asked for, and received, English troops to protect them.

In 1562, French Royalist troops recaptured Rouen and pillaged it for three days. In 1572, Protestants were murdered by crowds of Catholics. Rouen was also attacked on several later occasions by French forces but, thanks to help from the Spanish army, it was not captured.

The 16th to the 18th centuries brought prosperity to Rouen through the textile trade and the increased demand for its port facilities. The city specialized in the sale of wool and of faience (glazed ceramic ware). It also began to produce books and became an intellectual center for medical studies.

During the 19th century, steamships with their increasingly deeper drafts had trouble getting up the Seine to Rouen. At the same time, this venerable port had to cope with the challenges posed by increased railroad cargo-carrying traffic.

The net result was that Rouen entered a period of decline, emerging from it only by carrying out major improvement projects in the Seine, e.g., dredging a deeper channel in the river, and by leveling the nearly 30 small islands downstream of Rouen which hindered safe navigation.

In the 19th and 20th centuries, Rouen got caught up in warfare. This included the Franco-Prussian War of 1870–1871, when it was occupied by the Prussians; World War I, when the British used Rouen as a supply base with many military hospitals; and World War II, when the city was occupied by the Germans until it was liberated by the Canadians in 1944. After the war, a new estuary channel dredged in 1960 would allow Rouen to evolve into becoming Europe's most important grain-shipping port.

The best short summary of the history of Rouen and the Seine that we have seen makes the following points:

- Rouen was the heart of the Roman province of Normandy. Politically and commercially, Normandy was completely dominated by Rouen, with its large population and position on the Seine. Rouen boasted roughly 30,000–40,000 inhabitants, and via the Seine it had good contacts with Paris, with its population of 80,000–120,000 people....
- The Seine area was thus a rich trade center, and was visited by numerous merchant ships every year.... The Seine estuary especially was a dynamic area, and several large town clustered around it profited from trade.[4]

The Port of Paris

What can be called Haropa Port's unusual "triangular marriage"—linking Paris, Le Havre, and Rouen—has been a clear success. Haropa Port is now the No. 1 logistics hub for France; the No. 1 inland port worldwide for river transport; and the No. 1 world port for the export of wines and spirits.

The only bad news is that all three of the components of Haropa Port have varying but significant levels of pollution. In rough "order of pollution" they are: (1) the Greater Paris area is, as might be expected, by far the worst; (2) the Rouen area, which has about 50 percent less pollution than Paris; and (3) the Le Havre area, which has about half of Rouen's total.

Paris itself is now the leading French port complex for the transport of goods and is a major maritime complex at the pan–European level. In the Greater Paris area, river traffic has increased markedly, due chiefly to four major infrastructure projects which are now underway there.

In addition, several industrial and logistics companies are studying prospects for setting up new operations on port lands there. Moreover, a new port in the Greater Paris area, located at the confluence of the Seine and the Oise Rivers, is also now being discussed. When and if all these ambitious enterprises ever see the light of day, a reasonable guess is that the pollution in the Seine in Paris itself is likely to increase further over time.

28

The Likely Future of the Seine

By the early 1960s, the number of commercial boats using the Seine had increased rapidly. The banks of the river had become far more congested, too, and were less and less people friendly.

One very "creative" solution to this problem—fortunately, it was never put into effect!—was to make it possible for pedestrians to *Rouler ou flâner sur la Seine* ("Roll or stroll on the Seine") itself. This was a project suggested by the French architect Paul Maymont in 1960–1962.[1]

Far-fetched as it may seem today, it involved building a number of totally dry new "floors" or "levels" dug into in the bedrock of the Seine. Protected from the river that would be on top of them by an impervious "roof" above them, these floors or levels would, in theory at least, allow people to live, work, bicycle, and play *under the river,* which would continue to flow and to carry boat traffic above them.

On a much less visionary and far more practical anti-pollution level, however, Paris has been trying to clean up the Seine for many years.

It now hopes to make so much progress on this front that diving and swimming in the Seine will be possible during the 2024 Summer Olympics, but the jury is still out on this matter. Our own guess is that this radical improvement will not come to pass. Let us now look at some of the causes of the Seine's environmental problems and at the difficulties involved in trying to cure them any time soon.

Working with what is potentially one of the most attractive urban rivers in the world, Paris has, alas, fallen very far short of the over-ambitious promise that Jacques Chirac, then the mayor of Paris, made in 1998 when he promised to swim himself in the Seine within five years. (Although officially forbidden since 1923, swimming in the Seine in Paris nevertheless continued until about 1950.)

It is recognized that pollution levels in the river are now appreciably

28. The Likely Future of the Seine

lower than they were in the 1980s and 1990s and that there are now many more fish in the river. Nevertheless, swimming in the Seine, which was a popular social pastime in the 1888s, is illegal in the Seine's urban stretches due to the high bacteriological levels and the dangers posed by boat traffic.[2]

Remedial plans have been studied, some timed to be online for the 2024 Summer Olympics. One idea is building a huge subterranean water tank near the Gare d'Austerlitz train station on the left bank of the Seine. This would store stormwater and prevent sewage from spilling into the Seine when the drains of Paris overflow during heavy rains.

With a capacity of over 12 million gallons, it would hold the contents 30 Olympic-sized swimming pools. At an estimated cost of $1.6 billion, it would be invisible at the surface level and would have trees planted in the topsoil of the garden above the tank. Connected by underground pipes to sewers on both sides of the Seine, the polluted water collected by the tank would be pumped into these sewers for treatment once the heavy rains have ended.

All this being known, however, there is still no guarantee that such a tank would in fact be able to prevent large amounts of sewage from flowing into the Seine during rainstorms. At present, approximately 528 million gallons of sewage-contaminated wastewater run into the river each year, and it remains to be seen what impact such a tank would really have.

One of the main factors historically responsible for the pollution of the Seine is sewage-mixed-with-rainwater, which is often the source of the harmful-to-humans bacteria found in the river. In addition to sewage pollution, there are also assorted industrial pollutants and illegal discharges of contaminated water from barges and boats which are not good for people, either.

The Seine's water, due to its long history of receiving large amounts of pollution from industrial sources, still contains high levels of heavy metals such as copper, cadmium, lead, and zinc. Toxic pollutants in surface run-offs also include mercury, nickel, chromium, toluene, DDT, and other pesticides and herbicides. Nutrients, sediments, and bacteria often end up in the Seine, too.

These pollutants appear in much greater amounts whenever there is a great deal of rain. This is due not only to the higher level of surface runoff caused by rainfall falling on Paris roads and other impervious urban surfaces, but also because the old sewage systems of Paris are very prone to what is called "sanitary sewage overflow." This means that whenever untreated sewage leaks into the river—a frequent occurrence during rainstorms—it will cause pollution there.

The Seine is now in better environmental condition than it was in the past. One key reason is that the heavy industrial, old-fashioned, pollution-prone manufacturing processes have either been closed entirely or have been forced by public opinion and by new laws to clean up their environmental acts. As a result, today French mass industrial processing on the scale of the past has almost ceased entirely between the source of the Seine and Rouen.

Moreover, over the past 25 years, the treatment of city-sewage has improved to the point where it no longer needs the "fatal fish skeleton" symbol that in the past had warned consumers of the gross pollution of the Seine which was the river's hallmark in the 1980s and 1990s.

Paris has now only one large sewage treatment facility (at Achères) that receives much of the city's drainage. The sewers are combined sewers that accept both the human wastes of the population and the rainwater that falls on the whole area. The banks of the Seine in Paris have no storm water drains, so when the sewers can no longer cope with the volume of its mixed load of watery wastes, they erupt from the lowest points of the city's drains along the Seine and flood into the river.

When this occurs, the only partial remedy is that the water authorities can now station barges at points along the river. These can pump oxygen into the polluted water, which can to some extent improve its degraded quality.

In order to look at the future of the Seine it is also a good idea to look at its past. Readers will find that this is best done by consulting François Beaudouin's definitive 1993 book on *Paris/Seine: Ville Fluviale—Son histoire des origins à nos jours* ("Paris and the Seine: A river city—Its history from its origins down to our own day"). This book may be the single best source on the visual history of Paris as recorded by contemporary painters who knew Paris well.

Finally, readers who are boaters themselves, or who want to learn something about navigating the Seine, will profit greatly from the multilingual *Waterways Guide to the Seine*, and from Edwards-May's *Inland Waterways of France*. Both these hands-on reference books are listed in the bibliography of the present book.

Looking ahead, the greatest environmental threat to Paris is likely to be climate change, e.g., global warming.

Global warming is occurring and increasing the prospect of heavy rains that can generate floods in Paris and elsewhere. The reasons are very simple and very clear. In a nutshell:

- Global warming is caused by increased concentrations of greenhouse gases in the atmosphere.
- Higher ocean water temperatures and higher air temperatures lead to more evaporation and cloud formation.

28. The Likely Future of the Seine

- For every degree of warming, the atmosphere can hold about 7 percent more moisture.
- Under these conditions, when it does rain, it can really pour.

Fortunately, at this writing, no floods in the Seine river basin have come very close to the high-water mark of what is still remembered in Paris as "the Great Flood" of 1910, which was 28 feet above the normal water level. Its closest competitors have occurred in 1955 (23 feet above normal); in 1981 (20 feet above normal); and 2018 (19 feet above normal).

29

The Seine and the English Channel

The English Channel is the arm of the Atlantic Ocean that separates southern England from northern France. Linked to the southern part of the North Sea by the Strait of Dover at its northeast end, it is the busiest shipping area of the entire world and is the terminus of the Seine.

About 350 miles long and varying considerably in width from 150 miles to 21 miles, it was a key factor in Britain becoming a naval superpower and has long been used by Britain as an anti-invasion defense. The Strait of Dover lies between England and France, is the narrowest part of the Channel, and marks the boundary between the Channel and the North Sea.

The weather near the Seine had a major impact on medieval shipping: it controlled or even overruled the best-laid political and military plans by both England and France. The prevailing south-westerly winds, for example, forced ships onto the coast of Flanders and of France north of the Seine.

As a modern author tells us,

> Time after time, continental [French] attempts to invade England were frustrated not by the English but by the weather. Fleets which had been assembled at great expense at Sluys ... or in ports near the mouth of the Seine were thwarted in their plans for crossing the Channel.... Conversely, the same south-west winds were a great benefit to the English when their fleets set out in the opposite direction.[1]

As noted earlier, in France the Channel in known as *la Manche* ("the sleeve"), which refers to its perceived shape. The eastern part of the Channel along the French coast between Cherbourg and the mouth of the Seine at Le Havre is called the Bay of the Seine (*"Baie de Seine"*).

This bay is a wide rectangular inlet of the Channel, bounded in the west by the Cotentin Peninsula, in the south by the Normandy coast, and

29. The Seine and the English Channel

in the east by the estuary of the Seine at Le Havre. The coast here alternates between sandy beaches and rocky promontories, with virtually no shelter for coastal shipping. Today the Channel coast is far more densely populated on the English shore than on the French shore, the largest French city there (Le Havre) having only about 268,000 inhabitants.

Because it is such a busy shipping lane, the Channel is always vulnerable to environmental problems, e.g., accidents involving ships carrying toxic cargo or oil. An updated ship traffic collision avoidance system has now reduced the frequency of such accidents, but it can never prevent them entirely, especially when human errors are involved.

Each year more than 4,000 cargo vessels, loaded with 20 million tons of freight, make the voyage on the Seine between Le Havre and Rouen. The administrative limit between sea waters and inland waters is an imaginary but well-understood legal line which prevents boats registered only for inland waterways from going down the Seine estuary all the way to the historic port of Honfleur.

The official name of the urban community of Le Havre is now "Le Havre Seine Métropole" (the "Metropolis of Le Havre-Seine"). It is located in the west of Seine-Maritime department in the Normandy region; was created in 2019 by a merger of the towns of Caux Estuaire and Cruquetot-l'Esneval; and has, as noted earlier, a population of about 268,000 people.

In an interview of 18 December 2022 on Le Havre, the Deputy Chief Executive Officer of HAROPA Port, Florian Weyer, made some key points along the following lines:

- As a maritime gateway handling 75 percent of HAROPA Port's traffic, Le Havre plays a major transportation role. By dealing with more than three million containers, we remain a driving force in the import of hydrocarbons [oil]. Unlike other major ports in Europe, Le Havre contains to expand its market share.
- Our growth will permit us to absorb traffic that our competitors cannot handle. In 2025, for example, a new 5,905-foot-long dike at the entrance to the port will promote faster river service to our port.
- At present, only 10 percent of the barges (the vessels carrying oil) are able to approach the port closely at all times because of adverse sea conditions during part of the year. The new dike will be sheltered and will thus provide permanent all-weather access for all vessels. Since each barge carries the equivalent of 250 truckloads of oil, this means there will be less truck traffic on the French highways.

- HAROPA Port is committed to improving its energy efficiency. The Seine axis accounts for 20 percent of industrial carbon emissions in France; we are working with manufacturers to decarbonize their activities. In addition, Le Havre is now home to a major project to utilize offshore wind power.
- We are also working on the electrification of docks to allow ships to shut down their engines when they are moored in port.

30

Suburban Villages Along the Seine

The diet of most Parisians was, historically, quite varied, consisting of cereals, vegetables, fruits, meat, milk, and wine. As the population of Paris grew ever bigger, however, the amount of its land that could be devoted to food production shrank as densely built-up urban areas began to increase in size and began to sprout houses rather than crops.[1]

The net result was that the rural villages around Paris increasingly had to take up what we might call the "agricultural slack" by producing, chiefly for Paris consumers, much more bread, wine, fruits, vegetables, and flowers than they had ever done before.

A good example of this is an undated but probably eighteenth-century illustration which shows, on the upper half of the page, a rural scene in which one couple (a farmer and his wife) are using a ladder to shake down a few apples from their one apple tree. The lower half of the illustration shows, much later, the many different kinds of fruits and vegetables later being unloaded from boats on the Seine and then sold on the quays by market women and hand-cart vendors.[2]

At the end of the 18th century, reports of annual Paris consumption levels were available only in a French measurement known as "livres par an" ("livres per year"). Rather trying to convert them into modern French measurements, however, it is much easier here simply to say that Parisians consumed very large amounts of fruits, vegetables, meat, and cereals grown around Paris.

A modern map showing what was grown in the suburban villages at that time, both along and close to the Seine in Paris, reveals that in central Paris itself there were still some market-gardens and woods.

The broader region around the capital, however, contained a large number of fruit trees, vineyards, vegetable fields, flower-growing areas, and woodlands—with the Seine making a big "U"-shaped turn, heading downstream, in the midst of all this agricultural plenty.

Perhaps the best illustration showing the well-ordered and prosperous villages of this broader region is the one of the Seine by Nicolas-Jean-Baptiste Raguenet in 1757 entitled *Le Quai et le village de Passy vus de la rive gauche* (*The Wharf and the village of Passy as seen from the left bank of the Seine.*)[3]

This painting of the Seine at Passy (a village located on the Seine, west of Paris) shows in the foreground five river boats. Four of them are long, graceful, narrow, open-deck Marne boats, which are probably carrying farm products or general cargo. The fifth is a much shorter cargo boat with a cloth cover over its hold. It was probably carrying a load of hay, which had to be kept quite dry.

The most famous resident of Passy was the French writer Honoré de Balzac, whose former home is now a museum in his honor. Noted residents at other times included the lord of Passy; a princess; a locally famous doctor; and the Turkish Ambassador.

Until the middle of the 19th century, transport on the Seine focused more on moving people, not on moving heavy commercial cargos from one point to another. Later improvements in river traffic technology lead to improvements in the banks and the ports of the river.

Since the 17th century, the Paris port of Saint-Paul had welcomed passenger-boats drawn by teams of horses. Beginning in about 1820, the first steamboats appeared. They won many Paris passengers by scheduling early morning departures from the port near the Quai de la Tournelle for destinations along the Yonne River, and from the port of the Quai d'Orsay for Rouen from 1836 to 1838.

In the same era, a dam-and-lock combination was devised to regulate water levels in the river, which made it much easier and safer for boats to navigate the Seine. Another valuable invention used a heavy steam-powered chain, resting on the bottom of Seine, to tow cargo boats. This allowed them to carry coal from the mines of northern France to distributors in the Paris area.

Finally, as if all this were not enough, the usually very muddy banks of the Seine in Paris were converted into what were called the "lower ports," simply by deepening them and facing them with stone, thus providing a total of 53 mooring places along the Seine in Paris where goods could safely be bought and sold.

The success of these efforts could be seen in the tonnages of goods moved on the Seine. Using contemporary French estimates, these were as follows: 520,000 tons at the end of the 18th century; 1,260,000 tons in 1824; 2,220,000 in 1843; and 3,200,000 in 1862. During this whole process, French roads were getting better, and the railroads made their appearance. As a result, the river transport on the Seine shifted: it now carried more heavy goods, e.g., wood and coal.

31

New Crews for European River Transport

Today, the profession of river transport requires increasingly well-qualified men and women.[1] In the past 10 years, for example, freight traffic on the rivers of Western Europe has increased by 40 percent, and water-based tourist activities, e.g., river cruises and river walks, have developed considerably, too.

There are now more than 23,000 miles of inland waterways in the European inland waterway network, and the opening of new wide-gauge river and canal links will enable France to better connect with this system. The inland waterway profession itself is becoming far more complex in terms of the electronic and other equipment in service now; the diversification of river traffic; the need to understand and to use the large European waterway network; and the growing importance of safeguarding the environments of the waterways in different countries.

The advantages of freight transport by waterways are clear. It can respond to the changing logistical needs of industrialists; reduce the saturation of automobile and truck traffic on the highways and roads; and adjust to the requirements of high-tech societies now increasingly in favor of sustainable economic and social development.

On the personnel level, in the future there are likely to be more job opportunities on the waterways for able, well-trained men and women who are willing, in return for good pay, to deal with the good and the bad aspects of professional life on the waterways. The constant growth of this sector of the economy, coupled with the retirement of many experienced personnel, means that there should be frequent openings in this challenging line of work.

They will range from deck hands and bosuns to masters, captains, and senior businessmen in waterway transport companies involved with the movement of both goods and people. The new Seine-Nord Europe project, which will link the Paris Basin to six seaports in the Le Havre-Rotterdam area by 2030 via a wide-gauge waterway, should generate many jobs, too. It is worth saying something about it now because of its likely importance in the future.

The Seine-Nord Europe Canal is a major regional development project which is designed to combine engineering expertise with respect for safety and for the environment. By 2030, it will link Compiègne on the River Oise, which is the main tributary of the Seine after the Marne and which rises in Belgium and flows into the Seine at Conflans-Sainte-Honorine, to Aubencheul-au-Bac in the north.

This large-gauge canal, which will be 66 miles long and 59 yards wide, will be an essential link in the Seine-Scheldt river network. It will provide continuous wide-gauge inland transport from Le Havre to Antwerp and will thus be part of the 12,427-mile network of European waterways. It will offer a creative and ecologically viable solution for some of the problems facing freight transport in this heavily populated area.

Each cargo ship, for example, will be able to carry the equivalent payload of 220 individual trucks, thus reducing truck traffic on the highways. The Seine-Nord Europe Canal can, at least in theory and under ideal conditions, be navigated by a ship in as little as 16 hours, compared to the roughly 30 hours needed to travel via the present river network.

The cost of this ambitious project will be more than 5 billion euros, financed by the European Union, by France, and by the local authorities that oversee the Société du Canal Seine-Nord Europe as its project manager.

Like any other major construction project, this one has both plus and minus aspects. According to François Manouvrier, the director of a French school that trains men and women for jobs on the waterways, the positive and negative qualities of this canal include the following:

- This new waterway will lessen the heavy truck traffic on the major French highway that links the Paris area and the north of France to the ports of Belgium and the Netherlands by diverting some of it to the canal. These ports are today already near the point of saturation.
- Although some French transport companies fear competition from foreign firms, the canal will be a good opportunity for them to expand their scope of operation beyond the Seine. Even if the canal does not benefit from them directly, it will nevertheless be *un puissant levier* ("a powerful lever") reenforcing river transport in general.
- That said, however, the canal may also increase the appeal of the

northern ports, especially Antwerp in Belgium and Rotterdam in the Netherlands, at the expense of Le Havre, for shipments to the Île de France area.
- Moreover, it is possible that some of the bridges and other logistic facilities enroute may be too low to permit the passage of cargo boats carrying two levels of shipping containers, thus limiting their rentability.
- Finally, the changing climate, which we have witnessed in recent years, with longer and more frequent periods of drought, raises problems for keeping the new canal full of water. If so, this may make waterways transport more uncertain.

To return now to manpower and womanpower matters, in France alone there are now three institutions which provide hands-on training for young men and women who wish to work on the inland waterways.[2]

The programs in all three of these French inland waterways schools are essentially the same: a total of 360 days of learning and practice. Students will emerge with the basic qualifications needed to work as a *timonier* ("helmsman") on an inland waterways vessel. Later, once they have had some experience, they can take the examination necessary to become the captain of an inland waterways ship.

There are now only two bits of bad news about this profession in France itself.

The first is the present lack of reliability of some of the locks and other infrastructure on the Seine. They are subject to frequent and random breakdowns, basically due to a shortage of the funds needed to keep them in good repair. However, according to another French inland waterways expert, François Bouriot, remedial projects are now being undertaken to resolve these problems.

The second bit of bad news is that there is now a shortage of captains and rivermen and river women on the inland waterways. M. Bouriot believes that new steps need to be taken to make this profession more attractive and thus to increase entry levels by newcomers.

Conclusions
The Jewel in the Crown

Guido de Bazoches (c. 1146–c. 1203), who was introduced in earlier pages of this book, was a medieval French canon [cleric] whose many books and letters were so well written that they became models for later writers.

In 1190 he famously referred to the Île de la Cité as "the head, heart, and marrow of Paris." It now seems impossible to improve on this definition, but in this final chapter we will look ahead a bit to see what the future might possibly hold for the Île la Cité, which can still rightly be considered to be the jewel in the crown of Paris.

By about 1400, Paris—chiefly because of its location on the Seine—was the site of the royal palace. A great many boats and boatmen were needed on the Seine to transport all the food, drink, and other supplies needed each day for the approximately 600 guests and retainers who expected to dine with, and otherwise be close, to the king.

We will do well here simply to follow Guido's lead by giving this historic island the full prominence it deserves. It has already been mentioned several times in our text, but now a more detailed commentary on it may perhaps serve as a fitting conclusion to this book.

First, it is necessary to stress that the relatively clean and very well-ordered Seine of Paris today bears little relationship, visually and socially, to the ramshackle Seine of Paris in the past. For example, two seventeenth-century engravings of the Île de la Cité between the Pont-au-Change and the Pont Notre-Dame show the old wooden tanneries there and many small fishing boats and cargo vessels moored along the muddy shore.[1]

One of the most interesting but most tragic events on the Île de la Cité occurred in *le square du Vert-Galant* (Vert-Galant Square) in 1314 when Jacques de Molay, the last Grand Master of the order of the Templars, and two of his final surviving companions, were burned alive there.

The Jewel in the Crown

This event took place seven years after 53 other Templars had been executed at a castle in Vincennes, about five miles from Paris, all of them on trumped-up charges generated by the king himself. Jacques de Molay and his two companions were falsely convicted under similar charges, and the Templars' story is worth recounting very briefly here.

The Templars (monk-soldiers of the Order of the Temple in Jerusalem) had been organized to protect Christian pilgrims en route to, within, and while leaving the Holy Land. The most important location there, in both Christian and Muslim eyes, was Jerusalem.

Christian military forces held Jerusalem itself from about 1099 to 1187 but after they eventually lost it to the Muslims, Christian pilgrimages to the Middle East dwindled and the Templars then had to look for new outlets for their energies.

In this process, being staffed with able men who were well-organized as international bankers and traders, and who held a "commandery" (a key administrative office) in Paris itself on the right bank of the Seine, the Order of the Templars had become extremely rich.

The French King Philippe the Fair (1268–1314) was always very short of money. He therefore decided to seize the great riches of the Templars by falsely accusing them of heresy—the gravest crime of the Middle Ages—and then having them convicted and put to death.

In so doing, he successfully enlisted the support of the weak and enfeebled Pope Clement V to destroy the Templars by bringing spurious charges against them. These ultimately resulted in the killings mentioned above.

Legend has it that, as the flames licked up around him, Jacques de Molay threw this curse at his murderers:

> "Pope Clement and King Philip: Before this year is out, I predict that all of you will have to appear before God to receive your just punishment! Curses on you! Curses on you! You will be cursed down to the thirteenth generation of your families!"[2]

To return now to the Île de la Cité itself, an excellent multi-color map of 1552 gives an outstanding bird's-eye view of all the buildings located there at that time.[3] Surrounded by the Seine, the spans of the various bridges over the river are all packed, cheek-by-jowl, with densely inhabited houses.

By the 19th century, the Seine, in its journey around the Île de Cité and elsewhere in Paris, was no longer simply an attractive and decorative water-gap between the east bank and the west banks of the river. Now it was instead a very busy *commercial channel* through the very heart of the capital, jam-packed with floating wash houses; *batteaux mouches* (passenger boats) carrying suburban commuters and tourists; barges full of building supplies and foodstuffs; and fishing boats.[4]

The modern French historians Danielle Chadych and Dominique LeBorgne have summarized very nicely the radical transformations made by Baron Haussmann on the Île de la Cité. As they explain, his ceaseless labors had *complètement bouleversée* ("totally overturned") the old architectural medieval order there.[5]

For example, the cathedral of Notre-Dame had been surrounded by the houses of the canons [clerics] and by more than 20 small religious sanctuaries. This was in good keeping with medieval practice, but almost all of them were demolished by Haussmann because he wanted instead to highlight the cathedral itself by installing in front it of a large traditional open space known as the parvis.

The net results of Haussmann's major interventions on the Île de la Cité were three new or reconstructed buildings there, namely, the Tribunal de Commerce (the Commercial Court), the Préfecture de Police (the headquarters of the police), and the Hôtel-Dieu (a large hospital). Three other major structures were left unaltered: the Conciergerie (the oldest remaining part of the former legal center), the Palais de Justice (the modern judicial center), and the Ste. Chapelle (the Holy Chapel).

Looking Toward the Future

In 2015, President of France François Hollande decided to give Dominique Perrault (architect and urban planner) and Dominique Bélaval (president of the National Center for Monuments) the assignment of thinking about what the Île de la Cité should look like in the year 2040.

A book on their findings, entitled *Paris—Île de la Cité—2040*, has been used in this chapter and is listed in the bibliography. It traces both the history of the heart of Paris and the planning for tomorrow by consulting archival documents, sketches, engravings, maps, photographs, and new ideas.

The need to upgrade the Île de la Cité was laid out by then–President Hollande in a 2015 letter to Perrault and Bélaval. He made points along the following lines:

- The situation on the Île de la Cité is not entirely satisfactory today. Despite the high level of tourist traffic and large number of users of the various services, with barely more than one thousand inhabitants it is not, strictly speaking, a lively place. The massed buildings of the Palais de Justice, the Préfecture de Police, and the Hôtel-Dieu seem like impenetrable blocks.

- It will be your responsibility to propose the main areas of intervention on the part of the different actors concerned with the multiple challenges of making the island a place to live and to restore it to its rightful place in the history of Paris and in the cultural and social life of the capital, and making it a part of the overall strategy of sustainable development for the city of Paris.[6]

The book mentioned above on "findings" is very detailed but for our purposes we need to focus only on its "Imagined possibilities," namely, the authors' creative ideas for architectural possibilities on the future of the Seine at the Île de la Cité.

They make the basic point that these possibilities require us to think about the island as a whole—that is, as a living and open neighborhood—turned toward the two banks of the Seine, thus bringing together economic activity, a warmer welcome for tourists, and the improvement and enhancement of an unrivaled concentration of French national heritage sites.

The most feasible of the possibilities shows what the southern arm of the Seine could look like in the future. At present, looking downstream towards Notre-Dame, the river flows along a massive stone wall on the island whose only attraction is that visitors can now sit along its bank and look at the Seine and at several of the distant bridges which can be seen from there.

One of the "imagined possibilities" ideas shows a computer-generated variation which is a great improvement to the present reality. It consists chiefly of moving the stone wall inward towards Notre-Dame and, in the new open space thus created, installing an area where people can sit under an open-air lattice-work roof and perhaps have a cup of coffee or a picnic lunch.

Other creative suggestions include replacing the present Pont Saint-Louis bridge with a new "urban plaza" modeled after the Yokohama Port Terminal in Japan; building a new footbridge, modeled after one in Bilbao, Spain, over the Seine; and using new platforms and moored house barges to permit dining and other evening activities along the southern arm of the Seine.

The long, eventful partnership of the Seine and Paris has basically been positive and constructive for France. The only downsides we can see now are two-fold:

- First, the environmental problems mentioned in earlier pages of this book have not disappeared but they can be managed. However, they will need a higher level of government spending and political will in order to keep them under control.

- Second, the growing environmental awareness of our own generation—and most certainly of our children's generation—will call for further efforts to transform more of the Seine's riverbanks in Paris into accessible and people-friendly places.

Perhaps, in conclusion, we will not go too far wrong if we summarize three major historical points made at much greater length by Alexandre Arnaud and Stéphanie Boura in their excellent study, published in 2000, *La Seine et Paris* ("*La Seine and Paris*").

Translated, shortened, and annotated, these points run along the following lines[7]:

1. The Seine in Paris is a symbol of life, perpetually flowing and constantly renewing itself. It gives the city its economy and its architecture and, in the distant past, its protection from enemies. The Seine has always been the lifeline that permitted Paris to grow and to become a radiant city, appreciated by peoples all around the world.
2. From its beginnings and throughout the Middle Ages, the Seine has always been *une mère nourricière* ("a nourishing mother"), thanks to its ports and quays; to its ability to support and stimulate the growth of Paris; and to the artisans and business people from all walks of life who have devoted their lives to making this great city work smoothly.
3. In more recent times, the Seine has continued to be a source of considerable economic growth for Paris, symbolized by the arrival of steamships after 1816, the international exhibitions held in Paris from 1850 to 1937, and the creation of the modern Port of Paris in 1968 and its continuing upgrading in the years since then.

A Chronology

4200–500 BC: Archeological finds show that, during these years, some families lived along the Seine in what is now Paris.

1st century: Pilgrims leave offerings at the temple of the river goddess Sequanna, who bequeaths to us her name in the form of "Seine."

361–363: The Roman Emperor Julian enjoys his winter headquarters in Lututia, the Roman name of the town inhabited by the Parisii tribe. Thanks to them, it will later become known as "Paris."

508: During the reign of Clovis, the king of the Franks, Paris becomes his capital and does well economically, thanks to its excellent location on the Seine.

9th century: The Vikings raid Paris three times.

911: The Viking chieftain (named Rolf or Rollo) and his followers are officially accepted by the French king and thus become permanent settlers in Normandy, which they had conquered earlier.

987–1328: Under the leadership of the Capetian dynasty, Paris becomes the dominant center of France.

After 1053: Merchants use both the Seine and overland transport to cater to the crowds coming to Paris area for the large open-air religious celebration known as the Lendit fair. Later, the fair will be held in a big covered market there known as the *Halles*, which was about 500 yards from the Seine.

1079–1142: Life of the brilliant philosopher and lover Pierre Abelard, who taught students at a school he had founded in Paris overlooking the Seine, and whose torrid affair with his student Heloise becomes the stuff of legend.

1121: King Louis VI grants to the boatmen of Paris a sizeable bonus for each cargo of wine that arrives safely in the city during the wine harvest.

1163: Construction of the great cathedral of Notre-Dame de Paris begins under the leadership of Bishop Maurice de Sully; some of its building stones are transported via the Seine.

1170: The French king awards the valuable right of commercial navigation on the

Seine to the "water merchants"—the entrepreneurs who buy and sell goods to be transported along the rivers of France. He decrees that only they can carry on business between the two bridges over the Seine in Paris and the Mantes-la-Jolie bridge over the Seine about 30 miles downstream.

1190: The traveler Guido de Bazoches, who warmly praises the location and the prosperity of Paris, writes that the Île de la Cité is "the head, heart, and marrow of Paris."

By 1200: The right bank of the Seine, which is higher and drier than the lower and often-muddy left bank, is now crowded with the shops of many local traders, e.g., tanners, fishermen, and millers with their watermills.

1210: Paris boatmen, using the image of a single-masted ship known as a *nef* as their official seal and coat of arms, set up the *Hanse*, that is, a "corporation of merchants trading goods by means of the waterways." This commercial enterprise later becomes an important political body as well.

1242–1248: King Louis IX of France orders the Sainte-Chapelle (Holy Chapel) to be built in the Palace de la Cité (Palace of the City) in Paris. Some of its building stones probably came from quarries along the Seine.

1280: Destroyed by a flood during this year, the Grand Pont in Paris is rebuilt in stone and is packed high with side-by-side houses. Most of its arches are used as supports for watermills to grind grain.

1300–1450: The Seine basin becomes the most important regional commercial center during the Hundred Years War.

1317: An illuminated medieval manuscript contains excellent color illustrations of many contemporary boats, bridges, and watermills on the Seine.

1323: The French professor Jean de Jandun reports that the Seine is responsible for all the excellent foodstuffs and other good things that are delivered so abundantly to Paris.

1413: There are now about 60 professional boatmen living in Paris and working in the small upstream and downstream ports of the Seine.

1415: King Henry V's first expedition into Normandy seizes the undefended French port of Harfleur.

1416: A major English naval victory over the French in the Seine estuary near Harfleur is one of the biggest and bloodiest naval clashes of the Hundred Years War.

1423: Paris tax records show that the money-changers are among the richest people in Paris.

1431: Joan of Arc is burned alive at the stake in Rouen as a relapsed heretic; her ashes are dumped into the Seine.

c. 1452–1460: One of the earliest depictions of Paris—a medieval painting by Jean Fouquet, now in the Metropolitan Museum of Art in New York—shows God chasing away the demons who have congregated over the Seine and the boats on it; the cathedral of Notre Dame; and the Île de la Cité.

15th century: Separate ports have already been built along the Seine to make it easier to deliver all the wine, grain, plaster, paving stones, hay, fish, charcoal, firewood, and lumber needed by Parisians every day.

1530: The French magistrate Claude Fauchet explains that the Seine is so important because 17 local rivers help it transport cargo shipments to Paris, which as a result has access to all the commodities available in France.

1545: Francis I sends a French fleet of 150 ships and 25 galleys from the mouth of the Seine to invade England, but weather conditions and ship losses on both sides prevent any major naval battle.

1547: The first "trains" of floating logs, used for lumber and firewood, are rafted down the Seine and other French rivers to market areas.

1572: During the Wars of Religion in France, the French king Charles IX orders his men: "Kill them all [meaning kill all the Protestants] so that none [of them] shall reproach me [for the slaughter I am ordering today]." About 3,000 Protestants are therefore killed in Paris by Catholic rioters: the Seine is so swollen with their bodies that they float back onto the bank of the river almost as soon as they are thrown in.

1578–1607: Pont Neuf (New Bridge) is the oldest bridge in Paris across the Seine. Listed since 1889 as an historical monument, it was the first bridge in Paris to cross both arms of the Seine; the first not to have any houses built on it; and the first to have pavements installed on it.

16th century: The most important industry in Paris is no longer money-changing but the weaving and dyeing of textiles, which pollutes the Seine and other rivers.

1615: An early map of Paris shows that there are already 12 bridges over the Seine.

c. 1721: Senior inspectors list the difficulties they face at the port of Paris, e.g., frauds, clandestine deposits of goods, poor working conditions, and navigation problems.

1732: The French author Mercier describes the raucous shouts of the Paris market women, each trying to sell her wares. Much earlier, the French poet Villon had earlier told his readers: "*The only really good market chatter is the Paris market chatter!*"

1757: Place de la Concorde (the "Square of Harmony") dates from this year. It was center-stage for public executions, by guillotine, of commoners and nobles alike during the French Revolution. King Louis XVI himself was executed there by this method in 1793.

c. 1760: This was the high point of river-borne commerce in pre–Revolutionary France. In addition to Paris itself, about 20 small ports along the right and left banks of the Seine and on the Île de la Cité were also flourishing.

1775: French official confirm that the big river barges known as "water coaches," pulled by teams of horses, offer "the greatest convenience for the transport of passengers and goods, thanks to their low fixed prices."

1802–2018: Extensive flooding occurs in Paris, the 2018 rise being caused chiefly by climate change.

1830: The canalization of the Seine is well underway, thus improving navigation and river safety. From now on, most of the tributaries of the Seine will gradually be physically modified.

1816: The age of steamboat dawns on the Seine when the French paddle steamer *L'Élise* arrives at Paris from London via the English Channel.

1831: Victor Hugo's famous novel, *Notre-Dame de Paris* (*The Hunchback of Notre-Dame*), is instrumental in saving the cathedral from destruction by time and by human neglect.

1840s: Locks and weirs are built on the lower Seine, guaranteeing there will always be more than 5 feet of water there regardless of the weather—enough for safe navigation.

Mid-19th century: During repair work on the Seine, hundreds of lead or tin "tourist-badges" from religious sites in the Middle Ages are found. These had either been lost by pilgrims or had been "donated to the river" by them once their pilgrimages were over.

1853: Baron Haussmann is put in charge of upgrading the buildings of central Paris around the Seine.

1864: The City of Paris now owns the upriver land on which the Seine rises.

c. 1885 to present: Copies of the serene death-mask of "The Unknown Woman of the Seine," a young French woman who probably died in Paris in about 1885, become the source of inspiration for literary works, both in French and in other languages; a fashionable ornament in the apartments of bohemian Paris; and a "womanly dummy" who now widely used for first-aid training in mouth-to-mouth ventilation.

1889: The Eiffel Tower is completed and today is the most visited monument in the world that charges an entrance fee.

1900: The first river brigade (*Brigade Fluvial*) is founded with 40 divers recruited from the ranks of the Paris police. There are now 14 river brigades, consisting of about 100 police officers, some of whom are equally well-trained women.

1900: French postcards jokingly depict hypothetical scenes of "Paris as a seaport."

1945–1975: "The Thirty Glorious Years" witness the rapid economic and demographic growth of France, especially in the Seine valley, following the end of World War II.

1949: Founded in this year, the Compagnie des Bateaux Mouches (Bateaux

Mouches tour boat company) today has 15 tour boats in Paris, which every year navigate a distance equivalent to traveling around the world five times.

1990s to the present day: Water quality in the Seine has improved significantly from pre–1990 days thanks to urban and industrial wastewater treatment, but the ecosystem still remains fragile due to agricultural pollution.

1991: UNESCO names a 3½-mile long stretch of the Seine in Paris, with its scenic 37 bridges and footbridges, as a World Heritage Cultural Site.

1991: On the eastern edge of the right bank of the Seine, an urban-renewal project unearths 10 long shallow Neolithic dugout canoes.

2019: Only huge amounts of river water, pumped up non-stop from the Seine, manage to save the cathedral of Notre-Dame de Paris from complete destruction during a horrific fire.

2022: "Haropa Port" is an acronym coined this year from the merger of three key French ports, namely, Le Havre, Rouen, and Paris, into a single mega-port.

Appendix 1
The Seine and Architecture in Paris

Historically, as indicated earlier, Paris has grown and expanded chiefly in roughly circular areas of human habitation and development from the Gallo-Roman era down to modern times. It is essential to remember that the Seine cuts right through the middle of the Paris region in one vast, gentle, curve in the shape of an inverted "U."

On outline maps of the region, these concentric areas are known in French as *enceintes* (enclosures). They were at first delineated by stone walls but now radiate outward from the heart of Paris, beginning at the Île de la Cité. They can be summarized in chronological terms as follows:

Enclosure of the late Roman Empire, 4th century
Enclosure of the 11th century
Enclosures of Phillip Augustus, 1190–1209/13th century (right bank of the Seine) and 1200–1215/1670–1685 (left bank of the Seine)
Enclosures of Charles V (1365–1420 and 1670–1685)
Enclosures of urban fortifications (1634–1647 and 1670–1685)
Enclosure of the tax collectors (1785–1860)
Annexation of the village of Austerlitz (1818)
Last defensive wall of Paris is finished (1846/1919)
The official expansion of Paris comes to an end (1929)[1]

The vibrant architecture of Paris has always been linked to the civil life of the city. For our purposes here, it can be addressed, albeit only very briefly, under a few selected themes in rough chronological order, which directly or indirectly have involved the Seine.[2] These themes are as follows:

1. Medieval times

Ever since the Middle Ages, Paris has been a unique political, economic, and cultural showcase. It has even imposed its own rules and conventions on the artists and architects flocking to it from many different parts of the world.³

Much later, Paris would become the beating political and cultural heart of the kingdom of France. At first, however, it was only a small and insignificant island located in the middle of the Seine and known as the Île de la Cité.

Because of its strong ties with the ruling leaders, however, this little island gradually gained importance, in part because it was defended by two small wooden bridges over the Seine, which linked the island to the mainland for the first time.

At the top of a local hill known as Mont Sainte-Geneviève, which overlooked the left bank of the Seine, a modest cathedral was built in the 4th century, followed by several later churches there.

2. Romanesque architecture

Beginning after 987, the rise of the Capetian dynasty extended the inland French government's influence to the very banks of the Seine. The resulting prosperity generated a new city there, known as Paris, and restored and expanded the river's political and economic role in the region.

In this era, many shipping installations and numerous mansions were built along the Seine. Paris thus began to win equality with the other big cities of Western Europe which had also been founded on water-borne commerce.

By 1144, architects in France had created designs which now permitted much more public space to exist in churches and in other new buildings. This "opening-up" made the new buildings much more spacious, more welcoming, and less claustrophobic for the faithful.

3. Gothic and radiant architecture

By the 1200s, Paris was widely recognized as the most beautiful city of Europe, the richest, the most densely populated, and the most modern. Lords, feudal barons, and senior leaders of the Church all had lovely *hôtels* (large private townhouses) or other fine buildings erected there.

Maurice de Sully, the Bishop of Paris from 1105 until his death in 1196, for example, built what would become the world-famous cathedral of Notre-Dame. A key reason was that he wanted to be able to work so conveniently close to the key transportation corridor provided by the Seine.

Another architectural jewel in Paris is the Sainte-Chapelle ("Holy Chapel")—a royal chapel in the Gothic style. It is located in a *creux* (literally, a "hollow space") between two arms of the Seine within the medieval

Palais de la Cité on the Île de la Cité. The Palais de la Cité was the residence of the kings of France until the 14th century.

4. Kings and Paris

The building of the Louvre after 1546 gave the French kings an urban dwelling-place in Paris very suitable for powerful sovereigns. In addition to their residences, French kings also paid special attention to the fortifications and the road-layout of Paris.

The construction of handsome and very practical quays along the Seine in Paris at this time confirmed it as the chief artery of Paris and gave the river an esthetic uplift. In addition, the kings also encouraged other major architectural projects in the city. Impressively large townhouses (hôtels) such as Cluny and Sens, neither of them far from the Seine, flourished during this period. The cloister of the Celestines (a monastic branch of the Benedictine Order) is a fine example of classical religious design.

5. Paris architecture in the 17th century

Two contemporary paintings, both by André Callot, depict the very busy commercial and social life of the men and women who worked and lived along the Seine at that time.[4] His pictures show the river as being full of well-equipped oared vessels near the Pont Neuf (the river was too narrow and fast-flowing there to permit the use of big sailing ships), and even more crowded with cargo boats and busy workmen near the Louvre.

It was during the 17th century that many Parisians began to think of their city as becoming the "New Rome." This was mainly due to its many paved streets, flourishing squares, vibrant hôtels, new churches, and a more extensive urban "openness" stemming from large, planted, and carefully tended boulevards.

6. Modernization

The modernization of Paris accelerated during the 18th century. An improved method of numbering street addresses was introduced in 1805 and made it easier to find people and places. There were now more paved roads and some effective sewers. Gas lamps to light the otherwise very dark streets at night became more common in the 1830s.

Better management of the quays along the Seine, coupled with the new canal Saint-Martin (which, using steamboats and bigger canal boats, soon became a very active commercial waterway in Paris), and the development of railway terminals (1836) all made life much easier, more efficient, and more prosperous for most Parisians. A postcard of 1908, for example, shows a very high concentration of cargo-carrying boats active in the Canal Saint-Martin.[5]

7. New ideas in the mid–19th century

French architecture was quite dynamic in this period and delighted in challenging the established order.

For example, a drawing by the artist Gustave Doré, published in 1860 in *Le Nouveau Paris* ("The New Paris"), shows an enthusiastic crowd on a Paris street cheering the departure of a heavily laden horse-drawn cart which, symbolically, is dragging away the abandoned carcass of a huge and now useless medieval building.[6]

Another unflattering drawing of the old order in Paris, this time by an unnamed artist, depicts big clunky buildings and a darkly ominous bridge at the Pont des Tournelles on the Seine, where the first of several later bridges was built in 1370. The drawing is entitled *Le Vieux Paris au milieu du XIXes.* ("Old Paris in the middle of the 19th century"). By implication, this illustration questions whether these "leaden" structures still have any legitimate place in the new (post–1800), lighter, and more vibrant Paris.

Appendix 2
The Mona Lisa

The *Mona Lisa* is not only an accurate likeness of a real woman but also is—and far more importantly—the very embodiment of a Renaissance ideal. A brief description of it may therefore be some interest here.

Painted by Leonardo da Vinci between 1503 and 1506 (he may have continued working on it until as late as 1517), the *Mona Lisa* is the best known, the most frequently visited, and the most parodied work of art in the whole world. Today it is still appreciated by experts and lay viewers alike because of its warm, calm, enigmatic focus; its gentle monumentality; and its evocative background.

This is almost certainly a painting of the Italian aristocrat Lisa Gherardini, who was the wife of the prosperous Florentine silk merchant Franceco del Giocondo. The Italian name for the *Mona Lisa* is *La Gioconda*, which means "the jocular one," that is, that she is happy or playful. Its name in French is *La Joconde*, which means the same thing. Acquired by King Francis I of France, it is now the property of the French Republic and has been on permanent display in the Louvre since 1797.

There is of course no shortage of literary commentaries on this celebrated work of art but here we will draw only on one essay written by the English essayist, art and literary critic, and fiction writer Walter Horatio Pater (1839–1894). It appeared in his most frequently reprinted book, namely, *The Renaissance: Studies in Art and Poetry*, which was published in 1873.

In it, Pater advocated an intense inner lifestyle which was known as Aestheticism and which was single-mindedly focused on art. His account of the *Mona Lisa* has a unique, other-worldly, spiritual quality to it. Indeed, it describes Lisa Gherardini in phrases suggesting that, figuratively speaking, she is in fact *immortal*.

The key section of Pater's description, lightly edited, reads as follows:

Appendix 2

She [Lisa] is older than the rocks among which she sits; like the vampire, she has been dead many times, and learned the secrets of the grave; and has been a diver in deep seas, and keeps their fallen day about her; and trafficked for strange webs with Eastern merchants....

The fancy of a perpetual life, sweeping together ten thousand experiences, is an old one.... Certainly Lady Lisa might stand as the embodiment of the old fancy, the symbol of the modern idea.[1]

Appendix 3
The Paris-Area Canals

Canals have been mentioned in previous pages but it is worth saying something now about four such canals, namely, the Canal de la Haute Seine (the Upper Seine), the Canal Saint-Denis, the Canal Saint-Martin, and the Canal d'Ourcq. Like the neighboring Seine, they, too, have carried their share of boat traffic over the years. Their stories, very briefly, are as follows.[1]

Since Roman times, small boats had gone down the Seine towards Paris, loaded with the fine wines and the other much-in-demand products of Burgundy and Champagne. The bad news, however, was that navigation was always very tricky because parts of the upper reaches of the Seine were shallow and sinuous. For this reason, in 1676 a royal official was authorized to improve navigating conditions between Paris, Nogent, and Troyes.

This project was so successful that after 1703 a regular passenger service was established between Troyes and Paris. Such local products as cereals, hemp, charcoal, and building timber were soon being shipped to Paris. In 1709, however, a cold winter damaged many of the port structures, and more damage to the ports was caused by the heavy log rafts that were then lumbering down the River Aube and the Seine.

Napoleon therefore ordered, in 1805, the digging of the Canal de la Haute Seine, which would not be finished until 1846 under the reign of Louis-Philippe. The new canal ran for 27 miles across the plains of the Bassée but due to the gravelly soil near Troyes it would not reliably hold water there. The bottom line is that since 1957 this canal has been officially closed and its towpath has been turned into a bicycle trail.

One of Napoleon's most successful urban renewal projects was the Canal d'Ourcq, which brought new trade and new life into the heart of Paris. The Seine itself was still of critical importance to the Parisians, but in 1801–1802 a series of Seine floods had waterlogged parts of the city and killed a number of people in the process.

The construction of the Canal d'Ourcq proved that Napoleon understood the symbolic importance of flowing water to the tempo of life in Paris, e.g., by having 56 ornamental fountains built, whose water came from the Canal d'Ourcq.[2] When a few critics complained that too much water was flowing into this canal, Napoleon joked that his only regret was that he had not been able to channel the entire flow of the Marne River into this very canal![3]

The Ourcq river flows into the River Marne and, thanks to its favorable position adjacent to Paris, it was always important in waterborne transport. By the beginning of the 17th century, for example, it had a series of 21 different river-structures designed to make it navigable. Small boats descended the river laden with timber, charcoal, cereals, and paving stones for the streets of Paris.

At the start of the 19th century, Paris badly needed clean drinking water that was kept totally separate from the streets of the city because they were such perfect breeding-grounds for disease. The Seine may have been the life-blood of Paris, but it also carried such potentially fatal diseases as dysentery and typhus.

Moreover, each quarter of the city had its own abattoirs. Animals destined for markets were always slaughtered in the streets; their blood and guts slowly inched their way through broad gutters and then oozed into the Seine. It was now so polluted in Paris that its water was no longer safe to drink.

The solution, thanks to a bright French engineer, was to redirect the clean waters of the River Ourcq into a new canal to be used both for drinking water and to transport cargo boats. It also brought both new trade and more excitement into the city. In 1839, improved models of locks, coupled with better steam engines for boats, were introduced, too.

This combination was so efficient it was said a passenger could now travel between the locks "at the speed of a galloping horse." Two pumping stations were installed in 1869 to lift more water into the canal. They had huge and very handsome iron wheels, 32 feet and 36 feet in diameter respectively, which today are helped by electric pumps.

At the start of the 19th century, navigation conditions on the Seine itself were still dangerous because of the enormous loop the river takes when flowing through Paris. Serious problems then included the need to pass under too many bridges, where headroom could be a problem; shallow river depths; and the presence of floating mills, which were much cheaper to build directly on the river itself than on the expensive and very limited open land along the Seine's banks.

It was therefore decided to dig a new canal between the Arsenal and the Paris village of Saint-Denis. This opened for business in 1821; a second canal company was created to dig the nearby Saint-Martin canal. When the lower part of this canal was later closed, however, the companies failed and in 1830 then Paris regained its official ownership of both of them. A French postcard dating from 1908 shows the Saint-Martin canal doing a very brisk cargo-handling business then.

Today, navigating along the Canal Saint-Denis and the Canal Saint-Martin will permit the boater to avoid the intense river traffic in the center of Paris. He or she will then have to cover only 6 miles, rather than 18 miles by the Seine itself. The problem, however is the heavy traffic and big wakes of the sand-carrying barges which have priority over leisure boats and must be given a very wide berth.

Appendix 4
Tug Boats on the Seine

By the end of the 19th century, the heavy horses which had traditionally hauled cargo barges on the Seine and on its tributaries were gradually being phased out by steam—namely by coal-burning tug boats.[1]

In this era, business on the rivers was quite brisk and many boat companies competed for the right to have their tugs tow the heavy convoys along the Seine and other inland waterways.

Among the boats used in this trade were the little Guèpes ("Wasps"); the vessels called the Bleus (painted blue in honor of the Virgin Mary); the Barnum (a powerful barge named after the massive horses of the Barnum & Bailey circus); and the passenger boats known as the Hirondelles ("Swallows").

The last of these famous old tug boats was converted into a "pusher" in 1955—a maritime style much less attractive but much more efficient at moving heavy convoys by pushing them rather than by towing them. One of these old boats has been restored and is now moored in front of the Conflans-Sante-Honorine waterways museum near the junction of the Seine and the River Oise.

Appendix 5
Shipping Along the Seine in Paris

Past and present river shipping offer many points of historical and current interest.[1]

Early Days

The Seine and its tributaries, e.g., the Marne, the Yonne, and the Oise, were the first commercial transportation artery in the northwest of France.

Along these waterways, river cargo was moved by horsepower; by the winds; and—above all—by the currents. As mentioned earlier, a key location for all shippers on the Seine was Paris—especially the gently sloping sand-and-gravel beach of the Port de Grève at the Place de Grève (this is today's Place de l'Hôtel-de-Ville, the city hall), located on the mainland opposite the Île de la Cité.

All sorts of products were sold in this area for many, many years. A photo of 1908, for example, shows a floating apple-market there, where apples from Normandy were sold from barges—boats fitted with tent-like covers over them to protect the apples.[2]

An illustration of the Hôtel de Ville and of the Place and the Port de Grève, dating from about 1780 and painted at a quiet moment in the early morning because there are so few people about and only one boat is then underway, shows a well-organized, prosperous, formal layout of buildings, with cargo boats getting ready for a busy new day.[3]

This port was located in central Paris and was often so congested with cargo and with workers who were entirely dependent on the current of Seine, e.g., the leather tanners, that all of the workers had to compete with each other to find enough working space on the Seine.

The Port de Grève was also a very good place for medieval workers who were *en grève*, which at that time meant that they were looking for a job. Eventually, however, its meaning changed radically and evolved into an important factor in modern French culture today: namely, the process not of *looking for a job*, but rather the process of *being on strike*.

An engraving of this port, made in 1680, shows that it was very busy indeed: shipments of charcoal, wheat, and hay all are much in evidence along the riverbanks, their owners waiting impatiently for their turn for their products to be on- or off-loaded into the many boats moored there.[4]

A map of the Port de Grève itself and of some of its small neighboring ports shows that this region was the main port of Paris in the Middle Ages and would become the site of the city hall of Paris. Goods flowing through this port came in from, or were bound for, such regional ports as Meaux, Sens, Laon, Noyon, and Amiens. Wine was the specialty of this port, highlighted by the presence of two big floating pontoons—one holding the wine of Burgundy, the other holding wine from other parts of France.[5]

The port also attracted a wide range of shore-bound workers. The main market there was known as the "Apport Paris"—a traditional term evoking the old gates *(portes)* of the city, where, sitting or standing, locals could offer for sale all their fresh fruits, vegetables, and herbs. Butchers, fish merchants, wine dealers, tanners, and dyers all knew that the Seine could help them by disposing of their offal and other wastes free of charge—all they had to do was to dump it into the river.

Their cargoes included wines from Burgundy; wheat; hay from Picardy; logs and kindling from Gentilly; sandstone road-pavements; building stones; plaster; salt; and charcoal. There was also a very active trade in many varieties of fish, e.g., herring from Rouen, and a wide range of markets, taverns, and hotels catering to producers and boatmen alike.

Boats heading down the Seine towards Paris had to follow the main navigation channel between the many small islands of the Seine and then moor at one of the landing places on the right bank of the river.

In the 18th century, the Seine was dotted by hundreds of islands of various sizes. Few of the little ones still exist today (most of them were merged or destroyed in the interests of safer navigation) but, writing in 1865, the French poet Nicolas Boileau described them in their heyday as he saw them from an unidentified village somewhere along the river. A translation of his poem runs along the following lines:

> It is a small village, or rather a hamlet,
> Built on the slope of a long range of hills,
> Where the eye roams over the nearby plains.
> The Seine, at the foot of the hills which are washed by its flow,

Sees, rising from the heart of its waters, twenty islands that,
  separating the main current in different ways,
Shape there twenty many rivers from just one single river.[6]

Hauling cargo upstream, either by animal or human power and with up to six boats forming a watery "train," was harder and more expensive.

It required, for example that the riverbank being used for this purpose must be kept entirely clear of any obstacle that might hinder transport along the towpath. Because of the greater costs involved, cargo sent upstream usually had to be more compact and more valuable than the less-expensive goods (high volume/low value items, e.g., hay) heading downstream.

Moreover, earlier in the Seine's transport history, the towpath used by horses to pull cargo boats upstream came to a full stop in central Paris at the port called the Ecole Saint-Germain.

Contrary to what the name of this port might suggest (École means "school" in French), there was no school there. The name of the port was simply a deformation of an archaic word that was used to give some indication of the "scale" or "size" of this port.

By the time of King Philip Augustus, the port of Grève was not big enough to handle all the river commerce. As a result, the king granted to the league of river merchants a sum collected from each shipload of salt, herring, hay, and grain that arrived in Paris. He used the income from this trade to build a new port, called "de l'Ecole," which was located where the Place de l'École stands today.

Initially, this port was preferred by merchants who specialized in fish from the sea; in lumber and firewood from the extensive French forests; in cider from Normandy; and in hay from the lower valley of the Seine. By about 1822, an illustration shows that it was then more devoted to boats carrying passengers rather than natural products.[7]

Beyond the port, a fortified bridge prevented boat traffic from continuing to the large defensive fortress known as the Grand Châtelet. This was an infamous twelfth-century French government stronghold surrounded by deep ditches filled with flowing white water from the Seine. It contained a court; the police headquarters; prisons; and, until it was transferred to the Place de Grève in 1357, the office of the *Prévot des marchands*, the senior merchant-official of Paris, who was elected by his peers.

In addition, it was also an active commercial and social center. A large two-page illustration of it at the end of the eighteenth-century shows a very active courtyard full of open-air stalls selling foodstuffs to large numbers of men and women, some of whom who are not only shopping, carrying water, and chattering away gaily, but are also actively flirting with each other.[8]

After many years of heavy-duty service as a boat-landing stage, tannery, slaughterhouse, junk-dealers' yard, brothel, and open-air market, in order to improve the flow of traffic on the Seine and to remove a public health eyesore, the Grand Châtelet was eventually demolished in 1792–1802. It was replaced by a public square now known as the Place du Châtelet.

The Grand Châtelet was designed to protect the Grand Pont and the Petit Châtelet was designed to protect the Petit Pont. Both date from the 9th century and the Petit Pont has two especially vivid stories associated with it:

- In 886, a great flood in the Seine washed away the Petit Pont fortress during a long siege by Norman invaders. In the process, the flood also isolated 12 of the surviving French defenders in what little remained of the tower of the fortress. Although they fought very fiercely to the very last man, they all were massacred by the Normans.
- In about 1719, the Petit Châtelet still retained the memory of a very old and very strange tale. According to this story, the Petit Châtelet was the traditional meeting place for an assorted group of musicians, buffoons, jugglers, pigs, and a billy goat. They were all subject to a fine of some sort for a now-unknown reason and had to pay their fines in what was then called "monkey money."
- By demonstrating their special skills, all of them—with the exception of the billy goat—were exempted from their fines. The billy goat, however, was executed by a hammer-blow between his horns.[9]
- The tale does not give any explanation of why he was killed. Our own guess is that this tale is simply a garbled version on some ancient folk-legend.

There are reasons why the broader Paris region of this and later eras can variously be thought of either as an ugly "wart on the river" because its congestion and pollution, or as "an invigorating commercial node" because it so profitably transshipped wheat and other cereals, wines, fruits, hay, fish, charcoal, plaster, and heavy construction materials so far and wide.

The sources of many of these essential goods included the French regions of Bourgogne, Morvan, Champagne, Brie, and Beauce. A map of Paris in 1615, for example, identifies twelve important Seine-related transshipment points in the central portion of the city.[10]

Modern Times: The Port de Gennevilliers

Today this large commercial port is one of a group of inland harbors run under the overall direction of the French government. It is one of the biggest river-port complexes in Europe and was constructed in the 1930s under the leadership of Fulgence Bienvenüe, who also built the Paris subway system. Remarkably, he used the rubble from the subway excavations to build the quays for the Seine ships.

The port now handles about 3.4 million tons of merchandise each year, receiving not only containers from Le Havre but also shiploads of cereals, gravel, and steel products. Located at the upstream limit of cruises by river shipping, its landing stages are also used by river vessels.

Île Saint-Denis

In the 10th century, part of the long narrow Seine island outside of Paris bearing this name was owned by a scoundrel known to history only as Bouchard le Barbu ("Bouchard the bearded"). He capitalized on this favorable location by taxing all the boats passing around the island. He thereby earned a good deal of money, but in 998 these lucrative rights were stripped from him and were given instead to his principal victims, namely, the monks of the nearby Abbey of Saint-Denis.

Today, the island is the site of two big modern shipyards, namely, Chantier Van Praet, and Chantier Van den Bosche, plus a number of live-aboard moorings for private boaters. These shipyards have a long and distinguished history. Chantier Van Praet, for example, was founded in Belgium in 1727.

La Défense and the Big Ships' Supplies Store Azura Marine

The name of this quarter of Paris, La Défense, comes from a statue named "The Defense of Paris," which is dedicated to the soldiers who defended the city during the Franco-Prussian War of 1870. Thanks to its large number of modern office buildings, however, this quarter is now the biggest business center in Europe.

It is also the site of Mazura Marine, which sells a complete stock of boating gear for both large and small vessels plying fresh and/or salt water. Customers can even moor their own boats at the pontoon located directly in front of the store itself.

Appendix 6
The Tidal Wave of the Seine

Writing in 1821, the French author Jean-Baptiste-Balthazar Sauvan reported this from the Seine estuary: "One immense wave rolled on majestically foaming from bank to bank, leaving everything in uproar in its train, while all before was perfectly calm."[1] He was referring here to the tidal bore—the tidal wave, which in the past arose four times a year at Causebec-en-Caux, where the Seine runs into the sea. This great wave was a very popular tourist attraction until the early 1960s, when the Seine was dredged and the bore disappeared.

The bore was known locally as the *mascaret* and began in the Seine estuary when the spring tide rose high. It came about because sea water was then pushed up the Seine channel at 15 miles per hour, overflowing the narrow channel and generating in a single wave up to 13 feet high.

The bore was first mentioned in the Latin chronicles of the Abbey of Saint-Wandrille as slowing the raiding longboats of the Vikings and thus helping the local villagers to defend themselves. As late as the 19th century, the bore would wreck commerce along the lowest reaches of the Seine. Indeed, between 1789 and 1850, more than 200 ships are said to have been capsized and sunk by it.

With the coming of the railroad, the bore became such a must-see sight that tourists in Paris even scheduled trips to be at the estuary when the tides were at their highest near the equinoxes. After the Seine was "tamed," however, by being dredged and having locks, dams, and a canal built along it, the bore passed permanently into the Seine's long history.

Appendix 7
Medieval Transport of Wine and Grain by River

A modern map has been used here to approximate how wine and grain (and many other products, too, e.g., logs, bread, animals, hay, fruits, and fish) could all be sent to markets by river, which in medieval times was usually the cheapest way to ship anything.[1]

The modern scholar Susan Rose has pointed out that

> As more and more varied evidence [on the transport of medieval wine] becomes available, particularly from France, from the eleventh century, the fact that many vineyards were producing for the [distant] market becomes increasingly obvious. One important indication of this is that most vineyards [in France] were situated near navigable waterways.
>
> To be a successful wine producer it was essential to be able to transport wine to the consumers. Transport on a clumsy lurching ox cart of heavy wine barrels was not only slow and expensive but was bad for the wine especially in hot weather. It was much better to take the wine down a river often on flat-bottomed barges to a trading city or to a port with access to the open sea. From the ports increasing quantities of wine could travel overseas to northern lands, especially the British Isles and Flanders....
>
> It is notable how many [wine-growing regions in France] are north of the Loire or in the Seine-Marne valley... [Mediterranean wines] lacked the easy access to profitable markets which stimulated the growth of vineyards within each reach of Rouen, La Rochelle and, at least at a later date, Bordeaux and the estuary of the Gironde.[2]

Most of these items could also be sent by overland transport, at higher cost and with more delays, but, in the interests of simplicity, their overland trajectories will not be included below.

Our river discussions will begin on the northern upper reaches of the Seine and will end on the southern lower reaches of the river.

To start with the river journey made by wine, the first leg of the journey for wine from Bourgogne was for it to be transported down the Seine to Melun and thence to Corbeil, where other wine came down to the Seine via the Essonne river.

Continuing further downstream, wine from the Orge river joined the wine on the Seine at Villenuve-Saint-Georges. Beyond Choisy, more wine came onto the Seine transportation route via the Marne river. Continuing downstream far beyond Paris, yet more wine shipments joined the Seine downstream of Pontoise and Cergy via the Oise river. No other wine-bearing rivers, however, joined the Seine beyond the Meulan area.

The river journey made by grain began in Bourgogne at Saint-Germain-Laval; picked up more grain at Villeneuve-Saint-Georges via the Yerres river; and then basically followed the wine river route down to the Seine's juncture with the Oise.

Appendix 8
The First Iron Steamship to Reach Paris

The first iron steamship to go to sea and up the Seine to Paris was *Aaron Manby*, constructed by shipbuilder Aaron Manby (1776–1850) at the Horseley Ironworks in England. The story of this unique vessel is worth outlining briefly here.

The ship was the brainchild of an eccentric but visionary English naval officer, Charles Napier (1786–1860), who had the idea of building a fleet of steamships for service on the Seine. Launched in 1821, *Aaron Manby* was the first iron steamship ever to go to sea.

Of 120 tons burthen, she was 106 feet long, with a beam of 23 feet counting her big paddlewheels; an extremely tall (47-foot-high) funnel set forward of amidships (the center-point of the boat); a 30-horsepower oscillating cylinder steam engine; and, finally, two paddlewheels (each 12 feet in diameter and 2 feet 6 inches wide). Her average speed was 9.2 miles per hour.

Defying the conventional nautical wisdom of the day, this iron-hulled vessel not only floated safely but also floated relatively lightly: in fact, she drew one foot less water than any other steamboat then afloat.

After nautical trials in the U.K. in May 1822, she crossed the English Channel under Napier's command and arrived safely at Le Havre on 10 June, carrying passengers, a cargo of linseed, and iron castings. She then steamed up the Seine to Paris, where she generated no end of favorable comments, and would be based there for the next decade.

During that period, she was used by a steamship company, the *Compagnie des bateaux à vapeur en fer* (the "Iron steam boat company") to operate its business between Paris and Le Havre, and for the pleasure trips it arranged up and down the Seine.

When Napier's business failed in 1827, *Aaron Manby* was sold to a

French company, which operated her on the River Loire until she was finally scrapped in 1855. Napier had foresightedly conceived of his ship being the first step towards an iron warship, and to a certain degree he was right: the Royal Navy's first iron warship, HMS *Warrior*, was built in 1860, the year of Napier's death.

Appendix 9
The Inland Waterways Museum on the Seine

The founder of this museum—it is known as *le musée de la Batellerie*—was François Beaudouin, who grew up on a boat that his parents had built on the Seine. This vessel was named *Belle Lurette* (*Beautiful Lurette*); he later wrote of it that these "semi-wild" years of his youth had given him a real love for the river.

While in secondary school he "discovered the sea" and then spent 12 years in the French Navy and working for a French ship-building company. He was always quite interested in nautical research, however, and found that very little scholarly work had been done so far on traditional French boats and their navigation.

He therefore decided to work closely with two well-established French nautical experts in this field. As a result, he was invited in 1967 by the town of Conflans-Sainte-Honorine to set up a waterways museum there.

In 1993, he published a definitive and very well-illustrated book on *Paris/Seine: Ville Fluviale—Son histoire des origines à nos jours* (*Paris/Seine: A River-Oriented City—Its history from its origins to our own time*). Most of the illustrations and the documentation in this book come from the waterways museum. We believe that the book should be required reading for anyone interested in this subject.

Appendix 10
Mercenaries Along the Seine

The role of mercenaries in medieval and Renaissance Europe has been discussed by Hunt Janin and Ursula Carlson in a book published in 2013 and listed here in the bibliography. It did not, however, have anything specific to say about mercenaries along the Seine itself. This appendix tries to fill a bit of that gap.

The use of mercenaries along the Seine is not well-documented. They appear to have been used there only from time to time, depending on specific military campaigns and on the tactical problems associated with them.

Of all the mercenary bands pillaging France in the era of the Hundred Years War, by about 1360 the most fearsome group was known simply as "the Great Company."

These mercenaries, in raiding parties, were sent from the upper Seine valley to attack the towns of Troyes, Provins, Château-Thierry, and Châlons-sur-Marne. Other mercenary groups conducted raids into the lands located between the rivers Seine and Loire, under the leadership of a thug called Ruffin. Another mercenary leader, Pierre de Sault, captured the fortress of Moulineaux on the south bank of the Seine below Rouen.

Using mercenaries, King Charles V evicted Charles of Navarre from all the latter's lands in the Seine basin. The mercenary chieftain du Guesclin was put in charge of all the territory between the Seine and the Loire rivers. A mercenary force of 4,000 men crossed the Seine upstream from Troyes and then spread out into Champagne. Mercenaries later conducted skirmishes and ambushes near the Seine.

These men drifted in and out of France depending on the tides of war, serving either the French or the English as fortune favored them. For example, when the English and the French got involved in a war in Spain, they paid mercenaries to join them there. When a relative peace broke out, the mercenaries had to look for combat opportunities anywhere else that seemed more promising, e.g., in Italy, crusades in what is now known as the Middle East, or conflicts in Switzerland and in the Holy Roman Empire.

Chapter Notes

Epigraph

1. Hussey, *Paris*, p. 13.

Preface

1. Lacordaire, *Les Inconnus de la Seine*, p. 299.
2. Favier, *Paris*, p. 15.
3. Favier, *Paris*, p. 9.
4. This term seems to have come from two different historical sources: the prominence of the philosophic movement known as the Enlightenment, and a new lighting system which made it possible to illuminate all the streets of Paris for the first time in their long history.
5. Lestel, "The evolution of the Seine Basin Water Bodies Through Historical Maps," p. 1.
6. Lambert and Septet, *Paris sur Seine*, p. 1.
7. Translated from Beaudouin, *Paris/Seine*, back cover of book.

Introduction

1. Both these illustrations are from Pérouse de Montclos, *Paris*, pp. 16–19.
2. Friel, *Henry V's Navy*, p. 80.
3. Flatman, *Ships and Shipping in Medieval Manuscripts*, p. 55.
4. Lacordaire, *Les Inconnus de la Seine*, p. 150.
5. Lorenz and Sandron, *Atlas de Paris*, p. 21.
6. *Seine, Waterways Guide*, p. 96.
7. Alexandre and Boura, *La Seine et Paris*, p. 55.
8. Lambert and Septet, *Paris sur la Seine*, p. 56.
9. Adapted from Chadych and Leborgne, *Atlas de Paris*, p. 39.
10. Evans, *Life in Medieval France*, pp. 14–15.
11. An official French publication of 1500 shows a strong young man poling a skiff upstream under a Seine bridge with houses built on it. (Source: Alexandre and Boura, *La Seine et Paris*, p. 71).
12. Hussey, *Paris*, p. 167.
13. These historical examples are taken from the *Waterways Guide to the Seine*, p. 137.
14. Lacordaire, *Les Inconnus de la Seine*, p. 92.
15. Lacordaire, *Les Inconnus de la Seine*, pp. 148–149.

Chapter 1

1. Quoted by Roi-Tanguy, *Paris, Metropole sur Seine*, p. 141.
2. Carpentier, "Quality of dredged material from the River Seine basin," Abstract, p. 1.
3. Edwards-May, *Inland Waterways of France*, p. 268.
4. Beaudouin, *Paris/Seine*, p. 18.
5. Favier, *Paris*, p. 166.
6. Rol-Tanguy, *Paris, Metropole sur Seine*, p. 141.
7. Adapted from the Waterways Guide to the Seine, pp. 92–93.
8. Brettentot, *Atlas de la Vallée de la Seine*, p. 8.
9. Lorentz and Sandron, *Atlas de Paris*, p. 22.

10. Lorentz and Sandron, *Atlas de Paris*, p. 25.
11. Van Deputte, *Ponts de Paris*, p. 79.
12. Lambert and Septet, *Paris sur Seine*, p. 125.
13. Rol-Tanguy, *Paris, Metropole sur Seine*, back cover.
14. Roi-Tanguy, *Paris, Metropole sur Seine*, p. 54.
15. Éditions du Breil, *Seine*, p. 76.

Chapter 2

1. Sciolino, *The Seine*, pp. 71–75.
2. Lorentz and Sandron, *Atlas de Paris au Moyen Âge*, p. 16.
3. Lambert and Septet, *Paris sur Seine*, pp. 6, 7.
4. Lorentz and Sandron, *Atlas de Paris au Moyen Âge*, p. 11.
5. Chadych and Leborgne, *Atlas de Paris*, p. 25.
6. Brennetot, *Atlas de la Vallée de la Seine*, p. 16.
7. Lorentz and Sandron, *Atlas de Paris au Moyen Âge*, p. 10.
8. Chadych and Leborgne, *Atlas de Paris*, p. 26.
9. Musée d'Archéologie Nationale," "Saint-Denis's markets and fair: The Lendit fair," pp. 1–4.
10. Chadych and Leborgne, *Atlas de Paris*, pp. 37, 58.
11. Comments on these three occupations are drawn in part from Alexandre and Boura, *La Seine et Paris*, pp. 65–77.
12. Beaudoin, *Paris/Seine*, p. 60.
13. Annotated after Alexandre and Boura, *La Seine et Paris*, p. 74.
14. Adapted from Lacordaire, *Les Inconnus de la Seine*, pp. 68–70.
15. Lacordaire, *Les Inconnus de la Seine*, p. 127.
16. Alexandre and Boura, *La Seine et Paris*, p. 51.
17. Eddison, *Medieval Pirates*, p. 54.
18. For a good illustration of the Petit Pont in the 18th century during its reconstruction, see Baudouin, *Paris/Seine*, p. 65. This shows that a bridge worker has fallen into the Seine and is using a broken beam from the bridge to stay afloat.
19. Lacordaire, *Les Inconnus de la Seine*, p. 11.
20. Hussey, *Paris: The Secret History*, p. 108.
21. Beaumont-Maillet, *L'Eau à Paris*, p. 26.
22. Beaudouin, *Paris/Seine*, pp. 49–51.
23. Beaudouin, *Paris/Seine*, p. 59.
24. Beaudouin, *Paris/Seine*, p. 80.
25. Lorentz and Sandron, *Atlas de Paris au Moyen Âge*, p. 188.

Chapter 3

1. Heath, *The Vikings*, p. 4. A vast amount has been written about the Vikings; Heath's book is a good introduction to this interesting but complicated subject.
2. McGrail, *Early Ships and Seafaring*, p. 148. *Sea Stallion* is the modern name for a reconstruction of a Viking ship discovered in Denmark in the 1960s. Built c. 1070–1090, the original ship was one of the most impressive Viking longships ever created and would have had a crew of 70 or 80 very strong and very well-trained warriors. See Flatman, *Ships & Shipping in Medieval Manuscripts*, p. 74.
3. The longest Viking ship ever found was the *Roskilde 6*. Built in about 125, it was 123 feet long and is now in the Viking Ship Museum in Roskilde, Denmark.
4. The source for this quote is given by Wikipedia as https: books.googleusercontent.
5. Verbruggen, *The Art of Warfare in Western Europe During the Middle Ages*, p. 13.
6. No source for this quote is given but it was quoted in an undated Wikipedia article on the "Siege of Paris (856–857)."

Chapter 4

1. Adapted from Bove and Gauvard, *Le Paris du Moyen Âge*, p. 12.
2. Beaumont-Maillet, *L'Eau à Paris*, p. 18.
3. Beaumont-Maillet, *L'Eau à Paris*, pp. 10–11.
4. Astic-Heisserer, *Paris médiéval*, p. 20.
5. Roux, *Regards sur Paris*, p. 51.
6. Beaumont-Maillet, *L'Eau à Paris*, p. 100.
7. Beaumont-Maillet, *L'Eau à Paris*, p. 141.

8. Beaumont-Maillet, *L'Eau à Paris*, p. 207.
9. Beaumont-Maillet, *L'Eau à Paris*, p. 207.
10. Beaumont-Maillet, *L'Eau à Paris*, p. 209.
11. Arnaud and Boyra, *La Seine et Paris*, p. 144.
12. Hugo, *Notre-Dame de Paris*, pp. 133–134.

Chapter 5

1. Janin and Carlson, *Mercenaries in Medieval and Renaissance Europe*, p. 23.
2. Many of the points used here on the role of the Seine in the Hundred Years War are variously sourced to Favier, *La Guerre de Cent Ans*; Allmand, *The Hundred Years War*; and "Weapons and Warfare."
3. Grummitt, *The English Experience in France*, pp. 1–2.
4. Flatman, *Ships and Shipping in Medieval Manuscripts*, p. 110.
5. *Froissart's Chronicles*, pp. 136–137.
6. Fowler, *Medieval Mercenaries*, p. 3.
7. Quoted in Urban, *Medieval Mercenaries*, p. 101.
8. Backouche, *La Trace du Fleuve*, p. 31.
9. Lacordaire, *Les Inconnus de la Seine*, pp. 42–51.
10. VanDeputte, *Ponts de Paris*, p. 163.
11. Pounds, *An Economic History of Medieval Europe*, pp. 391–392.
12. Since big ships drew too much water to be able to land troops directly on shore, small boats had to be used for this purpose. See Flatman, *Ships and Shipping in Medieval Manuscripts*, p. 109.
13. Rodger, *The Safeguard of the Sea*, p. 145.
14. Barker, *Agincourt*, p. 176.
15. Barker, *Agincourt*, p. 175.
16. Friel, *Henry V's Navy*, p. 125.
17. Weapons and Warfare: The Battle of the Seine, pp. 1–2.
18. Burl, *Danse Macabre*, p. 3.
19. Pernoud and Clin, *Joan of Arc: Her Story*.
20. Pernoud and Clin, *Joan of Arc*, pp. 136–137.
21. Contamine, *War in the Middle Ages*, p. 110.
22. Quoted by France, *Mercenaries and Paid Men*, p. 17.
23. The source of this translated citation is unknown because it was not identified in the reference work used, but it may come from a French website on Château-Gaillard (lesandelys.com/chateau-gaillard).

Chapter 6

1. Ville de Paris, *À Paris*, p. 23.
2. Larbodière, *Ponts de Paris*, back cover.
3. UNESCO, *Paris, Banks of the Seine*, pp. 12–13; see bibliography.
4. In modern times, the Autonomous Port of Paris has evolved into a public institution of the government of France. Its job is to encourage waterway transport of goods and passengers in the Ile-de-France region. It does so by developing, maintaining, and operating the port facilities of Paris and the surrounding region. The three main infrastructures of the Autonomous Port of Paris, all linked to road and rail networks, are located in Gennevilliers, Bonneuil-sur-Marne, and Limay. In addition, in 2012 a new port grouping was set up, which ties the administration of the three major Seine ports (Le Havre, Rouen, and Paris) more closely to each other.
5. UNESCO World Heritage Center, "Paris, Banks of the Seine," p. 12.
6. Beaumont-Mailler, *L'Eau à Paris*, pp. 218–219.
7. Favier, *Paris*, pp. 178–179.
8. For some excellent photos, see the book by Jean-Marc Labordière, *Ponts de Paris*, listed in the bibliography.
9. Some of the points in this chapter are drawn from Sciolino, *The Seine*, pp. 89–96.
10. Beaudouin, *Paris/Seine*, p. 135.
11. Chadych and Leborgne, *Atlas de Paris*, p. 128.
12. Beaudouin, *Paris/Seine*, p. 130.
13. Beaudouin, *Paris/Seine*, pp. 122–123.
14. Beaudouin, *Paris/Seine*, pp. 118–119.
15. Adapted from Beaudouin, *Paris/Seine*, p. 15.
16. Lambert and Septet, *Paris sur Seine*, p. 80.
17. Van Deputte, *Ponts de Paris*, p. 57.
18. Adapted from Van Deputte, *Ponts de Paris*, p. 78.

19. Astic-Heisserer, *Paris Medieval*, p. 52.
20. The following discussion is sourced to Beaudouin, *Paris/Seine*, pp. 54–55.
21. Alexande and Boura, *La Seine and Paris*, p. 93.
22. Pérouse de Montclos, *Le Guide de Patrimoine: Paris*, pp. 50–51.
23. Beaudouin, *Paris/Seine*, p. 55.
24. Adapted from Chadych and Leborgne, *Atlas de Paris*, p. 63.
25. For excellent illustrations of a *cagnard* (vaulted gallery), see Beaudouin, pp. 61–62 and p. 73. They show a boating family and friends and washerwomen all hard at work in the cold gloom of the gallery where their poverty forces them to live.
26. See Beaudouin, *Paris-Seine*, p. 79, for a good copy of this picture.
27. Beaudouin, *Paris/Seine*, p. 49.
28. Rol-Tanguy, *Paris, Metropole sur Seine*, p. 14.
29. Adapted from Lambert and Septet, *Paris sur Seine*, p. 49.
30. Lacordaire, *Les Inconnus de la Seine*, pp. 58–59.
31. Beaudouin, *Paris/Seine*, pp. 168–169.
32. Lanbert and Septet, *Paris sur Saine*, p. 77.

Chapter 7

1. Van Deputte, *Ponts de Paris*, pp. 64–65.
2. Beaudouin, *Paris/Seine*, p. 120.
3. Laundry boats, often moored permanently in the Seine, usually had men aboard in addition to laundry-women. These men were workers who had other jobs afloat or ashore as well. Listings of 1723 to 1780, for example, mention men who variously broke up old boats for firewood; specialists in getting boats through the arches of bridges; wood dealers; ferrymen; mariners; businessmen; wine merchants; carpenters; and fishermen. (Source: after Backouche, *La Trace du Fleuve*, pp. 42–43.)
4. For a good photo of this lovely building, see Beadouin, *Paris/Seine*, pp. 126–127.

Chapter 8

1. Adapted from Erlande-Brandenburg, *Notre-Dame de Paris*, p. 7.
2. Erlande-Brandenburg, *Notre-Dame de Paris*, p. 147.
3. Favier, *Paris*, p. 25.
4. Musée de Cluny, "Pillar of the Boatmen," p. 1.
5. Alain Erlande-Brandenburg, *Notre-Dame de Paris*, pp. 51–53.
6. Beaudouin, *Paris/Seine*, p. 77.
7. Hugo, *Notre-Dame de Paris*, 1831.
8. Krailsheimer's translation of *Notre-Dame de Paris*, pp. xxiv–xxv (see Bibliography).
9. Adapted from Inglis, "Gothic Architecture and a Scholastic: Jean de Jandun's *Tractatus de laudibus Parisius*."
10. Willshire, "We want it to come alive," pp. 1–6.
11. Adapted from Georgetown University, "Notre Dame Cathedral North Rose Window," p. 1.

Chapter 9

1. Leniaud and Perrot, *La Sainte Chapelle*, pp. 17, 21.
2. Leniaud and Perrot, *La Sainte Chapelle*, rear cover of book.

Chapter 10

1. Rol-Tanguy, *Paris, Metropole sur Seine*, p. 22.
2. Hussey, *Paris: The Secret History*, p. 151.
3. Pérouse de Montclos, *Paris*, p. 182.

Chapter 11

1. Rol-Tanguy, *Paris, Metropole sur Seine*, pp. 141–142.
2. Rol-Tanguy, *Paris, Metropole sur Seine*, p. 141.
3. Rol-Tanguy, *Paris, Metropole sur Seine*, p. 142.
4. Adapted from Lambert and Septet, *Paris sur Seine*, p. 12.
5. In 1545, Francis I sent a large French fleet from the mouth of the Seine to attack England, but bad weather and ship losses

on both sides prevented any major naval battle.
  6. History, "August 10, 1793," pp. 1–2.

Chapter 12

  1. The Hays Foundation, "About Marlene and Spencer Hays," pp. 1–2

Chapter 14

  1. Rol-Tanguy, *Paris, Metropole sur Seine*, p. 28.

Chapter 16

  1. Toureiffel.paris, "monument/history," pp. 7–8.
  2. *The Guardian*, 4 July 202, pp. 1–2.

Chapter 17

  1. See Beaudouin, *Paris/Seine*, p. 136.
  2. Rol-Tanguy, *Paris, Metropole sur Seine*, p. 43.

Chapter 18

  1. Many of the observations in this chapter are drawn from Travelwithart, pp. 1–22.
  2. Tate Gallery, "Impressionism," pp. 1–9.
  3. Adapted from Lacordaire, *Les Inconnus de la Seine*, p. 295.

Chapter 19

  1. Quoted in Janin, *The University in Medieval Life*, p. 180.
  2. Pernoud, *Abélard et Héloïse*, p. 67.

Chapter 20

  1. Rol-Tanguy, *Paris, Metropole sur Seine*, p. 4.
  2. Lacordaire, *Les Inconnus de la Seine*, p. 122.
  3. Lacordaire, *Les Inconnus de la Seine*, p. 133.

  4. Lambert and Septet, *Paris sur Seine*, pp. 18–19.
  5. Alexandre and Boura, *La Seine et Paris*, p. 47.
  6. Quoted by Sciolino, *The Seine*, pp. 204–205.
  7. Alexandre and Boura, *La Seine et Paris*, p. 153.
  8. Reproduced by Alexandre and Boura, *La Seine et Paris*, p. 149.
  9. Beaudouin, *Paris/Seine*, p. 172.
  10. Beaudouin, *Paris/Seine*, p. 128.
  11. Lacordaire, *Les Inconnus de la Seine*, p. 146.
  12. Beadouin, *Paris/Seine*, pp. 112–115.

Chapter 21

  1. The information in this chapter is drawn from the National Police of France publication on "River and Nautical Brigades of the Police and Gendarmerie," which is listed in the bibliography.
  2. Much of the following account of the role of the Seine in the great Notre-Dame fire of 2019 comes from Sciolino, *The Seine*, pp. 329–338.

Chapter 22

  1. This account of the St. Bartholomew's Day massacre is drawn from Hussey, *Paris: The Secret History*, pp. 119–121.
  2. Hussey, *Paris: The Secret History*, pp. 120–121.

Chapter 23

  1. A good source on the "Unknown of the Seine," is Felice, "The most famous unknown girl," pp. 1–5.
  2. Hussey, *Paris*, 273–274.

Chapter 24

  1. Brennetot, *Atlas de la Vallée de la Seine*, pp. 36–37.
  2. Brennetot, *Atlas de la Vallée de la Seine*, p. 44.

Chapter 25

1. Some of the points made in this chapter come from Lestel et al. on "The Evolution of the Seine Basin Water Bodies Through Historical Maps," pp. 1–57.
2. Lacordaire, *Les Inconnus de la Seine*, p. 10.
3. Backouche, *La Trace du Fleuve*, p. 9.
4. Lestel *et al*, "The Evolution of the Seine Basin Water Bodies Through Historical Maps," p. 6.
5. Lacordaire, *Les Inconnus de la Seine*, p. 258.
6. Garnier *et al*, "Continental Atlantic Rivers: the Seine River."

Chapter 26

1. Alexandre and Boura, *La Seine et Paris*, p. 52.
2. These points are variously drawn from Lacordaire, *Les Inconnus de la Seine*, and from Alexandra and Boura, *La Seine et Paris*.
3. Alexandre and Boura, *La Seine et Paris*, p. 81.
4. Beaudouin, *Paris/Seine*, pp. 109 and 114–115.
5. Alexandre and Boura, *La Seine et Paris*, p. 91.
6. Beaudouin, *Paris/Seine*, p. 171.
7. Alexandre and Boura, *La Seine et Paris*, pp. 52–53.
8. These examples are drawn from Evans, *Life in Medieval France*, p. 49.
9. Backouche, *La Trace du Fleuve*, p. 163.
10. Chadych and Leborgne, *Atlas de Paris*, p. 97.
11. Backouche, *La Trace du Fleuve*, p. 164.
12. The following points on Paris as a seaport are drawn from Alexandre and Boura, *La Seine et Paris*, pp. 123–126.

Chapter 27

1. Many of the points made here are taken from the Haropa Port Press Kit of 28 January 2022.
2. Heebøll-Holm, *Ports, Piracy and Maritime War*, p. 44.
3. *Seine*, Waterways Guide No. 21, p. 46.
4. Heebøl-Holm, *Ports, Piracy and Maritime War*, p. 71.

Chapter 28

1. Lambert and Septet, *Paris sur Seine*, p. 29.
2. O'Sullivan, "Paris Has a New Plan to Make the Seine Swimmable," pp. 1–2.

Chapter 29

1. Eddison, *Medieval Pirates*, p. 25.

Chapter 30

1. The key source of this chapter is Chadych and Leborgne, *Atlas de Paris*, pp. 116–147.
2. Beaudouin, *Paris/Seine*, p. 94.
3. Chadych and Leborgne, *Atlas de Paris*, p. 117.

Chapter 31

1. This chapter is largely drawn from information provided by companies offering training for apprentices inland navigation; see the bibliography.
2. Private communication of 27 March 2023 from F. Manouvrier, the head of an inland waterways training school in France.

Conclusion

1. Beaudouin, *Paris/Seine*, p. 60.
2. Astic-Heisserer, *Paris Médiéval*, p. 42.
3. Alexandre and Boura, *La Seine et Paris*, p. 55.
4. Hussey, *Paris: The Secret History*, p. 293.
5. Chadych and Leborgne, *Atlas de Paris*, p. 163.
6. Bélaval and Perrault, *Paris—Île de la Cité—Mission 2040*, pp. 7–8.
7. Adapted from Arnaud and Boura, *La Seine et Paris*, pp. 8, 33, 79, 111, 155.

Appendix 1

1. Adapted from Chadych and Leborgne, *Atlas de Paris*, p. 9.
2. These themes are stated in or implicit in pp. 40–86 of *Le Guide du Patrimoine: Paris* by Jean-Marie Pérouse de Montclos, which is cited in the bibliography.
3. In modern times, one of the artists who moved to Paris was the American painter Louise Janin (1873–1997), the aunt and great-aunt of the coauthors of this book.
4. Pérous e de Montclos, *Le Guide du Patrimoine: Paris*, pp. 54–55.
5. Beaudouin, *Paris/Seine*, p. 136.
6. Pérouse de Montclos, *Le Guide du Patrimoine*, p. 73.

Appendix 2

1. Pater, *The Renaissance: Studies in* 86 of *Le Guide du Patrimoine: Paris* by Jean-Marie Pérouse de Montclos, which is cited in the bibliography ; see *Art and Poetry*, p. 8.

Appendix 3

1. This appendix is drawn in part from the *Waterways Guide* to the Seine, pp. 138–158.
2. Hussey, *Paris: The Secret History*, pp. 216–217.
3. Beaumont-Maillet, *L'Eau à Paris*, p. 142.

Appendix 4

1. This chapter follows the "Tug Boats on the Seine" chapter of the Waterways Guide to the Seine, p. 84.

Appendix 5

1. Chadych and Bourgorne, *Atlas de Paris*, pp. 36–37, and *Waterways Guide to the Seine*, pp. 84–89.
2. Rol-Tanguy, *Paris, Metropole sur Seine*, p. 21.
3. Backouche, *La Trace du Fleuve*, p. 48.
4. Chadych and Bourgorne, *Atlas of Paris*, p. 36.
5. Favier, *Paris*, p. 234.
6. *Épitres* by Nicolas Boileau, cited by Wikiquote, p. 227.
7. Beaumont-Maillet, *L'Eau à Paris*, p. 75.
8. Beaudouin, *Paris/Seine*, pp. 40–41.
9. Beaudouin, *Paris/Seine*, p. 67.
10. Lambert and Sepet, *Paris sur Seine*, pp. 3–4.

Appendix 6

1. Sciolino, *The Seine*, pp. 271–272.

Appendix 7

1. Lorentz and Sandron, *Atlas de Paris au Moyen Âge*, p. 193.
2. Rose, *The Wine Trade in Medieval Europe*, pp. 13–14.

Bibliography

Alexandre, Arnaud, and Stéphanie Boura. *La Seine et Paris*. Paris: Action Artistique de la Ville de Paris, 2000.
Allmand, Christopher. *The Hundred Years War: England and France at War C. 1300-c. 1450*. Cambridge University Press, 1994.
Astic-Heisserer, Sophie. *Paris Médiéval*. Paris: Taride, 2015.
Backouche, Isabelle. *La Trace du Fleuve: La Seine et Paris (1750–1850)*. Paris: École des Hautes Études en Sciences Sociales, 2000.
Baldwin, John W. *Paris, 1200*. Stanford University Press, 2010.
Barker, Juliet. *Agincourt: The King, the Campaign, the Battle*. London: Abacus, 2006.
Beaudouin, François. *Paris/Seine: Ville Fluviale—Son Histoire des Origines à Nos Jours*. Paris: Éditions de la Martinière, 1993.
Beaumont-Maillet, Laure. *L'Eau à Paris*. Paris: Hazan, 1991.
Bélaval, Philippe, and Dominique Perrault. *Paris: Île de la Cité—Mission 2040*. Paris: Éditions Norma, 2017.
Bove, Boris, and Claude Gauvard. *Le Paris du Moyen Âge*. Paris: Belin, 2014.
Brennetot, Arnaud. *Atlas de La Vallée de La Seine: De Paris à la Mer*. Paris: Éditions Autrement, 2019.
_____, Françoise Lucchini, and Claire Maingon. *La Seine: Une Vallée, des Imaginaires…: Perceptions et Représentations de la Seine au Moyen Âge à Nos Jours*. Rouen: Presses Universitaires de Rouen et du Havre, 2015.
Burl, Aubrey. *Danse Macabre: François Villon—Poetry & Murder in Medieval France*. Thrupp: Sutton, 2000.
Carpentier, S., R. Moilleron, C. Beltran, D. Hervé, and D. Thévenot. "Quality of Dredged Material in the River Seine Basin (France). I. Physio-chemical Properties. the Seine River Basin—France and Waterways That Must Be Dredged." https://pubmed.ncfi.nim.nih.gov/12186280/#. Accessed 29/06/2022.
Cassard, Jean-Christophe. *L'Âge d'Or Capétien: 1180–1328*. Paris: Belin, 2014.
Chadych, Danielle, and Dominique Leborgne. *Atlas de Paris: Évolution d'Un Paysage Urbain*. Paris: Éditions Parigramme, 2022.
Connecting Citizen Ports. "Port of Paris." https://www.citizenports.eu/partners/partner/port-of-paris. Accessed 28/05/ 2022.
Contamine, Philippe. *War in the Middle Ages*. (Trans. Michael Jones.) Oxford: Basil Blackwell, 1986.
Cushway, Graham. *Edward III and the War at Sea: The English Navy, 1317–1377*. Woodbridge: Boydell Press, 2011.
Douglas, David C. *William the Conqueror*. New Haven: Yale University Press, 1999.
Eddison, Jill. *Medieval Pirates: Pirates, Raiders and Privateers 1204–1453*. Stroud: The History Press, 2013.
Edwards-May, David. *Inland Waterways of France*. Eighth Edition. Cambridgeshire: Imray, Laurie, Norie & Wilson, 2010.
Erlande-Brandenburg, Alain. *Notre-Dame de Paris*. Paris: Éditions de la Martinière, 2015.

Evans, Joan. *Life in Medieval France.* London: Phaidon Press, 1957.
Favier, Jean. *La Guerre de Cent Ans.* Paris: Fayard, 1980.
_____. *Paris: Deux Mille Ans d'Histoire.* Paris: Fayard, 1997.
Felice, Andrea. "The Most Famous Unknown Girl." https://wwww.felicecalci.com/la-belle-italianne-the-most-famous-girl/?lang:en. Accessed 23/06/2022.
Flatman, Joe. *Ships and Shipping in Medieval Manuscripts.* London: British Library, 2009.
Fowler, Kenneth. *Medieval Mercenaries:* Volume I: *The Great Companies.* Oxford: Blackwell, 2001.
France, John. (ed.) *Mercenaries and Paid Men: The Mercenary Identity in the Middle Ages.* Boston: Brill, 2008.
French Waterways. "The 5 Iconic Paris Sights You Can See Best from the River Seine." https://www/french-waterways.com/5-iconic-sights-can-best-see-river-seine. Accessed 15/08/2022.
Friel, Ian. *Henry V's Navy: The Sea-Road to Agincourt and Conquest 1413–1422.* Stroud: The History Press, 2015.
Garnier, Josette A., Michel Meybeck, and Sophie Ayrault. "Continental Atlantic Rivers: The Seine Basin." https://www.resarchgate.net/publication/357854611_Continental_Atlantic_Rivers_the_Seine_Basin. Accessed 15/09/2022.
Georgetown University. "North Dame Cathedral North Rose Window." http://repository.library.georgetown.edu/handle/10822/5544233#. Accessed 25 February 2022.
Germain, Arthur. "From the Source of the Seine to Havre by Swimming." https://arthurgermain.fr/mes-defis/la-descente-de-la-scene-a-la-nage. Accessed 13/09/2022.
Grummtt, David. (ed.). *The English Experience in France: War, Diplomacy, and Cultural Exchange, C. 1450–1558.* Aldershot: Ashgate, 2002.
Hays Foundation. "About Marlene and Spencer Hays." https://haysfoundation.org/about-marlene-and-spencer-hays. Accessed 6 March 2022.
Heath, Ian. *The Vikings.* London: Osprey Publishing, 1987.
Heebøll-Holm, Thomas K. *Ports, Piracy and Maritime War: Piracy in the English Channel and the Atlantic, c. 1280-c. 1330.* Boston: Brill, 2013.
Histoires de Paris. "Les Difficultés de la Navigation Sur la Seine." No URL, 2/07/2017. Accessed 26/03/2023.
History. "This Day in History: August 10, 1793—Louvre Museum Opens." https://www.history.com/this-day-in-history/louvre. Accessed 1 March 2022.
Hugo, Victor. *Notre-Dame de Paris.* (Alban Krailsheimer, trans.) Oxford University Press, 2009.
Hussey, Andrew. *Paris: The Secret History.* London: Penguin, 2006.
Hutchinson, Gillian. *Medieval Ships and Shipping.* London: Leicester University Press, 1997.
Imray, Laurie & Wilson. Nautical Chart C12 of St. Ives. St. Ives: www.imray.com, 2014.
Imray, Laurie, Norie & Wilson. Passage Chart: Eastern English Channel. Cambridge: 2014.
Inglis, Erik. "Gothic Architecture and a Scholastic: Jean De Jandun's *Tractatus* de Laudibus Parisius," in *Gesta,* 42, 2003, pp. 63–85.
Institut Fluvia. "River Training," France, 2022.
Institut nationale de recherches archéologiques préventives. 18 January 2017. No place of publication given. Accessed 27 January 2022.
Janin, Hunt. *The University in Medieval Life, 1179–1499.* Jefferson, NC: McFarland, 2008.
_____, and Ursula Carlson. *Mercenaries in Medieval and Renaissance Europe.* Jefferson, NC: McFarland, 2013.
_____, and Ursula Carlson. *Medieval Monks and Monasteries.* Jefferson, NC: McFarland, 2023.
Joint Research Center. Paris: "Fact Sheet: Seine River Basin." https://water.jrc.ec.europa.edu/pdf/seine-fs.pdf. Accessed 2/10/2023.
Jolliffe, John. (trans. and ed.) *Froissart's Chronicles.* London: Penguin, 1967.
Koenigsberger, H.G. *Medieval Europe 400–1500.* Harlow: Longman, 1998.
Lacordaire, Simon. *Les Inconnus de La Seine: Paris et Les Métiers de L'eau eu XIII au XIV Siècle.* Rungis: 1985.
Lambert, Guy, and Cécile Septet. *Paris Sur Seine.* Paris: Éditions du patrimoine, 2019.

Larbodière, Jean-Marc. *Ponts de Paris: Découverte & Histoire*. Issy-les-Moulineaux: Éditions Massin, 2017.
Le Guide du Patrimoine: Paris. (Jean-Marie Pérouse de Montclos ed.). Paris: Hachette, 1994. www.imray.com.
Le Petit Palais. "Building History." https://www.petitpalais.paris. Accessed 10 March 2022.
Leniaud, Jean-Michel, and Françoise Perrot. *La Sainte Chapelle*. Paris: Éditions du Patrimoine, Centre des Monuments Nationaux, 2007.
Lestel, Lawrence, David Eschbach, Michel Meybeck, and Frédéric Gob. "The Evolution of the Seine Basin Water Bodies Through Historical Maps." https://springer.com/10.1007/698_2019_396. Accessed 21/08/2022.
Lorentz, Philippe, and Dany Sandron. *Atlas de Paris au Moyen Âge » Espace Urbain, Habitat, Société, Religion Et Lieux De Pouvoir*. Paris: Éditions Parigramme, 2021,
McGrail, Seán. *Early Ships and Seafaring: European Water Transport*. Barnsley: Pen and Sword Archeology, 2014.
"Medieval battle." *Weapons and Warfare: Battle of the Seine*. https://weaponsandwarfare.com/2009/02/11/battle-of-the-seine-1416. Accessed 11/01/2022.
Michelin. "Le Quartier Latin," *Paris: Le Guide Vert*. Paris, 2010, pp. 247–265.
Michelin Travel Partner. Boulogne Billancourt: *Paris—Short Stays*. January 2020.
Musée d'Archéologie Nationale. "Saint-Denis's Markets and Fairs: The Lendit Fair." https://archeologie.culture.gouv.fr/saint-denis/en/endit-fair. Accessed 29/06/2022.
Musée de Cluny. "Pillar of the Boatmen." https://www.musée-moyenage.fr/en/collection/pillar-of-the-boatmen.html. Accessed 19/06/2022.
National Police of France. "River and Nautical Brigades of the Police and the Gendarmerie." https://www.police-nationale.net/brigade-fluviale/. Accessed 14/06/2022.
Office du Tourisme de Paris. "Focus on the Rives de Seine Park." https://www.parisinfo.com/visiter-a-paris/tourisme-duragle-a-paris/le-nouveau-parc-rives-de-seine. Accessed 25/05/2022.
Olson, Lynette. *The Early Middle Ages: The Birth of Europe*. Basingstoke: Palgrave Macmillan, 2007.
Orsay Museum. "Exhibitions." https://www.musee-orsay.fr/fr. Accessed 6 March 2022.
O'Sullivan, Feargus. "Paris Has a New Plan to Make the Seine Swimmable." https://www.bloomberg.com/news/articles/2021-12-04/how-parus-plans-to-make-the-seine-swimmage-by-2024. Accessed 13/9/2022.
Paris Fire Brigade (Sapeurs Pompiers de Paris, Nautical Means). https://pompiersparis.fr/type-engin/moyens-nautique/. Accessed 17/06/2022.
Paris: Official website of the Convention and Visitors Bureau. "Musée du Louvre." https//en.parisinfo.com/paris-museum- monument/71065. Accessed 01/032022.
Pariscityvision. "The Seine and Its Painters." https://www.pariscityvision.com/en/paris/seine-river-cruise/seine-painters. Accessed 14/03/2022.
Pater, Walter Horatio. *The Renaissance: Studies in Art and Poetry*—Leonardo da Vinci. https://www.gutenberg.org/files/239/2398-h/2398-htm#leonardo. Accessed 05/03/2022.
Pernoud, Régine. *Héloïse et Abélard*. Paris: Éditions Albin Michel, 1970.
_____. *Lumière Du Moyen Age*. Paris: France Loisirs, 1981.
_____, and Marie-Véronique Clin. *Joan of Arc: Her Story*. (Jeremy duQuesnay Adams, ed. and trans.). London: Phoenix Press, 2000.
Pérouse de Montclos, Jean-Marie. *Le Guide du Patrimoine: Paris*. Paris: Hachette, 1994.
Porter, Catherine. "Olympic Swimming in the Seine? How Paris Is Remaking a River." *New York Times*. https://www.nytimes.com/2023/05/12/sports/olympics/paris-olympics-seine-cleanup.html. Accessed 15 May 2023.
Potter, David. *France in the Later Middle Ages*. Oxford University Press, 2006.
Pounds, N.J.G. *An Economic History of Medieval Europe*. Second Edition. New York: Routledge, 2013.
Power, Eileen (trans. and ed.) *The Goodman of Paris* [a prosperous male citizen of Paris]: *A Treatise on Moral and Domestic Economy by a Citizen of Paris, C. 1393*. Rochester: Boydell & Brewer, 2006.
Rebours, C. "Haropa Port Press Kit." Overview of 2021—Outlook for 2022. Paris, 28 January 2022.

Rendu, Jean-Baptiste, and Jacques Guillard. *Abbayes & Monastères de France*. Issy-les-Molineaux: Éditions Massin, 2013.
Rodger, N.A.M. *The Safeguard of the Sea: A Naval History of Britain, 660–1649*. London: Penguin and National Maritime Museum, 2004.
Rol-Tanguy, Francis (ed.). *Paris, Metropole sur Seine*. Paris: Les Éditions Textuel, Paris Project #40, Atelier Parisien d'Urbanisme, 2010.
Romero, Estela (ed.) "Long-term Water Quality in the Lower Seine: Lessons Learned Over 4 Decades of Monitoring." Environmental Science & Policy 58, 2016, pp. 141–154.
Rose, Susan. *England's Medieval Navy, 1066–1509*. Barnsley: Seaforth Publishing, 2013.
_____. *The Medieval Wine Trade in Western Europe 1000–1500*. London: Bloomsbury, 2011.
Roux, Simone. *Paris au Moyen Âge*. Paris: Hachette, 2003.
Roux, Simone. (Jo Ann McNamara, trans.). *Paris in the Middle Ages*. London: Folio Society, 2014.
_____. *Regards sur Paris: Histoires de la Capitale (XII–XVIII Siècles)*. Paris: Éditions Payot & Rivages, 2013.
Russon, Marc. *Les Côtes Guerrières: Mer, Guerre et Pouvoirs Au Moyen Âge—France-Façade Océanique XIII–XV Siècle*. Rennes: Presses Universitaires de Rennes, 2004.
Sciolino, Elaine. *The Seine: The River That Made Paris*. New York: W.W. Norton, 2020.
"Seine." Waterways Guide No. 21. (Anne Ackermans, ed.). Castelnaudry: Éditions du Breil, 2016.
Seine River. "Water Quality and Pollution." https://seineriver7g2.weebly.com/water-quality-and-pollution.html. Accessed 14/09/2022.
Steves, Rick. *Paris*. Berkeley: Avalon Travel, 2021.
Tate Gallery. "Impressionism." https://www.tate.org.uk/art/art-terms/i/impressionism. Accessed 15/03/2022.
Thornton, Tim. *The Channel Islands, 1370–1640*. Woodbridge: Boydell Press, 2012.
Toureiffel.paris. "The Monument and Its History." https://www.toureiffel.paris/en/the-monument/history. Accessed 12/03/2022.
Training Centre for Apprentices in Inland Navigation (CFANI). "River Transport." Tremblay-sur-Maurice: cfani@free.fr.com. No date of publication given.
Travelwithart. "The River Seine Paintings—Capturing French Life on the River in the 19th Century." https://wwwtravelwithart.com.river-seine-paintings-of-the-impressionists. Accessed 14/03/2022.
UNESCO. "Paris, Banks of the Seine." https://whc.unesco.org/en/list/600/. Accessed 20/02/2022. pp. 1–16.
Urban, William. *Medieval Mercenaries: The Business of War*. Barnseley: Pen & Sword, 2015.
Van Deputte, Jocelyn. *Ponts de Paris*. Paris: Edition Sauret-Paris-Musées, 1994.
Verbruggen, J.F. *The Art of Warfare in Western Europe During the Middle Ages from the Eighth Century to 1340*. Second Edition. Rochester: Boydell & Brewer, 2002.
Vespierre, Bernard. *Guide du Paris Médiéval*. Paris: L'Harmattan, 2006.
Ville de Paris. "À Paris: Le Magazine: Entrez en Seine!" Automne 2022, # 79.
Visitor Guide. Musée de la batellerie et des voies navigables. Conflans Sainte-Honorine. https://www.musee-batellerie-conflans.fr/fr/visitors-guide. No date of publication given.
Weapons and Warfare. "Battle of the Seine (1416)." https://weaponsandwarfare.com/2009/02/11/battle-of-the-seine-1416. Posted on 11/02/2009. Accessed 01/11/2022.
Willsher, Kim. "Eiffel Tower Riddled with Rust and in Need of Repair, Leaked Reports Say." *The Guardian*. https://www.theguardian.com/world/2022/jul/04/eiffel-tower-riddled-with-rust-and-in-need-of-repair-leaked-reports-say#:~:text=Now%2C%20however%2C%20confidential%20reports%20leaked,2024%20Olympic%20Games%20in%20Paris. Accessed 05/07/2022.
Willsher, Kim. "'We Want It to Come Alive'": architect's plan to transform Norte Dame area." https://www.theguardian.com/world/2022/jul/02/architect-bas-smets-plan-to-transform-notre-dame-cathedral-area-paris. Accessed 06/07/2022.
World in Paris: Travel Tips by Locals. "15 Curious Facts About the Pont Neuf, Paris." https://worldinparis.com/pont-neuf-paris. Accessed 27/02/2022.

Index

Abelard, Peter (French polymath and lover) 123, 124, 125, 181

Balzac, Honoré de (French novelist) 172
Bateau Mouche (tourist excursion boat) 117, 135, 184
Berthier, Karine (French expert on Seine-related occupations) 35
Bièvre (a Paris river heavily polluted in the past by textile mills) 13, 16, 47, 48, 49
boat crews 129
Boileau, Étienne (leader of the merchants of Paris) 198
Bonaparte, Louis-Napoleon III 20
Bonaparte, Napoleon 18
booksellers along the Seine 97, 98, 130, 131
bourgeois of Paris (businessmen who profited from their trade along the Seine) 32, 55
Bove, Boris and Claude Gauvard (modern French medievalists) 46
bridge(s) (the 37 bridges and footbridges over the Seine in Paris) 46, 49, 52, 54, 63, 65, 66, 67, 69, 71, 73, 74, 75, 77, 81, 84, 94, 96, 97, 101, 111, 121, 127, 128, 129, 147, 177, 179, 182, 183, 185, 188, 190, 214
Brigade Fluviale (River Police) 135, 137

canals of the Seine 113, 118, 133, 145, 193, 195
Capetian dynasty 30, 118, 181, 188
Château-Gaillard (a fortress in Normandy) 60, 61, 213
Clovis (king of the Franks) 29, 30, 181
cog (a medieval cargo boat) 42
Conciergerie 7, 94, 119, 178

Daumier, Honoré (French artist) 132
de Jandun, Jean (French university professor) 48, 90, 182
de Maupassant, Guy (French novelist) 122

de Molay, Jacques (leader of the Templars medieval order) 97, 176, 177
de Ronsard, Pierre (French poet) 38
Devil's Arch (arch of a bridge that caused numerous accidents to boats on the Seine) 19, 40
du Camp, Maxime (French historian) 13

Eiffel Tower 22, 63, 64, 65, 83, 106, 114, 115, 116, 119, 130, 184
enclosures ("enceintes"—i.e., concentric circles of human habitation in Paris) 187
English Channel 205

Fauchet, Claude (Seine river expert) 1, 183
Favier, Jean (French medievalist) 1, 88
floods 6, 9, 16, 18, 19, 22, 35, 50, 63, 70, 74, 77, 80, 101, 166, 194
Froissart, Jean (French historian) 54, 55
future of the Seine 1, 164, 165, 166, 167, 179

Grand Palais 6, 7, 64, 83, 112, 113
grèves (traditional boat-landing-areas along the Seine) 9
Guido de Bazoches (medieval French cleric) 9, 176, 182

Les Halles (major covered market on the bank of the Seine) 31, 39
Hanse (major interest group of Paris merchants) 32, 182
Harfleur (harbor on the Seine) 29, 53, 57, 58, 59, 156, 157, 158, 182
Haropa Port (the combined ports of Le Havre, Rouen, and Paris) 156, 163, 169, 170, 185
hauling boats up the Seine 14, 56, 129, 199
Haussman, Baron Georges Eugène (French official in charge of the Seine) 20, 21, 65, 178, 184

223

Index

Le Havre 136, 142, 143, 146, 151, 155, 156, 157, 158, 159, 160, 163, 168, 169, 170, 174, 175, 185, 201, 205
Hidalgo, Anne (Mayor of Paris) 23
Hollande, François (President of France) 178
Hugo, Victor (French novelist) 52, 78, 87, 89, 184
Hundred Years War 53, 54, 55, 57, 58, 59, 60, 61, 157, 161, 162, 182, 208

Île de la Cité (the Island of the City of Paris) 7, 8, 9, 16, 18, 20, 26, 28, 29, 30, 32, 43, 46, 47, 67, 69, 70, 72, 84, 86, 87, 88, 94, 96, 97, 98, 106, 133, 139, 150, 176, 177, 178, 179, 182, 183, 187, 188, 189
Île San Louis (one of the most elegant neighborhoods of Paris) 23, 65, 67, 71, 72, 83, 84, 85
illustrations and descriptions of the Seine 120, 121
inconnus de la Seine (the "unknown people", i.e., the forgotten people, of the Seine) 3, 140
Inland Waterways Museum of the Seine 4
iron-hulled ships (steamships) on the Seine 205

Janin, Louise (American artist) 102, 217
Joan of Arc 60, 61, 161, 182
Julian (Roman Emperor who wrote about a little island in the Seine which later became Paris) 28, 29, 18

Latin Quarter of Paris 14, 47, 123, 124, 125, 139
locks (navigation locks used to regulate water levels on the Seine) 14, 15, 16, 18, 19, 22, 146, 175, 184, 194, 202
London 20, 36, 51, 100, 155, 184
Louis VII (French king who encouraged trade along the Seine) 32
Louvre 52, 64, 65, 76, 79, 83, 96, 100, 101, 102, 103, 105, 106, 119, 121, 138, 139, 151, 189, 191
Lutèce or Lutetia (later known as Paris) 26

massacre of Protestants 138
medieval seal of the water merchants of Paris 8
mercenaries along the Seine 54, 208, 209
Mercier, Louis Sébastien (French author) 38, 101, 102, 183
Mona Lisa (painting by Leonardo da Vinci) 102, 140, 191
money-changers on the bridges of Paris 39, 40, 182

monks 41, 43, 46, 48,, 77, 124, 201
mooring ring on the Seine (a humorous account of the follies of a Paris miller) 36
Musée d'Orsay 7, 83, 106, 130

nef (traditional Seine wooden boat, depicted both on the seal and the coat of arms of Paris) 32, 182
Neolithic period 6, 26, 156, 185
Notre-Dame de Paris (world-famous cathedral) 19, 20, 24, 29, 33, 34, 38, 47, 48, 49, 52, 64, 74, 75, 76, 84, 86, 87, 88, 89, 90, 91, 92, 93, 94, 101, 118, 131, 136, 176, 178, 179, 188, 184

occupations of Seine workers in Paris (e.g., tanners, fishermen, and millers with their windmills) 32

Parisii (the earliest inhabitants of Paris) 7, 28, 64, 66, 181
Paris Plages (banks of the Seine transformed in summer into temporary beaches) 23
Petit Palais 64, 83, 111, 112, 113
Place Dauphine 98, 99, 121
pollution of the Seine 133, 137, 146, 148, 149, 163, 164, 165, 166, 183, 185, 194, 200
Pont Neuf (oldest bridge across the Seine in Paris) 10, 63, 64, 71, 75, 78, 83, 96, 97, 98, 99, 101, 119, 126, 128, 183, 189
port of Gennevilliers (and smaller ports) 148, 155, 200
Prévert, Jacques (French poet) 3

Raguenet, Nicholas-Jean-Baptiste (French artist of the Seine) 75, 76, 172
riverbanks of the Seine 126, 127, 129, 130, 131, 133, 133, 135, 147, 198
Rouen 2, 17, 18, 30, 42, 43, 44, 45, 53, 54, 56, 58, 60, 61, 100, 136, 142, 143, 146,, 151, 156, 157, 160, 161, 162, 163, 169, 172, 182, 185, 198, 203, 208

Sainte-Chapelle (the Holy Chapel) 47, 48, 83, 94, 182, 188
Seine River Basin 167
sequential parts of the Seine (for navigation purposes, the Seine is divided into five parts) 17
shipping on the Seine 13, 14, 15
"the society of the street" and "the society of the river" in Paris 75
steam 17, 49, 51, 52, 56, 70, 117, 155, 159, 162, 172, 180, 184, 189, 194, 196, 205

Index

"tidal wave" of the Seine 202
"trains of logs" floating down the Seine 11, 83, 113, 152
transport of wine and grain by river 203, 204
Les Trente Gloriouses ("The Thirty Glorious Years of Paris" between 1945 and 1975) 142

UNESCO's 3½-mile-long World Heritage Cultural Site in Paris 9, 12, 63, 64, 83, 114, 115, 185
University of Paris 10, 48, 124, 125
Unknown Woman of the Seine 140, 184

Van Gogh, Vincent (Dutch painter) 106, 121, 133

"Very Rich Hours of the Duke of Berry"— Les Trés Riches Heures du duc de Berry (painting) 105
viking(s) 64, 181, 202
villages along the Seine 171, 172
Villon, François (medieval poet) 38, 183
Voies Navigables de France (the navigable waterway system of France) 25, 136

water pumps and water venders (both delivered drinking water to Paris) 51, 65, 91
watermills 19, 28, 33, 35, 38, 145, 182

Zouave (a large stone statue on the Seine used informally to measure flood levels on the river) 16, 80

www.ingramcontent.com/pod-product-compliance
Lightning Source LLC
Chambersburg PA
CBHW032040300426
44117CB00009B/1134